Woodbrooke College

200 33725

D0551563

The Last Man in Russia

OLIVER BULLOUGH

The Last Man in Russia

And the Struggle to Save a Dying Nation

ALLEN LANE
an imprint of
PENGUIN BOOKS

ALLEN LANE

Published by the Penguin Group
Penguin Books Ltd, 80 Strand, London WC2R ORL, England
Penguin Group (USA) Inc., 375 Hudson Street, New York, New York 10014, USA
Penguin Group (Canada), 90 Eglinton Avenue East, Suite 700, Toronto, Ontario, Canada M4P 2Y3
(a division of Pearson Canada Inc.)
Penguin Ireland, 25 St Stephen's Green, Dublin 2, Ireland (a division of Penguin Books Ltd)
Penguin Group (Australia), 707 Collins Street, Melbourne,
Victoria 3008, Australia (a division of Pearson Australia Group Pty Ltd)
Penguin Books India Pvt Ltd, 11 Community Centre,
Panchsheel Park, New Delhi – 110 017, India
Penguin Group (NZ), 67 Apollo Drive, Rosedale, Auckland 0632, New Zealand
(a division of Pearson New Zealand Ltd)
Penguin Books (South Africa) (Pty) Ltd, Block D, Rosebank Office Park,
181 Jan Smuts Avenue, Parktown North, Gauteng 2193, South Africa

Penguin Books Ltd, Registered Offices: 80 Strand, London WC2R ORL, England

www.penguin.com

First published 2013
001

Copyright © Oliver Bullough, 2013

The moral right of the author has been asserted

All rights reserved.
Without limiting the rights under copyright
reserved above, no part of this publication may be
reproduced, stored in or introduced into a retrieval system,
or transmitted, in any form or by any means (electronic, mechanical,
photocopying, recording or otherwise) without the prior
written permission of both the copyright owner and
the above publisher of this book

Typeset by Firstsource Solutions Ltd

Printed in Great Britain by Clays Ltd, St Ives plc

ISBN: 978-1-846-14373-1

Contents

Introduction: We will bury you

Misha, a journalist friend, rang me around noon on 1 January 2004. I assumed he was calling to wish me a happy new year. For Russians, New Year is a more important holiday than it is in the West. Presents are exchanged and toasts drunk for success in the year ahead. It is normal to call or text friends if only to laugh with them.

Misha, however, had something different in mind. He had, I later discovered from his girlfriend, been drinking – with breaks only to pass out – solidly for two days already, and he went on to drink for two more.

'Oliver, listen, I need your help. What is the meaning of the word zombie hedgehog?'

He was speaking Russian, heavily slurred, but still intelligible. He said the last two words in English, however, and clearly wanted me to translate them. I was baffled, and asked what he meant. There was a pause at the other end, then he swore at something or someone in the room with him and hung up. I waited for him to call back, but he never did. When I next saw him, a week or two later, he had no recollection of the call and I never did find out why he had asked.

Misha had an alcohol problem. On a trip to Chechnya a few months later, we got up at around five-thirty in the morning to be sure to arrive in Grozny with plenty of time to work. I had arranged that the hotel would make breakfast for us early. I was drinking tea and waiting for my eggs when Misha walked into the dining room. The waitress asked him what he would like to drink, and he looked around at me.

'Do you want to drink?'

I shook my head. I needed it clear to work.

'Give me a bottle of brandy,' he told the waitress. She brought it, with a single glass, on the same tray as his breakfast. He drank it, shot by shot, while he ate his fried eggs, sausage and bread. He bought another bottle as we were leaving. By the time we reached the Chechen border, he had drunk that too – a litre of brandy before nine in the morning – and insisted we stop for vodka.

This is not one of those stories of journalistic excess that end with the drunkard doing his job despite being barely coherent. (There is an apocryphal Fleet Street photographer who is said to have fallen off his stepladder and still to have shot three perfect frames before hitting the ground.) No, Misha was by turns abusive and sentimental as I tried to get some kind of work out of the day. By evening, he was comatose and a few of us cobbled together some material to send to Moscow under his name.

Although this was an extreme episode, it was not in itself unusual. Many of my colleagues would drink spirits when out of the office, and managers across Russia have learned to incorporate into their plans time lost through drinking. The culture of drinking is so entrenched that the language has a multitude of words to describe the different stages of alcohol abuse. *Zapoi* means the kind of multi-day bender Misha had survived over the New Year. *Opokhmelitsya* is a verb meaning to have a drink in the morning to remove a hangover (it is a crucial element of a *zapoi*, but exists in other contexts too). *Peregar* is the smell of alcohol from a mouth in the morning.

This is a habit not only of the destitute. Misha was a successful, talented and well-paid journalist. He and his colleagues drank in ways I had never seen before. And, although Russian men do drink more than women, this is not by any means a uniquely male problem. Anyone travelling to work on the Moscow metro in the morning will see well-dressed, made-up young women drinking beer out of cans. In Russia, buying alcohol is easier than buying bread. Kiosks have whole walls of vodka, which they sell for as little as £3 for a half-litre.

While hiking in the wilds near Siberia's Lake Baikal, my brother and I met a small group of fellow outdoor enthusiasts and we decided to camp together for the night. They were the first people we had seen for a couple of days, and we brought out a bottle of vodka we had been saving for just such an occasion. Our offer was met not with alacrity, however, but with scorn. One of the group, a professor from a university in Novosibirsk, explained, as if talking to a child, how real hikers behave. Real hikers watch every gram they carry, he said. They have no space in their rucksacks for such indulgences as vodka. I was wondering whether perhaps Tom and I should find somewhere else to camp, when he reached behind him.

'This is what you need,' he said, drawing a brown bottle out of his rucksack. It was what the Russians call *spirt*, pure alcohol. I saw his point. If you want to get drunk, why waste space carrying vodka – with its 62.5 per cent of water – when you can carry the same volume of alcohol and get the water from a stream?

The evening of the day when Misha overdid it in Chechnya, we were cooped up on a military base. It was then illegal for foreign journalists to travel in Chechnya without an escort (this was both for our protection and to stop us getting any work done), and we had to be in the barracks long before the sun set and the violence started. Misha was asleep but I was not, so another journalist and I passed the hours before bed chatting to Ilya Shabalkin, a colonel who acted as spokesman for the federal forces, and a couple of other officers. Shabalkin brought out a two-litre bottle of Dzhelka, a cheap but not undrinkable brand. I had contributed a small bottle of Green Stamp, a brand then fashionable in Moscow.

I quickly fell behind. How much you can drink is a sign of your masculinity, and Russians have a multitude of sayings to ridicule anyone who tries to stop early or to skip a round ('If you won't drink with us today, you'll betray your homeland tomorrow' is one example). Fortunately, foreigners tend to be exempt, it being understood that we are already inferior. I could only watch as these four men – three of them holding high rank in the Russian armed forces, and the other a successful reporter – drained the bottles like an ebbing tide. By the time I crept away to bed, there were three empty bottles on the table, and they had started on a fourth. That is more than six litres of vodka among five people, one of whom was barely drinking, on a weekday. And they had not yet finished.

When Russians drink vodka, they do not sip it, or mix it with juice. They drink shot after shot, each one followed by a quick bite of gherkin or bread. Russian vodka normally tastes chemical, like an unsuccessful science experiment. Unlike with whisky, wine or beer, there is no effort to make the drink itself enjoyable. It is a means to an end, a vehicle to get you drunk. I will drink vodka if I have to, but rarely out of choice. When I can, I drink beer instead, which means I can usually remember the night's events the next morning.

Russians have always had a reputation for drinking. One of the first mentions of them in the historical record features their king rejecting Islam because of its prohibition on alcohol. The average Russian drinks three times the volume of spirits drunk by a German, and four times that of a Portuguese, and that's only the official figures. No one has any idea how much self-distilled moonshine is drunk, but it must be a lot, for every traveller in Russia has a story about it.

I was once on an overnight train from St Petersburg to Moscow. I had bought the cheapest ticket, and was one of eight passengers sitting bolt upright in a dingy compartment as the train crawled through a dark forest. We had all brought beer to drink, but the bottles were finished now, and lay littered around our feet. We were semi-drunk and morose, staring ahead at the gloomy outline of the person opposite.

An old woman sitting by the window stood up, rummaged around in her bag on the luggage rack and brought forth a two-litre plastic bottle and a light-blue cup. Holding up the cup, she offered us all a drink. It was too dark to read, and I was too uncomfortable to sleep, so I agreed. So did everyone else. The cup went up her row of four passengers, crossed over to me and came back down our side. We each downed our share in a gulp, then breathed through our sleeves to take away the burn. The last man before the window passed the cup over the table and back to her, so she could pour out some more.

It tasted like white spirit, but the effect was spectacular, a rush of well-being to the back of the head. Conversation was kindled, and we became rowdier as the light-blue cup's journey continued. Stopping once I had started was apparently not an option, and I got drunk very fast. It was a relief when I saw the old woman drink the last glassful. I had not disgraced myself. No one could say the foreigner had failed to keep pace. That was when she stood up again and reached to the luggage rack, whence she pulled down a jerry can.

She could barely manage it, and I could hear the liquid sloshing around inside. She rested it on the table and carefully filled the bottle up again before lifting the can back on to the shelf. There would be no escape. The drinking went on until I passed out.

Something like that happens every night on trains all over Russia. Done once, it is an amusing anecdote. Done daily and it is a disease, and it is killing the nation. Between 1940 and 1980, Russian consumption of all alcoholic drinks increased eightfold. The nation decided, apparently as one, to go on a huge *zapoi*, and the consequences have been disastrous.

All across what is the Russian heartland, old Muscovy, the land where the Russians held out against the Mongols, Napoleon and Hitler, the picture is of destitution. Thousands of villages are empty. Thousands more are home to a handful of pensioners, and will be empty too within a couple of decades. Some towns have halved in population in twenty years. In 1950 – when Stalin was at his most erratic, when the country was still half destroyed by World War Two, when terrible sacrifices were being demanded from the population – births outnumbered deaths by 1.7 million.

In 2010, deaths outnumbered births by 240,000, and that was the best year for a couple of decades. In 1991, the country was home to 148.3 million people. In 2010, that number had fallen to 141.9 million. The Russian nation is shrivelling away from within.

And it is not just that Russians are not being born. Russians are dying. The average Russian male born in 2010 was calculated to live less than sixty-three years. Russians of both sexes taken together are almost four times more likely to die of heart disease than a Western European, and more than five times more likely to be killed by an 'external cause' – murder, suicide, drowning, poisoning, car crashes. The comparable countries for violent death are Angola, Burundi, Congo, Liberia and Sierra Leone.

Russia is not the only country afflicted with a falling population. In Italy and Germany, for example, the average couple has fewer than two children, which will inevitably lead to population decline. Western European women are reluctant to have as many children as their mothers.

Western Europe's situation causes problems of its own, not least when it comes to affording the state pension system, since people are living longer thanks to improving healthcare and healthy living campaigns. The Russian situation is far more serious, however. It is driven by the death rate, and overwhelmingly by the death rate among working-age men. The average Russian man will not live to get his pension.

It is widely assumed that the drinking and the population crisis are a post-Soviet problem. It is true that the problem accelerated with the collapse of communism and the extreme economic dislocation that followed. Inflation wiped out pensions and savings, while factories closed and threw millions of people out of work. Russians drank to blot out the times they were living through. In truth, however, they were drinking before.

The years of the late 1950s and early 1960s when Nikita Khrushchev led the Soviet Union are little remembered today, but they were the high point of the state's achievements and self-confidence. It was not only people in Moscow who believed the Soviet Union would surpass the West in production and living standards. People in the West worried it would too. This was the era when sputnik, Laika the dog and Yuri Gagarin blasted into orbit. Gary Powers in his U-2 spy plane was shot down over the Urals and it seemed even the most advanced American weapons were at the Russians' mercy.

Armies of state employees controlled the production of ever greater volumes of steel and armaments, all checked by legions of statisticians. Soviet tanks stood poised on the borders of West Germany. Hungary's attempt to throw off Moscow's dominance in 1956 was ruthlessly crushed. The government could be forgiven for congratulating itself on its achievements. The future was red. Khrushchev, addressing Western ambassadors in 1956, showed his confidence and contempt with the phrase 'we will bury you'. Soviet citizens would outlive their Western rivals, and would dig their graves for them.

It was an ironic boast because, if Khrushchev had been alert and well informed, he would have noticed a worrying trend. At or around the same time that Gagarin became the first man in space – a triumph Russians boast of to this day – the Russian nation began to die out.

For a start, Russian women stopped having enough babies to maintain the population. For a nation to sustain itself, the average woman must have around 2.1 children. From 1965, Russian women gave birth to fewer than that. And that was when Russians started to die younger too. In the early 1960s, the average Russian and the average Austrian both lived for about sixty-nine years. By 2005, the Austrian was living for an extra decade and a half, the Russian for four years fewer.

I could speculate about why Russians were drinking so much. I wondered if it was a simple function of availability. The Soviet Union produced vodka, so Russians drank it. But that is not a real answer. No one drinks themselves to death just because they can. When a whole population takes to the bottle, something far more serious must have happened. Perhaps Russians felt their destinies were out of their control. The country was stagnant and would remain that way for as long as anyone could predict. If tomorrow will be no better than today, why not enliven today by getting drunk?

But speculation was all I had. Academics have largely overlooked Russia's 1960s and 1970s. There is no decent biography of Leonid Brezhnev, though he led the world's biggest country for close to two decades. Nor is there a good book about Yuri Andropov, though he headed the KGB for almost as long and took the top job too for a little while. Ambitious young historians look elsewhere to make their name. These are years of stagnation and decay, and far less sexy than the times of Joseph Stalin, when the Soviet Union was growing, or of Mikhail Gorbachev, when it was falling apart.

And there is another reason why that period is little written about. Although there are now detailed studies of the life chances of Russians, there was no equivalent work in the Brezhnev years. The Soviet Union produced millions of bound copies of its leaders' speeches and thousands of novels proclaiming how bright the future would be. But it published no books asking why the workers of the workers' state were anaesthetizing themselves to an ever greater degree. The government controlled publishing, and allowed Russians to read only books that told them how well off they were.

Even a book as plodding as *Dr Zhivago* proved electrifyingly controversial for the Soviet state. Its author, Boris Pasternak, was hounded to an early grave in 1960 for not conforming to the standards expected of a Soviet novelist, and for daring to have it published abroad. Despite the treatment of Pasternak, however, a small group of writers insisted on writing their own way. Smuggling their manuscripts abroad was their protest against the state's insistence on obedience in

7

all things. At that time, creative endeavours needed state approval, which meant these upstarts had to be crushed. In a defining moment, in February 1966, Andrei Sinyavsky and Yuli Daniel, two writers who had published books in the West, were put on trial to show their peers that such independence could not be allowed.

They were not pro-Western as such, but they hated being stultified by what was going on around them, and their trial is symbolic of what a whole generation was going through. 'The cost of obedience was a tension, an anxiety that only increased as the years went by. He was a born writer, not a soldier,' one friend wrote of Sinyavsky. Soldiers obey, but writers question, and the system would not tolerate questions.

The body of self-printed and distributed literature – *samizdat* – produced by these men and those that followed is a crucial source for what was going on beneath the veneer of success that the Soviet Union presented to the world. It was here, for the lack of anything else, that I began to look for the reasons why Russians began to drink in such quantities.

My research got me nowhere, however. The dissidents' concerns were lofty and admirable – freedom of speech, freedom to emigrate, the right to a fair trial – but did not seem the kind of thing to drive a mass epidemic of alcoholism. Then I found a book by Ludmilla Alexeyeva, a veteran of the human rights struggle who was forced into exile in 1978. Perhaps because she was living in the United States, she took a broad view of the country, and looked outside the capital.

She wrote how Russians everywhere had become depressed by the hypocrisy of corrupt officials who promised a bright future for others while enjoying the fruits of the present themselves. The Russian state was killing hope, and humans cannot survive without it. In the vacuum, people reached out for anything available, including God.

> The hunger for religion ... was not a result of the efforts of the church, but rather of the decay and corruption of official ideology. It spread over the entire country and affected all social groups. Enormous numbers of people tried to fill the resulting spiritual and intellectual vacuum with alcohol, others tried to fill it with the most diverse kind of activities, from gardening to philosophy.

The Russian Orthodox Church, like the official hierarchies of the Muslim, Jewish and Buddhist congregations in the Soviet Union, had been infiltrated by and subordinated to the state. Although communists had begun by assaulting religion and imprisoning priests, Stalin realized during World War Two that the patriotic appeal of defending the faith was a useful mobilizer of men.

The Orthodox Church was not a monolith, however. Among its priests were some who did not support the government slavishly in all things, as their bishops did. And among those priests was a man called Dmitry Dudko – Father Dmitry, to his friends. Alexeyeva described him in her book, so I read his work. He, I realized quickly, was an exceptional man.

While the state was engaged in producing reports on how well it was doing, and the dissidents were engaged in proving it wrong, Father Dmitry was quietly comforting the miserable and the downtrodden. And he was not just a compulsive comforter; he was a compulsive writer. He left notebooks and articles and sermons: hundreds of thousands of words. These ranged from accounts of parishioners' confessions to autobiographical sketches, to poems, to sermons. They are a priceless source for anyone seeking to understand how communism, a movement intended to perfect humanity, turned into a system of oppression and misery.

The communism he describes is not one that aims for a radiant future, despite its claims. The Soviet state was, in fact, almost perfectly designed to make people unhappy. It denied its citizens not just hope, but also trust. Every activity had to be sanctioned by the state. Any person could be an informant. No action could be guaranteed to be without consequence. Father Dmitry preached friendship and warmth and belief to his parishioners, and inspired a generation to live as humans and not as parts of a machine.

And Father Dmitry, I realized, as I read his books and delved into his world, was more than a witness and an agitator. His life story – from his birth in a Russian village after the revolution, to his death in Moscow in 2004 – is also the history of his nation. He lived through collectivization, the crushing of the 80 per cent of Russians that were peasants. He served as a soldier in World War Two, when millions of peasants died defending the government that had crushed them. He spent eight years in the gulag, the network of labour camps created to break the spirit of anyone who still resisted. He rose again to speak out for his parishioners in the 1960s and 1970s, striving to help young Russians create a freer and fairer society.

Those decades are little written about today, but they are central to Russia's population crisis, so those are the decades this book focuses on. It is not a biography of Father Dmitry, nor is it a history of the Russians' twentieth century. Instead, it is something in between. Father Dmitry's life, for me, is the life of his nation in microcosm. In tracing the life and death of Father Dmitry, I am tracing the life and death of his nation.

How did Russia become a country where my friend Misha considers it acceptable to drink a litre of brandy before embarking on a day's work? And how did it become a country where no one finds that strange – a country where brandy is on sale beside fried eggs, sausage and bread at breakfast time? One man's alcoholism is his own tragedy. A whole nation's alcoholism is a tragedy too, but also a symptom of something far larger, of a collective breakdown.

Public life in Russia is stubbornly dishonest. Transparency International's yearly survey ranks countries on a 10-point scale, where 10 is very clean and 0 is highly corrupt (New Zealand came top in 2011 with 9.5, Somalia and North Korea came last with 1). Russia has, since the survey began in the 1990s, consistently scored between 2.1 and 2.8, putting it in the company of Nigeria and Belarus, and below the likes of Syria, Pakistan and Eritrea. Russians consider themselves civilized Europeans, but have to endure the humiliation of daily encounters with officials that belong in a squalid dictatorship.

I once asked Kolya, a friend of mine, what he would do first if he became president. Kolya is jovial and loud, so I expected he would announce something funny. Perhaps he would legalize polygamy for people whose names begin with a K. He sat and thought for more than a minute. He stared at his glass of beer and toyed with a cigarette.

'I would kill myself,' he said at last, without a trace of a smile.

It is hardly surprising that Russians have long been unenthusiastic about politics. In one yearly survey from the Levada Centre, a polling organization, the options to choose from are 'life isn't so bad, you can survive', 'life is bad, but you can endure' and 'enduring our calamitous situation is impossible'. There has been a slow move from the third category to the second since the late 1990s, but the fact that those are the only categories does not suggest that this is a country happy about the future.

In this book, I ask how this came about. It is not only a journey into the past, however, because the Russian population crisis could have enormous consequences for the future. In the Chinese province of Heilongjiang there are more than 38 million people. In Russia's Maritime, Amur and Birobidzhan regions, which border it to the north and are collectively not too much larger, there are around 3 million people. If that number keeps falling, then it is easy to wonder if the Chinese might think the Russians do not want that land and decide to take it from them. The modern world has never had to confront a situation where a country does not have enough people to support itself any more.

In Father Dmitry's life story, therefore, I have sought other answers too: is there hope for the future? Is the damage inflicted on the Russians reversible? Can a new generation, raised without the dead dogma of communism, kindle a new kind of state, where people are free to be themselves?

It is possible to imagine the kind of state where Russians might be happy to live, work and have children: the only kind of state that could have a future. It is what Father Dmitry was trying to build when he preached in the churches of Moscow, and when he prayed in the KGB's camps. That is why I set off to follow the tracks of Father Dmitry and his friends, north to the gulag, east to the Urals, but first of all west to the village of his birth: Berezino, in the forests of Russia's ancient heart.

SUMMER

I

They took our grandfather's land

So one morning in summer 2010 I woke up in an old Soviet hotel in the city of Bryansk, far to Moscow's west.

It was hot. The buildings were wavering in the heat before I even left the bus station, where tanned, shirtless bus drivers shouted their final destinations as if they could persuade arriving passengers to cancel their travel plans and go with them instead. The route to Berezino was complex. First I sat on a packed minibus, which took me to a large shop. Then an elderly bus rattled to a town covered in grey cement dust. This was Fokino. Then another bus took me to Berezino itself. We stopped on the edge of a dusty yard, flayed by the sun and dominated by a five-storey apartment block. Two large-bosomed women stood beneath its balconies and argued.

My goal was to find Father Dmitry's surviving relatives, but I had not up to now given much thought to how I would do that once I got here. My normal approach is to turn up, look inquisitive and hope someone takes pity on me. I walked towards the two women, and idled past them. They ignored me. One or two people were still by the bus stop, so I walked back towards them, passing the two women once more. Again, no one looked at me.

'What are you doing?'

I turned to see a handsome woman of about forty, eyes crinkled with amusement, all dressed in black despite the weather. She was sitting on a bench in the shade of the bus station.

'I saw you come in on the bus, and then walk over there, and walk back here, and now you're standing around. What are you doing?'

She looked friendly, so I explained the nature of my quest: I was looking for relatives of Father Dmitry, and wanted to understand how his upbringing had made him the way he was. She shook her head. There were no Dudkos round here. But she had nothing much to do for the next few hours so she took my hand and marched me across the baked plain of the yard to meet her mother.

'I'm called Galya,' she said.

It was only after we had rung her mother's doorbell for some time that she remembered that it was a Saturday. Her mother, it transpired, was a Seventh Day Adventist and would be praying with her sister, Galya's aunt. We marched back down the staircase and across to a second apartment block – the ground in between was full of vege- tables ripening early in this intense heat – where we found the old women. They wore headscarves and cardigans, and were sitting on an old sofa with the Book of Revelation open in front of them.

They had never heard of any Dudkos, and had lived here all their lives. This was not good. Nonetheless, I decided to come away with something and got my notebook out anyway. Anna Vasilyevna, Galya's aunt, was born in 1922 – the same year as Father Dmitry. Nina Vasi- lyevna, who had twelve other children besides Galya, was three years younger. This, I thought, could at least be a chance to find out about life under occupation. This whole area was taken by the Germans at the very start of Hitler's war. Father Dmitry had spent two years under German occupation, and all old people would have shared his experi- ences of foreign rule.

Except they did not want to talk about that. They wanted to talk about their faith, and about grandchildren – in that order.

'I started to believe in God in the wartime. The bullets were flying. Our uncle Matvei brought the faith back from the army. He did not drink or smoke. He gave up vodka, and he stopped stealing or lying,' said the aunt.

I looked round at Galya, who was giggling silently. I began to suspect this was a practical joke she had set up to pass the time.

'They will burn everything. Now there is freedom of religion, if we live long enough the pope of Rome will come and kill us.'

She looked pleased, as if this would be a very satisfactory way to end her life. Then Galya's mother started reciting names.

'Vita, he's first. Write it down. Then Olya and Natasha.' I looked at Galya, confused. She mouthed the word 'grandchildren'. I blinked and wrote the three names down. 'Tanya, Sveta, Ira, Nina, Zhenya, Vasya, Yulia, Maxim, Igor, Denis.' The list went on and on until it finally finished: 'Nadya, Veronika, Misha. How many's that?'

I counted them. There were twenty-eight.

'Exactly. Twenty-eight. And eighteen great-grandchildren.'

An argument ensued about whether there were eighteen or nineteen. We went over the list thrice more. The aunt's husband had been killed in the war, so she had no grandchildren and she eventually tired of such a sterile debate. She turned back to the faith, and my mind drifted a little. I looked at the generations: thirteen children, twenty-eight grandchildren and eighteen great-grandchildren. That is the kind of contraction happening everywhere in Russia. If every couple has just one child, then the generation size halves, which is more or less what had happened here.

It could not have been more different when these two old women were born. Industry and railways had brought unprecedented mobility to Russia in the years before the revolution, but the villages where they started their lives had still changed little since the Middle Ages. The fertility level was high – comparable to that of Somalia today, where each woman has more than six children – and 80 per cent of Russia's population were peasants.

Although serfdom – the slavery that tied peasants to the villages and gave landlords almost limitless powers to punish them – was scrapped in 1861, the peasants were still not free to move. They had to pay off the debt incurred by buying their freedom, and were collectively liable as villages for the sum. Few wanted to leave anyway. The communal pull was so strong that successive well-wishers from both ends of the political spectrum retreated before their stubborn attachment to their old ways of life, the yearly division of land, the Church, folk medicine.

Death rates remained high. Mothers smothered unwanted babies in bed. Babies were left in the care of their siblings, who often rocked their cradles so hard they fell out and died. Diarrhoea was treated by hanging children up by their legs and shaking them violently. 'Outie' belly buttons were spread with dough so mice could nibble them off. In most homes, more than half the children died. The poorer families, according to one eyewitness account of life in a

Russian village in the late nineteenth century, often welcomed the deaths of infants with the words: 'Thank goodness, the Lord thought better of it.'

It was a life of superstition. Any outsiders were distrusted and opposed. Local officials could flog adults on their bare bottoms for the most minor of offences. The eyewitness, an aristocrat called Olga Semyonova Tian-Shanskaia, described how in one village near her home pigs dug up the body of a baby that had been murdered.

'No action was taken in the matter. Peasants do not like criminal investigations and keep quiet even when they know something.'

Officials could demand taxes before the harvest if they wanted, and would then confiscate property when the peasant in question could not pay. When the revolution came, the peasants rose up and seized the lords' lands, as well as that of any profitable neighbours who had made money from the few agricultural reforms imposed before World War One. The Bolsheviks, who understood nothing of the countryside, declared war on them, seizing their grain and causing famine. Somewhere between 10 and 14 million people died of hunger in the four years after 1917.

These old women were living witnesses to the history of their nation, its triumphs and its tragedies, but sadly they did not much want to talk about it.

'Now there is freedom of religion, but there is little time. When they smashed up the church, they imprisoned the priests,' said Galya's aunt, slapping my foot and chuckling.

Her sister chipped in: 'The pope of Rome will soon announce a census of religions.'

The aunt was not to be outdone. She summoned all the breath in her lungs and intoned: 'They will come and kill us.'

Both old women burst out laughing. Galya leaned over to kiss them on their pale cheeks. They adjusted their headscarves, and we left, leaving them sitting on the sofa companionably discussing their imminent demise. The photograph I took could just as easily be from a hundred years ago. Galya looked at me, shrugged and giggled.

I tried to give up the quest at this point and go back to Bryansk to regroup, but Galya was having none of it. Although born here, she visited rarely and wanted to show the peculiar Westerner off to all her old friends. So it was that we boarded another bus, which took us beyond the end of the metalled road, to Pupkovo.

There had been no rain for weeks, and the road was pale dust with a strip of yellowing grass up the middle. I could not imagine how anyone reached Pupkovo in the thaw, when a winter's worth of snow melted all at once, but then the thaw itself was hard to imagine in this brutal heat. Chunks of the fields on either side of the bus broke off into the air, floating on a wavering mirage.

When the bus stopped at the entrance to the village, there was desolation. A standing cross marked where the communists had knocked the church down. The church had stood until 1937, the cross said, so I wondered briefly if this was where Father Dmitry had worshipped as a boy. We strode down a slight slope into the village, where houses ringed an artificial pond. Most of the houses lacked glass in their windows; some of them lacked roofs. The place was all but abandoned and it was clear Galya was not the only person to have left Pupkovo.

'There used to be a club there,' said Galya, pointing at one building, which had been part of the collective farm. Now she was not smiling. 'But there's no one left to dance any more.'

We could hear laughter, however, and skirted the pond to a little cabin that had been built out over its surface. A shiny German car stood outside. A glistening fat man in tight shorts and nothing else waved us in, welcomed Galya by name and passed his bottle of beer into his left hand so that I could approach him and shake his right. He did not stand up or otherwise move. His was the expensive car parked on the lane. That and the large gold cross on a gold chain around his neck showed him to be a man of means. Galya explained my mission. The man turned to his two companions and to a child who was turning kebabs on the barbecue.

'Dudko? Who the fuck was Dudko? Wasn't he from the Kaluga region?'

The men simpered. The child stared.

'He was from the Kaluga region. Come on, we'll hire a forester's truck. Get some fucking beer, and some meat and have a barbecue. It's not fucking far through the forest,' he said with a grin, and a lunge towards Galya.

Galya's face was set. She declined without giving me a chance to come up with a plausible excuse. We had people to meet, she said, and took me by the hand once more.

'Galya, why aren't you wearing a fucking cross? Aren't you Russian? Where are you going? Have a fucking beer.'

She towed me out of the cabin and back on to the path. Her good mood, already soured by the sight of her home village, was gone.

'See that,' she said. 'Some example to his son. That was his son there, the one who said nothing. He's got a pregnant daughter at home with no husband, and he's sitting here drinking beer. No education. It was people like him who burned down my house, and look at him there with his cross. Oh, Russia, Russia.'

We turned left, her leading, on to a path across the fields, or what had once been fields. They butted on to the village houses but grew only rank grass.

'Everything used to grow here,' she said. Her voice was tight and her steps fast. 'See there: potatoes. Over there: tomatoes. Here was beetroot. And now, nothing. It's just ruined, like this whole country, and that man is there with his money and his beer.'

The sandy soil was exposed along the path, but otherwise this farmland had turned into wilderness. There was no human mark left.

'No one will even harvest this hay. Why bother? There's nothing to eat it.'

The path dipped down into some trees, where a small chapel sat in the shade. It was built of softwood planks and roofed with clear plastic. Inside was a well, made of circular concrete segments and choked with foul green slime. It was an evil-looking place to hold baptisms.

'He built it,' said Galya, with a jerk of her head back towards the pond. 'He's in the cement business.' She paused to make sure I had understood. 'Business,' she repeated with invisible inverted commas around it.

A man was clearing weeds from a path that approached the far side of the well. Galya greeted him as Vasilyevich – son of Vasily – and explained my goal. He shrugged at the name Dudko. No Dudkos here, he said, but he had some papers on local history at his house if I was interested.

It was the first lead all day, and I accepted with enthusiasm. So, we walked back past the pond, the fat man, his car and his gang, whose hails Galya ignored. News of Galya's visit spread quickly, and as we waited for Vasilyevich to bring out the papers, four or five women gathered: all of them were old friends of hers. There was no one else in the village. None of them had heard of the Dudkos. I was feeling a bit light-headed in the burning heat and began wondering whether Father Dmitry had existed at all.

The papers on the church were interesting, but Vasilyevich had no copies, so I looked through them, gave them back and turned to go. Galya and I would need to walk back to Berezino from wherever we were, so that I could find a bus back to Bryansk. There would be no further buses from here that day.

The earth track passed between further fallow fields. There was no cultivation here at all – just grass – and almost no livestock: only the occasional cow. The whole population seemed to have given up farming. We heard a car approaching from behind us. At the wheel was the man with the papers.

'A friend of my wife came after you left,' he said, addressing Galya instead of me. 'She used to work for the post office. Apparently, this used to happen to letters sometimes. There are two Berezinos in the Bryansk region. The other one is over by Unecha, near the border with Belarus, spelled Berezina, with an "a".'

It made sense. Berezino comes from the word for birch tree, and Russia has a lot of birch trees. It is a village name that could easily be repeated many times. Galya looked at me. The giggle was back.

'Two Berezinos? And you've come to the wrong one,' she said. She looked profoundly amused. The lines at the corners of her eyes were even deeper than before. She hooted with laughter and put her arm around me.

'How far have you come to go to the wrong village? From London?'

I stood stupidly in the sun. I could not help but smile. Galya's laughter was irresistible. I was probably already a local legend: the daft foreigner with a notebook who couldn't read a map.

'Get in,' the man said. 'I'll take you to the bus stop. You've got a long trip if you're going all the way to Unecha.'

Galya, who was still giggling, left me at the bus stop. She wanted to have a proper conversation with her mother and thought the old women might have calmed down by now. I could hear her still chuckling as she walked away. At last the bus came, and I was heading in the right direction.

When I finally found the narrow road to Father Dmitry's real home village, far to the west and a day's journey away, it was possible to imagine that nothing had changed here not only since he was born in 1922, but for centuries before that too. Conifers formed a spiky horizon all round. Potatoes sprouted from sandy fields. Sparse crops of barley ran right up against the walls of log-built houses.

But the impression was illusory. The peasants here in western Russia were some of the doughtiest enemies the Bolsheviks ever faced. They had to be prised away from their ancient customs like a child from its mother. The assault on them was merciless, their defeat was total, and their lives changed for ever. In the face of the onslaught, peasants clung to all that they could salvage: to their faith, Orthodox Christianity.

Orthodoxy is made up of ancient rituals and chants and processions that believers lose themselves in. Icons are objects of adoration, and churches have tiered screens to separate the priest conducting the mysteries from the waiting faithful. Orthodoxy claims descent from the faith of the earliest times, which is why it is so resistant to change – a characteristic reinforced in Russian villages where reform remains distrusted.

Father Dmitry never wrote much about his childhood, but from what he did record it is clear that his home was deeply religious. His father, an ordinary farmer with a stubborn face in photographs, kept a Bible in the house. His small son would secretly read it to himself. He played at being a priest, taking an ember and a candle, and filling the hut with smoke. He gave communion from a glass of water to all his friends, who treated the event, he said much later, with great solemnity.

Playing was not something they did much of, in those days, however. The Bolshevik state was only newly established, and its economy was wrecked by civil war and international blockade. Before the revolution, the government had barely troubled the peasants, beyond demanding taxes. Once the tax collectors were gone for the year, the only official they saw was the constable. The Soviets were different.

Communist officials confiscated the peasants' crops to feed the cities. They had machine guns and the farmers were powerless to resist them. One winter, troops came and took the last wheat from Father Dmitry's family: the grain they needed to live on and to plant for the next year. His father, the bearded tyrant who ruled his household and read the Bible, lay on the ground and wept. Dmitry, his brothers and his mother wept too.

His sister was married by then, but her husband left for Ukraine to try to find food for his wife and young child. He was not heard of again. Abandoned, she struggled into the nearby town of Unecha with her baby to beg for food from the townsfolk. The baby cried and cried. He needed to be fed, she said, as often as a kitten. Her milk dried up, and she tried to appease him with water but he cried still more.

Finally, the baby calmed and slept. Her begging had failed and she had fed him nothing, but at least he was not uttering the unignorable screams of a hungry infant. She struggled on in her fruitless quest for food. It was only when she got back home that she realized he was dead. Desperate with grief, she ran to her own mother. She walked around their hut in her grief, until she found an edible plant in the garden. She dropped to her knees to eat it, but Dmitry was too fast for her. He ran out into the garden and slammed her round the head with a pole.

'What did you do that for?' his mother demanded.

'We all want to eat,' he replied. He wrote later that he was pleased he had defended their food store, even from his own sister.

The family had planted rye, which they guarded jealously until it grew large enough to be eaten. The children awoke one day to find their grandmother had broken into their garden and was eating the immature seeds. She could barely walk she was so hungry, but the brothers drove her out of their crop like a cow. When they had pushed her out, they began to throw lumps of earth at her. She sank to her knees and cursed them.

Dmitry's grandfather was also a religious man, and he built his own church out in the fields where he recited what he could remember of the old services. He was hungry and begged food. Their neighbours beat him and he lost his mind. The children then teased him and laughed at him, throwing stones. Once he caught Dmitry and thrashed him.

When Dmitry was already in his teens, he and his father gathered to mark Easter, the holiest date in the Orthodox calendar. Dmitry held his homemade cross while his father read the holy service. Stalin's government wanted to force the peasants to give up their own property and merge it into a single collective farm. The new farms would be efficient and mechanized, and would provide the food surpluses the Soviet state needed so that it could industrialize. In effect, the peasants' labour, livestock and land would be taken from them and used by the government for someone else's benefit.

It is not surprising that many of the peasants wanted nothing to do with the new farms, but the government was determined. It sent squads of city folk into the villages to force the peasants to take part.

Recalcitrant peasants were taxed at a rate 70 per cent higher than their collectivized neighbours and, even after selling all their valuables, could rarely afford to pay what the state demanded. That is what happened to Father Dmitry's father, who refused to join the collective. He was charged with tax evasion. His insistence on maintaining the old religious rites was added to the charge sheet. He was, under the new legal code on the young judge's desk, conducting religious propaganda. He and Dmitry had to walk 3 kilometres to the courthouse in another village.

'Why have you not paid the state?' asked the judge.

'I have not paid, yes ... there's nothing to pay with ... I live badly,' his father replied.

'And why don't you join the collective farm? There you will live better.'

'Well, I can go into the farm, if I have to.'

The judge gave him two years in jail. He was one of the approximately 25 million Soviet citizens repressed – shot, deported, imprisoned, exiled – in the years between Stalin seizing power in 1928 and dying in 1953. That is an eighth of the Soviet population, approximately two people for every three families. Tens of millions more suffered by association. As relatives of 'enemies of the people', the families of the convicted prisoners too were denied many of the rights of citizens. Dmitry, the son of a class enemy, knew that his troubles were in many ways only now beginning.

After his father's conviction, they sat for a while but had nothing to say. When Dmitry returned home alone, his mother was inconsolable. The sentence was extended, and those two years became four. The boys begged and stole food to keep themselves alive.

The collective farms were key to Stalin's plans to turn the Soviet Union into a modern state capable of standing up for itself. They would break the old traditions, forcing the peasants to do the state's will and to become pliant proletarians. They would also create a surplus of food to be exported so the Soviet Union could import the tools and equipment needed to modernize the economy. In this they succeeded. By stealing the peasants' food, the government won its crash industrialization. As Stalin's supporters say: when he arrived, Russia had wooden ploughs; when he died, it had the hydrogen bomb. The collective farms were not a long-term success, however. By the end of communism, Moscow was paying as much for imported grain as it was earning from exporting oil. Grain yields per hectare were a third of those in Germany, although the Soviet Union had some of the richest land in the world.

From a cultural and social perspective, things were even worse. Or so I heard from Vasily Germangenovich Shpinkov, universally known as Germangenovich, from the village of Kazashchina. Kazashchina is a couple of kilometres to the west of Berezina. On my way to see him, I walked past a stork's nest, a dense umbrella of sticks. Storks are supposed to bring good luck, but this one did not seem to have helped the village. Almost every house was boarded up or rotting.

Germangenovich was born in 1926, making him four years Father Dmitry's junior. If he was busy when I arrived, he showed no sign of it, since he sat me down, squeezed on to the seat next to me and began to talk as if he had been waiting for me his whole life.

He had a strange twisted nose, scarred in the way I imagine a serious explosion would scar it. His grey hair was thick but chaotic. His eyes were bright. I had plenty of time to examine him since he believed in the bigger picture. His life story started with Peter the Great's victory over the Swedes at Poltava. That was in 1709.

He was a Cossack and proud of it, and he pointed out to me his reproduction above the door of a painting in which Cossacks are shown writing a rude letter to the Turkish sultan. He wanted me to know that the tsars had been good people, and told me so at length. I had to write it all down, since he waited for me to do so after every sentence.

As a result, my notebook is full of pages of information on tsarist-era serfs, when peasants were tied to their village and forced to give their labour to their lord for three days a week.

'In 1931, Stalin brought in a second serfdom. He took the land, he took the livestock and he left the people with just a quarter of a hectare. And people did not have to work only three days a week for their masters like under the old system, but all the time, plus the churches and priests were destroyed.'

He was talking directly into my face, so I had a close view of his nose. His eyes were alive either side of it.

'I remember how they forced people into the collective farm. The chairman of the village council sat at a table with a pistol which he said was for the enemies of the people, who were those who did not want to join the collective farm. I was six years old and was up on the stove.'

He gestured to the huge flat-topped stove that dominated the room. Traditional peasant houses such as this one are built around the stove. It projects into every room and keeps them warm in the wintertime. In very cold weather, the family sleeps on top.

When the chairman had finished his speech and everyone shouted 'Praise Stalin, praise the revolution!', Germangenovich's grandmother told them they were all fools, that nothing good would come of it; that it was not for life, it was for death. Her curses made no difference. The government took over all the barns, and all the livestock. It even took people's wedding rings, the state's desire for currency was so strong.

'We had to give our cow to the state, and my mother got two and a half metres of cloth, which she used to make shirts for my father. That was the payment for our cow: a couple of shirts. When my father took the horse to the collective farm, we cried, we children. He knew that the horse would die, because it would have no master, no one would look after it. Our horse went to the common barn, and they took our land, and this is where the starvation came from.'

There were seven people in his family: his parents, him, his three siblings and his grandmother. They ate herbs and weeds to stave off hunger. His father did not have the money to buy an exercise book, so they went semi-naked and barefoot to their lessons without anything to write in.

'The children were weak, many could not go to school. They were naked and hungry, and refused to leave the house. How can you walk when your legs won't move? At school, they gave out bread. They had a list, and they divided children up. The poorest got bread, but me and my brother were so-called middle peasants so we got nothing.'

Middle peasants were the group of people between kulaks – the supposedly rich oppressors, who were often ordinary farmers whose hard work had allowed them to own slightly more than their neighbours, and who were sent off to die in Siberia and the north – and the Bolsheviks' favoured poor peasants.

The classifications were based on a report that Lenin wrote in the late nineteenth century. He was a committed Marxist, and saw the laws of class struggle all around him. That led him to the erroneous conclusion that peasants were dividing into classes – kulak, middle and poor – thanks to the government's abolition of serfdom and various other limited agricultural reforms.

In fact, peasants distributed their land afresh every year, with families receiving a share proportional to the number of people in their household. That imposed equality and the differences Lenin observed were transient developments brought about by temporary increases in some families' sizes that would be erased when young men left home or old men died.

The peasants he labelled as rich were rarely rich enough to employ labour, and in any case distrusted the habits required to get ahead in business. Besides, as Olga Semyonova Tian-Shanskaia noted, any surplus wealth tended to go on vodka, which had the habit of returning the relatively rich to the ranks of the poor once more.

Even if stratification into classes did occur, it was wiped out by the revolution and subsequent disturbances. Peasants stole their rich landlords' belongings, then the Bolsheviks stole what was left. There were no kulaks, no middle peasants and no poor peasants. There were just peasants, and all of them were in dire condition.

For the Bolsheviks, however, what Lenin wrote was true, and the communist government set targets for how many kulaks needed to be 'dekulakized' so as to establish fairness in the countryside. In June 1931 alone, 101,184 families were resettled from their homes to remote areas. The population of the Narym territory in Siberia increased from 120,000 to 300,000 in less than three months as the kulaks poured in, with no allowances made to feed the new arrivals in the long Siberian winter.

The kulaks were often the peasants with the best handicraft skills. With their departure, the villages lost their most skilled and accomplished residents, as well as much of their livestock, since many peasants preferred to slaughter their animals rather than hand them over to the state. Lacking animals to work the land or supply manure for fertilizer, the peasants' grain crops collapsed, while grain seizures continued. That caused a new famine.

Germangenovich cut a piece off the loaf of bread on the sideboard – 9 centimetres square, a bit bigger than a packet of cigarettes, though not as deep. That was the ration that he did not get. The bread was on a tray in school, and only the poor peasant children got any.

'My brother asked for some and they refused him. So he just grabbed two bits of bread off the tray and ran. While they chased him, he ate one bit and the second he hid under his shirt and gave to me. That was a true brother.'

The government moved many of the villagers a few hundred kilometres into Ukraine, where there would apparently be work and food. They walked into the houses assigned to them, he said, to find the tables laid and the beds made. The Ukrainians had all died of hunger, and their fields were unworked.

In the winter of 1932–3, the death rate in some parts of Ukraine was thirteen times higher than normal. Russia was better off, but only just. In its worst-affected parts the death rate was nine times higher than normal.

In 1932–3, somewhere between 5 and 6 million people died, making it the worst single famine of the century until China surpassed it in 1958. Grain production that year was around 60 million tonnes, but the five-year plan demanded 106 million tonnes and the plan could not be changed, so grain seizures by officials continued despite the evidence of starvation. Desperate peasants fled the villages for the towns, where rations were better. The government, which had abolished internal passports with the revolution, sent the peasants back to their homes and reintroduced travel permits. Now only town-dwellers would have the right to live in towns, and peasants would be tied to the land by their lack of documentation. For Germangenovich, it was serfdom come again.

Stalin's lack of sympathy for the starving peasants, whom he referred to as 'peasants' in inverted commas as if to accuse them of being impostors, was shown when, in a private telegram, he said they were Polish agents seeking to blacken the Soviet Union's name. Ukrainian officials followed his lead and said the peasants were starving because they were lazy. Some 21,000 top officials, meanwhile, had access to special shops in the cities where delicacies were still available. Closed Shop No. 1 served the Moscow elite.

While officials ate caviar, the boy Germangenovich was killing vermin to try to stop them eating the grain that was left.

'We were ordered to kill mice, and we got given a book if we brought in a hundred mouse tails. It was a plague of mice,' he said. 'That is how we lived. Up to the war.'

On 22 June 1941, Nazi Germany attacked the Soviet Union, finding the Russian troops totally unprepared. The invaders' advance was quick and devastating. By 17 August, they had seized Berezina. The same disregard for logic that had led the Bolsheviks to starve millions of peasants had also persuaded them to purge the highest ranks of the army, leaving the officers untrained and scared to take the initiative.

The Germans took whole armies of Soviet troops prisoner, of whom 2.8 million would be dead by early 1942. It was one of the most spectacular military disasters in history, and it exposed Father Dmitry and Germangenovich to the German army and an entirely different culture.

'When the Germans came here in 1941, they looked at us and said ai-ai-ai. All these Russian children are naked. They were a badly fed army, and they asked my mother for eggs. And she said there were no eggs, because there was no grain for the chickens. They were soldiers just like ours,' said Germangenovich.

He could speak a little German that he had learned at school, so he often spoke to the soldiers, he said. They had nothing good to say for Hitler, or for Stalin. Neither side wanted to fight. They said they wanted to grab Hitler and break him over their knees.

The Germans, he said, took their pig. Before the Germans came the whole village had been called out to dig anti-tank defences around Unecha. 'We were digging anti-tank pits when suddenly there's a motorcycle, and then the planes, and then tanks with the black crosses on them. It was hot, like today. A German tank driver comes out, with a red scarf. He saluted and said "Guten tag."

'Then the general came and told us not to be scared, that he had come to free us from the Bolsheviks. Our people were very glad really, despite what you read in the history books now. There would not be a collective farm again. They gave us our land, and reopened our churches. And this general said they would not shoot Unecha if no one shot at them.

'The Germans gave us land, divided up the horses. We started to grow wheat. In 1942 and 1943 we had a great harvest, we kept it for ourselves, and the Germans took meat, chickens and pigs. They opened the churches, and people went to churches to pray. We chose our own mayors, police. The mayor was our neighbour. The Germans made us work sometimes, carrying wood or resurfacing the road, but it was not so bad.'

The Germans brought order, according to Germangenovich's account, which more or less tallies with most academic studies I have read. He described how the Germans shot one of his neighbours for stealing a pig. And, he said, they killed the Jews – a fact he related deadpan, as if it did not bother him. That was in November 1941 and March 1942 when Sonderkommandos 7b and 7a rounded up the Jews in Klintsy, Oryol and Bryansk.

'They killed the few Jews that we had here, and the gypsies. There was one young Jewish lad, but he left, so it was just the old ones left behind. All the Jews worked in the town, they traded, they didn't work with their hands. There were maybe a hundred in the city – they were killed.'

In a sudden rush of memory, he flicked back to the start of the war: 'The Germans had dropped all these leaflets on us. They published newspapers as well. They had agitators who worked hard. "Destroy the Yid politicians," the leaflets said. They threw leaflets from planes, I remember.'

Later I decided to look up those leaflets in the Lenin Library in Moscow. I found a section – formerly classified – of 'special materials', newspapers published by the Germans under occupation, which people like Germangenovich would have read. Sure enough there was a photograph of children and adults running after airdropped leaflets tumbling through the air. Perhaps he was among them.

The newspapers were a glimpse into a vanished life of a non-Stalinist Russia in the 1940s. There were jokes ('What is the punishment for bigamy? Two mothers-in-law'), lists of church services, and accounts of how the peasants were using their private land. Every issue had lists of people missing – wives, children, mothers – and the names of those looking for them.

'Konstantin Mitenkov from the village of Kamenki ... informs his wife that he is alive and healthy,' said one notice.

Most of the pages, of course, were filled with orders and propaganda. All typewriters were confiscated and town-dwellers were banned from venturing into the countryside. Jews were blamed for everything, over and over, particularly for the repression dealt out by Stalin's NKVD security service. A picture of an Orthodox priest featured the caption: 'When the healthy body of the accused person survived the six weeks of torment, he had to appear before the tribunal of the NKVD, which included in its make-up only Jews.'

Anti-Jewish campaigns in Slovakia, France, Norway and elsewhere were described in horrible detail, as was a build-up of anti-Semitism in the United States. Russians were exhorted to unite with the Germans against this supposed mutual enemy. It was clear that not everyone swallowed the message. A decree promised death to anyone who sheltered Soviet partisans, and deprivation of rations to anyone who did not register themselves with the authorities.

But some Russians did go along with the Nazis. There were photographs of Russians in German uniform. 'They know who is really to blame for the war,' one paper said; 'fighting alongside the German soldiers and their allies, they are aiming for one goal: to destroy Jewish Bolshevism and give peace to the Russian land.'

The Soviet troops returned to Unecha on 23 September 1943.

'I went to church. I was in the choir during the occupation,' said Germangenovich. 'Then the reds came back and closed the church and took the priest away and killed him. The priest was old, old, but he was taken away immediately when the reds came back. They took away our police too, and our mayor. Some got shot, some got sent to the north to die of hunger. All of us young people got conscripted into the army.'

It must have been a strange liberation for men like Father Dmitry and Germangenovich. Occupation had been – although fraught and dangerous – a time of unprecedented freedom and prosperity. Hitler's government hated the Russians, but the German army was keen to protect its rear and secure food supplies, so it treated civilians better than Hitler ordered it to do. It provided building material for churches, and doubled the size of the peasants' personal plots of land where they grew their food.

I wondered, after hearing Germangenovich, how much the German propaganda, with its relentless slurs against the Jews and the communists, had affected him.

'After the war if people had asked how the Germans were I would have said they were good. But no one ever asked me.'

Germangenovich and Father Dmitry were all immediately conscripted into the Soviet army, with its relentless demand for new soldiers. Father Dmitry arrived at the front as the rawest of recruits directly after the Soviet army had liberated Berezina. This was after Stalingrad, when the Soviets had broken the Nazis' back. But there was a lot of fighting still to come and the soldiers would need to march all the way to Berlin. That march was chaotic and brutal, as the Soviet troops delighted in avenging themselves on the Germans who had killed their comrades and destroyed their homes.

Again this is a time that Father Dmitry did not linger over in his memoirs, but he did write that he was revolted by the mass rape of women in newly taken towns, and by the obscene language used by his fellows. He wrote not of battle but of saving an icon from being destroyed, and about how soldiers at night cough like sheep. He refused to join the Komsomol, the Young Communist League, because he was a believer. He claimed never to have fired a shot in anger. Then he was injured. A shell fragment entered his leg and, while in hospital, he contracted typhus fever. His military career was over.

He returned to Berezina, but life had changed. Stalin was aware of the role the Orthodox Church had played in winning support for the war effort. He allowed the German-opened churches to remain open, so there was somewhere for Father Dmitry to worship.

He was a war veteran with a pension, but there was no work for him. Months went by. He reported to the military commission, but they had no orders for him. That was when he saw the advertisement that changed his life: an Orthodox seminary was taking applications for trainee priests in Moscow, the first such intake for decades. This was part of Stalin's bargain with the Orthodox Church. Father Dmitry applied, was accepted and left for Moscow. He was gone by the time his brother Vladimir returned from the front.

'He had gone to Moscow and gone to study in the seminary. This was in 1944, when the war was going on still,' Vladimir told me when I was in Berezina. 'It was very hard to study there, to get in there.'

I met Vladimir after church in Berezina one Sunday. I was late for the service so I sat outside, waiting for it to end. While I was sitting in the morning sunshine reading through Father Dmitry's memoirs, the priest unexpectedly stepped out into the sunshine. He was still holding the incense and a candle, but was talking into his mobile phone.

'We're still holding the requiem,' he told his caller, promising to call back later. He gave me a quizzical look and turned back inside. A chicken strutted round from the back of the church, pecking at the dust on the path.

At last, the service was over and the priest came out to ask who I was. I explained my interest in Father Dmitry, and he pointed out Vladimir. Vladimir in turn called over his daughter Maria. Maria hailed Lidiya, daughter of one of Dmitry's sisters, perhaps of the woman he had smashed round the head and driven out of their garden. We sat in the church building, which was deliciously cool now the day was heating up, and I asked them what had made Father Dmitry the man he was. Vladimir's hearing was bad, and his accent was thick. Lidiya had to repeat my question to him, her accent spongy with the soft 'g' of peasant Russia.

'Our parents were believers, and they implanted the faith in us children. I remember my father was reading the Psalms, I was small, but I learned Psalm number 50 by heart because I heard how he read it,' Vladimir said. He had very clear blue eyes, like a child's.

Lidiya filled in for him. She was born in 1938, so presumably she was repeating his memories anyway: 'They took our grandfather's land, his horse. They took everything. Life was bad then, though it's not much better now.'

Maria, a tall woman in a russet headscarf and violently patterned blue and green dress, had been quiet. She sat holding her father's hand, curls of hair emerging over her forehead. She had clearly felt she had nothing to say on the subject of the 1930s, but life today was a different matter.

'Life is poor, we don't live, we survive. We count pennies. One daughter studies in college, the other has finished eleven classes and needs to study in college too. And pay? Well, give health to my grandfather. You have to pay to study. The grandfather pays. I don't work. My husband earns 10,000 roubles a month. Can you really live on 10,000?'

A monthly salary of 10,000 roubles is about £200.

'Just for accommodation we pay 5,000. A kilogram of meat costs 260 roubles. How can anyone live on 5,000? Milk is 20 roubles a litre. And we need clothing. And everything. We don't live. We survive. The girls are beautiful, they want to look good. And milk is more expensive in winter.'

I pulled a new notebook out of my bag, and they began to talk among themselves. Even in the bad times, they said, children were born, but now the village was dying. Vladimir, who had a habit of laughing at things that did not seem funny, chuckled: 'The death rate is conquering the birth rate.'

Maria talked over him: 'There's no work. Most people work in Moscow on the building sites. That's men. Women work in shops. It's very hard to find work. My daughters finish school, and college, so as to get a job in a shop. God willing. One is working in marketing, the other in the commercial section. And without higher education you can't even work in a shop.'

Vladimir laughed again. 'The bad life left with the Soviet Union, but the good life did not come, it did not come.'

I took some photos of the family before leaving. Vladimir stood with his vulnerable, baby-blue eyes, flanked by the two cousins. I then walked out of the church and back down Berezina's street. Most of the houses were single-storey squares set in their own gardens. A five-storey block, of the standard Soviet design found everywhere from Armenia to the Arctic, towered over them, but most of its balconies lacked washing lines. They were empty.

The fields either side of the lane were mainly given over to potatoes, but one field of barley stood by the main road. I barely recognized it at first, being accustomed to barley how my grandfather grew it, in tightly regimented blocks surrounded by raw earth. Here the sandy soil was choked with grasses and wild oats that shaded into the barley with no clear division between crop and weed.

It was only when I stopped and looked up and down the road that I realized I had no clear plan how to get back to Unecha. I had got a lift here with a fellow guest at the hotel who was driving to Moscow, but now I would need public transport. There was a bus stop on the other side of the road: an open-fronted, heavy-roofed shed, which had lost its benches. A plank was balanced in a corner to be sat on. I sat on it for a while, and waited for a bus to come. It was uncomfortable.

Cars passed about every three minutes. A bus passed after twenty minutes, and another half an hour later. They ignored my waves. I read more of Father Dmitry's memoirs as I waited. He had little more than his brother to say about the German occupation.

The Germans dissolved the collective farms, he wrote, and the farmers worked for themselves again. The chairman and secretary of the collective farm, who had testified against his father's religious activities, even started to visit the newly reopened church. Life improved.

I put the papers away, and walked to the edge of the forest. There was a building there I wanted to look at. The fields were fallow, and the enormous barn was rusty and decaying. This had once been a major grain silo, with five hoppers controlled by switches, to load grain on to trucks. The electric circuits had been plundered long ago and the fuse boxes were clogged with old birds' nests, the copper wire stolen. Dozens of wagtails had set up home. They did not mind me, but another bird that I did not recognize complained as I poked about: 'Tut tut cheep tut tut cheep.'

Four rooks mobbed a buzzard on the margin on the trees, the dense saw-toothed wall of conifers. Swifts screamed overhead and mice scuttled in the long grass. The old collective farm was heaven for wildlife, but hostile for humans. No trucks had been driven here for years and years. I looked over to the bus stop and saw that a woman was now waiting, which made me suspect a bus was due.

In Unecha, I sought a ticket on the night train to Moscow. From the capital, I would find my way to the Orthodox Church's seminary near by. I was late at the ticket office, however, and only top bunks were available. Top bunks are torment when the weather is hot, since the heat in the carriage is trapped under the roof, but I took one anyway. I boarded the train at midnight and hoisted myself on to my shelf. I was quickly soaked in sweat, but I dozed. Perhaps hours later, I was dragged from sleep by the man from the lower bunk tugging at my arm and shouting.

'You're pissing on me, you're pissing on me,' he yelled.

Stung by guilt, I reached under the bedclothes. They were dry, and I denied it as forcefully as I could.

We looked at each other in the gloom, unsure of what to say next. He turned back and pulled his mattress off his bed, cursing. I was definitely not to blame, but I could see the dark patches of damp on his sheets. Then a savage flare of lightning lit the compartment and, almost instantly, thunder cracked directly overhead. The flash showed torrential rain pouring down the window of the compartment and, now I listened, I could hear the drumming of the drops on the roof, louder even than the rattle of the wheels.

Rainwater was pouring through the ventilation hatches on top of the carriage, through the ceiling, down the partition, through the gap between my bunk and the wall and on to his bed. I held out my finger to feel the water. It was already a substantial waterfall and the volume was increasing. I tucked my sheets away from the torrent, turned on to my right side and looked out at the storm. Every few seconds, a lightning flash would fix the conifers of the forest into a cutout, like the backdrop to a fairy-tale. The temperature had dropped with the storm's arrival, and I felt rather snug on my dry top bunk. I curled up in my blanket and dozed off, listening to the curses of my neighbour as more and more water drenched his sheets.

2

A double-dyed anti-Soviet

To Father Dmitry, fresh from his village, the capital of the Soviet Union was something wonderful. Moscow might have been semi-destroyed by World War Two, its people living in rags and surviving on porridge. But it was still the biggest and richest city he had ever seen.

'Moscow seemed to me to be a fairy-tale town,' he wrote later.

And the fact he could become a priest must have seemed a fairy-tale also. He had grown up at a time when religion was a secret activity, conducted in fields or at night. Churches still loomed over many towns and villages, but more often than not they were used as storerooms or factories or hospitals.

The seminary owed its rebirth to the deal struck between the Orthodox Church and Stalin at the height of World War Two. Although Stalin was by this stage marshal of the Soviet Union, responsible for the defence of the world's largest country in the worst war it ever fought, he summoned three of the surviving four bishops to a late-night meeting in September 1943, and insisted that they train new priests.

Stalin himself had studied at a seminary long before the revolution. He had got top grades and was even a highly praised choirboy for a while, which may have explained his enthusiasm.

'Why don't you have cadres? Where have they disappeared to?' he mused, according to a later history of the Orthodox Church. Presumably he was being sarcastic, since his own security service had arrested, imprisoned and shot them all. His sarcasm could have given the new patriarch Sergei a golden opportunity to protest that thousands of his fellow believers were in the gulag. The patriarch was too cautious, however, knowing that if he protested he might join them.

'One of the reasons is that we train a person for the priesthood and he becomes a marshal of the Soviet Union,' he said. He was referring to Stalin.

It was grotesque flattery, but appears to have worked in setting a jocular tone. The meeting lasted until three in the morning, with the dictator reminiscing about his schooldays in pre-revolutionary Georgia. That year, 1943, his government restored the Church as an official body. Some monasteries reopened when the war finished. And the seminary was opened too. At first it was based in Moscow, and then it was moved to a monastery in Zagorsk – a town 70 kilometres to the north-east of Moscow now known by its pre-revolutionary name of Sergiev Posad.

The train I caught to Sergiev Posad had none of the snug comfort of the sleeper from Unecha. It was one of the many electric suburban shuttles that take Russians from Moscow to their country houses in the forests and villages outside the great city. These dachas are a cult in Russia, and some Russians spend months growing vegetables or raising poultry like their peasant ancestors. Those farmers' descendants still love the taste of homegrown food.

It has long been lucky for the country that they do. In 1940, the private patches that peasants were allowed to keep produced almost all of the eggs and milk they consumed, as well as half of the potatoes and milk for everyone else, thus compensating for the inefficiency of the collective farms. By 1990, privately produced food made up more than a quarter of all the food produced in Russia, despite being grown on less than 2 per cent of the land area. In times of economic collapse, Russians have had the backstop of their own gardens to keep them alive.

Russians with jobs, who cannot flee the city all summer, head out at weekends. This Saturday morning, my carriage was packed with them and sweltering. Temperatures reached 39 degrees in late July 2010. In a few weeks' time, fires in the forests and in dried peat bogs around Moscow would choke the city.

As the train set off with a rattle, I sweated against the plastic seat back and resented the couple opposite me whose legs were trespassing into my space.

I had been at a dreadful party hosted by a British diplomat the night before and had, in a fit of revenge against everyone in the world, got drunk and boorish. This morning I was still irritable. My eyes itched and my brain ached. As we rumbled out of the Kursk station, a procession of hawkers entered our carriage and loudly failed to interest us in the items they had for sale: nylon socks, potato peelers, radios. A gypsy boy came and played the accordion so badly I was tempted to pay him to go away.

The sun shone on the forest as we left the city behind.

The seminary at Zagorsk did not open immediately after the restoration of the Orthodox Church. At first instruction was given in Moscow. The first time that Father Dmitry and his classmates got to see the ancient seminary buildings was in May 1947, when they took this same railway line to celebrate mass in the glorious Assumption Cathedral, built under Ivan the Terrible and the centrepiece of Russia's holiest monastery.

That was where I was going on that baking-hot train. The trees flicked past the window. The grass beneath them was dry and sparse. There was a lot of summer still to come, and it was already the hottest since records began. In a couple of weeks, Russia would ban wheat exports in anticipation of a disastrous harvest and the world's food prices would soar in response.

The couple opposite me whose legs I had resented were now asleep. They were middle aged and heavy set. He wore a light-blue shirt and flat cap, while she wore a flowery dress and looked hot and flustered even with her eyes closed.

I too tried to doze, but I kept being knocked by other passengers. They were fare-dodgers, pushing up the train in the hope we would stop soon and they could run down the platform around behind the ticket inspectors to the already checked rear of the train. Their chances were slim. The inspectors worked in a team of four: two women and two burly men to keep order.

The woman opposite had tucked her arm through her husband's. She did not remove it even when asked to show her ticket, as if she were worried he might be stolen. Their tickets checked, she closed her eyes and laid her head back on his shoulder. He did not wake up, and slept with a slight smile. Their fondness for each other improved my mood considerably.

After an hour and a half of slow rattling we pulled into Sergiev Posad, a little town with factory chimneys and apartment blocks. I could not face walking far in the heat, so I asked a taxi to drive me to the great walled fortress of the monastery complex, then felt stupid for paying 150 roubles when the journey took less than a minute.

The monastery was founded here more than six centuries ago, when a young man built a wooden chapel. He was St Sergei, after whom the town was named. His asceticism did not stop him networking with princes, however. They asked him to bless their armies, and he secured a reputation as a national religious leader.

The complex has come a long way since Sergei's day, having been ruled by a succession of equally canny hierarchs and thus endowed with land and wealth by generations of tsars and aristocrats.

Today, it is a perfect fairy-tale mix of heavy white walls – to guard the monks against the threats of the world, such as a Tatar attack in 1408 and a Polish siege 200 years later – then, soaring above them, the elegant gold bulb of the Assumption Cathedral, topped by a cross so heavy it needs guy wires. Either side of the entrance gate, which is as weighty as any castle's, the icons are sheathed in clear plastic marked by hundreds of lipstick smears where women on pilgrimage stop to kiss them. As I walked in, thousands of pigeons strutted among the feet of the faithful, occasionally flying up to their roosts in the arrow slits of the high walls.

I had asked Oleg Sukhanov, press officer at the seminary, to show me around and was already late. He was large and moustached and wore black. He did not seem to mind my lateness, however, and bustled me through the crowd flowing into this perfect little city of Orthodox architecture.

The seminary was off to our right, through a garden. Inside, stairs stretched up to the first floor. The stairwell was screened by heavy mesh, like in a prison, as if to prevent suicides. It struck a jarring note, but I had no time to ask about it, since at the first landing Sukhanov strode left down a dark corridor lined with photographs of the seminary's alumni.

He showed me the dormitory: vaulted roof, whitewashed walls, unvarnished parquet floor. Each bed had a chair at its foot. They were so close together only a narrow bedside cupboard could fit between them. A handful of students were relaxing, wearing high-collared jackets like military cadets. The room did not look like it had been redecorated since Father Dmitry's day. The only new furniture was a row of cheap laminated wardrobes, the doors of which were already hanging askew.

My tour was at high speed, and next stop was the chapel. According to legend, when King Vladimir, who was to become the Russians' first Christian ruler after his conversion in 988, wanted to choose a religion, he sent emissaries to investigate all the faiths of his neighbours: Latin and Greek Christianity, Judaism and Islam. The embassy that sailed to Constantinople was so dazzled by the gold and ritual and incense of Hagia Sophia that they rushed back to tell him all about it. Theirs was an experience that visitors to Orthodox cathedrals still revel in today.

'When we stood in the temple,' they are said to have told him on their return, 'we hardly knew whether or not we were in heaven, for, in truth, upon earth it is impossible to behold such glory and magnificence; we could not tell all we have seen; there, verily, God has His dwelling among men, and the worship of other countries is as nothing. Never can we forget the grandeur which we saw. Whoever has enjoyed so sweet a sight can never elsewhere be satisfied, nor will we remain longer as we are.'

That was convincing enough for Vladimir. He converted to the Greek version of Christianity in a decision no doubt helped along by the Byzantine emperor offering one of his daughters as a bride. On entering that chapel in Sergiev Posad, I could see what those envoys had meant. Sometimes Orthodox churches are gaudy and vulgar, but this one was sublime. A sky-blue vaulted roof glowed gently in sunlight pouring through a glazed lantern. Frescoes of angels and saints sucked my eyes towards the ranks of gold-framed icons on the screen. An elegant chandelier dominated the middle of the space. Two women bowed in their whispered prayers. Another woman carefully straightened narrow yellow candles that were bending slightly in the warmth of the day.

Father Dmitry, raised in a village faith of whispered prayers in homemade churches, would have been entranced by the majesty of this chapel. I craned my neck back and traced the paintings and the structure. It was magnificent: awe-inspiring and calming all at once.

In a classroom down the corridor, trainee priests stared and giggled at laptops like students all over the world. A sombre oil painting of an intense religious discussion loomed on the wall behind them, with peasants clustered around a cross in a dark room. The students were young, handsome and in high spirits.

Sukhanov and I returned to the corridor with the photographs. Father Dmitry's year was the first picture on the left, because they were the first students to enter the seminary after it reopened. All the other years had formal portraits of the students and teachers gathered together. This one had eighteen separate pictures, which had clearly been gathered after the students had already left. Some of them were identified by name but most were not, and I could not find Father Dmitry among them.

Later accounts relate how he always loved talking and debating, a trait he learned from the father and grandfather that had introduced him to Christianity. They had taught him that religion is a living thing, something to be discussed and celebrated. His father had taught him phrases from the Bible, and they had explored them, asking what they meant. He must have been a rambunctious presence in class, and that alone was enough to make him stand out. In 1940s Russia, people who wanted to survive did not talk openly to strangers. Even relatives needed to be treated with caution.

Soviet children were raised on the story of Pavlik Morozov, a young boy whose body was found on the edge of his village in the Urals in 1932. According to the story pieced together (some say, invented) by the police, Pavlik had informed the authorities that his father, a poor peasant, was forging documents allowing kulaks to pass themselves off as ordinary citizens. On the basis of the evidence, his father was exiled. Pavlik was then murdered. Four of his family members – his grandparents, a godfather and a cousin – were executed for the crime, which was said to have been a bloody act of revenge.

The story, which is likely to have been fabricated but which was passed off as true, was turned into an opera, songs, plays and biographies. School groups visited Morozov's grave, and children were encouraged to believe that snitching on your own father was valuable if your father was working against the state. Martyrdom in the service of communism was the highest ideal. Stories such as this one established a generation gap between new, young Soviet people and the old patriarchal villages of their parents.

As the historian Orlando Figes put it: 'for anyone below the age of thirty, who had only ever known the Soviet world, or had inherited no other values from his family, it was almost impossible to step outside the propaganda system and question its political principles'.

Father Dmitry, however, had inherited other values from his family, and that made him no Pavlik Morozov. He did not inform on his own father, although his father attended secret religious ceremonies, nor on his grandfather.

By the end of the 1940s, the gulag camps all across the Soviet Union contained more than 2.5 million people – a million more than in 1945 – and a similar number of people were in internal exile. From the second half of 1948 onwards, the police began rearresting former political prisoners by the alphabet.

'I have long noticed your anti-Soviet spirit. You have read one or two sermons, and you're already conceited. You want to reshape everything,' said the professor who taught the students how to preach. Dmitry, when asked his opinion of the Bolshevik killing of the tsar and his family, replied that it was brutal, and that he pitied the children. That was an unwise thing to say, and by now the authorities had their eye on him. He had always loved writing. Inspired by the Psalms, he used poems as a way of exploring the same issues he liked to debate: his country, history, God.

One older fellow student asked to read his poems. Dmitry, a village boy and untrained in the ways of the security services, assented. The student handed the poems to the KGB.

Prosecutors seized on a poem of his that described Stalin as an 'executioner' and the 'first destroyer'. Father Dmitry's brother Vladimir gave me a package of poems in Berezina, but I could not find this one among them. Perhaps he destroyed any other unwisely political ones long ago. The poems I was given had gently nationalist themes, but nothing so outspoken.

'Russia, I think of you always / and I am greatly concerned for your destiny,' says one. Another tells how he loves Russia for 'her tears, which she shares with him'. I wondered how many of these poems had been read by his fellow students.

In the corridor of photos, I took out a torch so we could better see the faces in the pictures. One of these men informed on him to the police. Who knows what reasons led him to denounce his fellow student? Often informers were people who were themselves at risk of arrest – children of kulaks, or members of supposedly suspicious minorities such as Jews or Poles – who were forced to denounce or be denounced.

Then again, a seminary with its concentration of believers was likely to have been a particular focus of suspicion, and agents would have kept a close watch on what was happening there. In the 1940s, there is said to have been at least one informer for every six or seven families in Moscow as a whole, and the Church would have been under still closer scrutiny. Perhaps then the man who sent Father Dmitry to jail was just doing it for money or a better flat.

The night before his arrest, Father Dmitry wrote later, he dreamed that a cross came towards him, that he carried it on his right shoulder and that it became heavier and heavier, until he woke up. He was arrested in central Moscow while calling on a sick friend.

He had to wait until Stalin's death before studying at the reopened seminary in Sergiev Posad. He was arrested before Easter 1948, and the seminary did not move out of central Moscow until the autumn.

His troubles are not mentioned in the official history of the college. Stalinism is too embarrassing an episode to be remembered at all in fact, and the book describes the 1940s simply as a busy time when the trainee priests had to share their premises with several educational establishments already based in Sergiev Posad. The chapel was home to a social club, the historian wrote, and students played ball on the open ground between the seminary and the cathedral.

'The schoolchildren with their cries and running about, the grown-ups hurrying about their affairs, the students playing their games – all of this created an atmosphere of vanity, of hubbub, having nothing in common with a monastery. On top of this was a club built next to our bedrooms and classrooms,' he wrote. A reader knowing nothing of the context would assume these were the only difficulties the priests faced, and the book does not record Father Dmitry's arrest or the undoubted lesson it must have taught the others of the dangers of speaking out.

43

The book does list Father Dmitry as graduating from the seminary, the first part of the institution. But he is not listed as having finished the second part of the college – the academy – until 1960. There is no explanation why it took him a decade longer than anyone else to complete his education, but those were the years he spent in the camps. I stepped out of the seminary, musing over the strange amnesia that had settled over the place. I walked out of the green gates and pushed through the crowds to the Assumption Cathedral, where the students worshipped and sang the liturgy on Father Dmitry's first visit here.

The sweet smell of perfume and the cool gloom were a comfort after the heat, glare and dust of the yard. Candles flickered, lighting the pillars as they towered up to the dome. A huge heavy gold screen bore rank after rank of saints in their strange, stylized clothing.

Jesus said, when asked whether it was correct to pay taxes, 'Render unto Caesar the things which are Caesar's, and unto God, the things that are God's.' It is an injunction that theologians have struggled to interpret ever since, as it apparently demands complete obedience to the government while also demanding obedience to God.

Western theologians come from a tradition where the pope ruled the Church and kings ruled countries. They are able to separate the two kinds of authority and create a doctrine of resistance to secular authority if conscience demands it. But Orthodox theologians have never had that luxury, making the bishops' task of relating to a government that explicitly wanted to destroy the Church very hard.

Orthodox Churches draw their lineage back to the traditions of the Byzantine Empire when the emperor was both the ruler of the state and the protector of the Church. There is no theological basis for rebelling against the government, since it is assumed to be from God, even when that government is sworn to the Church's destruction.

'Every religious idea, every idea of God, every flirting with the idea of God, is unutterable vileness,' said Lenin. 'Millions of filthy deeds, acts of violence and physical contagions are less dangerous than the subtle, spiritual idea of a God decked out in the smartest "ideological" costumes.'

Stalin's restoration of the Orthodox Church was marked by the almost complete penetration of the hierarchy by the security organs. Patriarch Alexy I, who headed the Russian Orthodox Church after its restoration, was highly valued by the KGB as an agent of influence, according to documents smuggled out of Russia by former KGB archivist Vasili Mitrokhin.

'The Russian Orthodox Church supports the totally peaceful foreign policy of our government, not because the Church allegedly lacks freedom, but because Soviet policy is just and corresponds to the Christian ideals which the Church preaches,' said Patriarch Alexy in 1955.

Bishops remained sycophantic to the end, praising Khrushchev and later communist leaders even while the KGB were arresting Christians. Where now the Catholic Church in Poland is able to praise believers who were oppressed by the communist government, and to expel collaborators, the Orthodox Church in Russia has a much harder time. This is partly because it does not have a core of leaders who resisted the government.

Anatoly Oleynikov, the last deputy chairman of the KGB, said in 1991 that only 15–20 per cent of priests refused to work with the security organs. Priests who refused to help the KGB were not promoted, and thus were denied access to the highest positions. The last two Soviet-era patriarchs – Pimen and Alexy II – were full KGB agents.

Even though the communist regime is gone, the Church is still unsure how to relate to those priests like Father Dmitry who were imprisoned for the faith. As the little history of the seminary shows, it often finds it easier to ignore the fact that they ever existed.

This identification of the Church with the state was not new of course. The Church had been almost completely suborned to the tsarist state as well. But, before communism, it could pretend to be serving God by doing so, since the tsarist government supported the Christian faith. The Soviet state was committed to eradicating religion, and expended considerable effort in attempting to do so. According to Father Dmitry, his fellow priests being trained in Sergiev Posad only very rarely put up a fight against the state's atheism.

'They made informers out of the students at the spiritual academy, and out of priests. They called them in and started to play on their sense of truth, on their love of the homeland, promised them better positions. Sadly, positions in the Church, although the Church is separated from the state, are assigned by the secular authorities,' Father Dmitry wrote later. 'I was never called in anywhere, not when I studied in the academy, nor when I became a priest. One academy student who gave in to them, a weak-willed but kind man, told me in secret that I was considered a double-dyed anti-Soviet, a desperate person.'

The name of the man who informed on Father Dmitry was Vasily Petrovykh. Petrovykh graduated in 1947 and served as a priest in a remote village in the Kostroma region to the east of Moscow, which was not much of a reward for co-operating with the security services. Still, he had a wife and two sons, so perhaps he was not given a choice. Besides, co-operation was so widespread that not everyone who helped the security services could be given a high-profile job.

Back on the station platform, cheap posters announced special church services in aid of those in prison; for those suffering from depression, apathy, desolation and suicidal thoughts; and for the dead. The Church, despite its long repression and then its close association with a brutal regime, has returned to its role as the comforter of the lowest in society.

After Father Dmitry's arrest, and while in detention, he dreamed of Stalin with an axe, teaching his friends how to kill people. He dreamed of being brought before Stalin in his underwear. 'My conscience would not allow me to admit my guilt,' he wrote later of his dream encounter with the dictator. 'To speak the truth would mean to undergo torture. I decided to speak the truth. How can I speak untruth when there is so much suffering, when I am standing before him with bound hands, and he continued to teach those around him how to punish? And I woke up with that feeling.'

He was not able to express such nobility at his real trial, though he won the small triumph of stopping his tormentors from swearing in his presence. He tried to justify his poem's criticism of Stalin by saying that atheists killed the spirit of people, but it was not an argument that won him much ground.

Eventually the prosecutor told him to write down his confession, to write the words 'I consider myself to be guilty. I slandered Soviet reality.'

But Father Dmitry refused. He said that he did not consider himself guilty: 'I spoke the truth. Come with me, and I will show you what is being done. I will show you my suffering father, I will show you the exhausted people.'

It did not sway his accusers. He got ten years in the gulag for distributing anti-Soviet poems. There was no appeal. The village lad had been through starvation, brutality, the imprisonment of his father, destitution, war, occupation, conscription, injury, arrest and now imprisonment. He was only twenty-six years old, and his life was still ahead of him.

As my train waited at one of the little stations on the way back to Moscow, an express thundered past in the opposite direction. Despite the noise they make, Russian trains are rarely very quick, and I had plenty of time to read the destination boards bolted to the side of each carriage: Vorkuta.

Vorkuta is in the far north and, if I wanted to retrace Father Dmitry's route into the camps of the gulag, I would need to take that train too. After his sentencing, he was sent up the rails to Inta in the Komi Republic, at the northern end of the Ural Mountains. By the late 1940s Komi was one vast prison, where the tundra took the place of a fence: frozen solid in winter, impassable swamp in summer.

Back in Moscow, the returning Muscovites from my train streamed on to the platform of the Kursk station. Progress was slow, held up by a crowd that had gathered to watch an old drunk arguing with three fashionable teenagers. He was furious at some slight, and two policemen had to hold him back as he tried to swing punches. The teenagers' smug smiles and the officers' chuckles simply enraged him all the more.

Eventually, the policemen tired of the game and released his arms, at which point he collapsed on to the grimy, soggy tarmac and wriggled like a turtle on a jar, shouting abuse as the three teenagers walked away. I went inside to buy my ticket north.

3

Father Dmitry was K-956

From my upper bunk, the forest shuffled past very slowly. Every kilometre a sign – a square of metal or a neat little lozenge of concrete – told me how far we were from Moscow, with smaller signs counting off the tenths of a kilometre in between. I mused about how much paint it must take to keep them bright and shining, and what on earth they were for. The only reasonable explanation was to provide something of interest for passengers on the train to look at, but it seemed an incredible amount of effort for such a minimal reward. After a kilometre or two, they lost their appeal almost entirely.

The town of Inta, where Father Dmitry served his sentence for writing poems, is 2,000 kilometres from Moscow. Getting there would take thirty-six sweltering hours. I scribbled a calculation, that is 55 kilometres an hour; another calculation: 34 miles an hour. If that was our average between Moscow and Inta, it was no wonder it felt like we were going slowly. You can drive more quickly in many built-up areas, and this was very far from being a built-up area. There were no houses of any kind. The trees were dense and monotonous: solid, prickly and dark.

Sometimes we would rattle through villages, clutches of log-built houses huddled close to the tracks. But fewer than half the houses had anything planted outside. Most were still secure against the weather, their roofs were whole, but no one lived there. If someone did, they would have filled every available hectare with potatoes against the winter. Outside the villages the fields were choked with weeds: no livestock, no crops. The only farm animals I saw all day were a dozen geese in a garden.

One of the most striking statistics about modern Russia is that, of the 153,000 villages in the country in 1989, some 20,000 have been abandoned. Another 35,000 have fewer than ten people. The population has fallen faster in cities, however, meaning that the proportion of Russians living in villages has actually gone up over that period. This is a practically unique example of a modern, developed country deurbanizing.

The economy of the far north has all but vanished. It was based on subsidized coal mines and, now the subsidies are gone, as are most of the factories that burned coal, so the mines have not been able to stay open. In Soviet times, workers received special high wages for working in the north, but those rates are gone too. The knock-on effect of the mine closures has touched everything the Soviets created in the Arctic. Shops cannot stay open without people to buy their goods. Factories cannot stay open so far from their markets. The railway line I was travelling on was built to tie the Arctic into the Russian economy but, that whole day, the only two other trains I saw were passenger trains. There were no goods being shipped either north or south.

Somewhere to the north-west of me, in 1923, the OGPU security service, which would later be renamed the NKVD, then the KGB, then the FSB, opened its first labour prison. That first link in what became the chain of gulag camps was on the Solovetsky Islands in the White Sea. It opened when Father Dmitry was just a year old. The island camp held several thousand men by 1925.

But feeding and guarding prisoners in such a remote location was expensive. The government in Moscow needed every rouble to build its new economy. The camps would have to pay their way. That meant that, over time, they were forced to evolve into profitable enterprises. They did this by a key innovation: feeding prisoners a quantity of food proportionate to the amount of work they did. This killed off weaklings early, meaning that non-productive inmates did not have to be carried by those strong enough to fell timber, make bricks, dig coal or do any of the other tasks left to prisoners in the fastnesses of the Soviet state.

It was economically successful, since it meant camps could be pushed into areas barely habitable and exploit their resources for the first time. Decades later, this expansion was chronicled by Alexander Solzhenitsyn, a Red Army officer jailed for making jokes about Stalin, who became the historian of the camp system. After his release in the 1950s, he collected accounts from other former inmates, and welded them together into a great sprawling epic of oral history that he called *The Gulag Archipelago*.

Solzhenitsyn compared the camp system itself to a cancer, spreading from its original point of mutation on the Solovetsky Islands – colloquially known as Solovki. Camp officials were aggressive cancer cells, the camps they set up were the secondary growths. Instead of voyaging up blood vessels and lymph canals as cancers do in the body, the metastasizing prison system spread up railways and rivers.

'In the summer of 1929 an expedition of unconvoyed prisoners was sent to the Chibyu River from Solovki,' he wrote. 'The expedition was successful – and camp was set up on the Ukhta, Ukhtlag. But it, too, did not stand still on its own spot, but quickly metastasized to the north-east, annexed the Pechora, and was transformed into UkhtPechlag. Soon afterwards it had Ukhta, Inta, Pechora, and Vorkuta sections – all of them the bases of great independent future camps.'

The conditions, he wrote, were 'twelve months of winter, the rest summer'. The camps expanded rapidly in the 1920s and 1930s, when the likes of Father Dmitry's father were imprisoned. But they became still worse in the 1940s when the war stretched the country's resources and left even free citizens hungry, let alone prisoners. Work norms increased, while food rations were cut. According to statistics published later, 352,560 prisoners died in 1942, which was one in four of the prison population. In 1943, the death rate improved slightly, and only one in five prisoners died: 267,826 people.

Solzhenitsyn wrote how nothing was wasted on human comforts, not even to honour the dead. 'At one time in Old Russia it was thought that a corpse could not get along without a coffin. Even the lowliest serfs, beggars, and tramps were buried in coffins,' he wrote. 'When at Inta after the war one honoured foreman of the woodworking plant was actually buried in a coffin, the Cultural and Educational Section was instructed to make propaganda: work well and you, too, will be buried in a wooden coffin.'

More than two million people died in the camps of the gulag during the war years, many of them building this railway line I was travelling on. When Nazi Germany invaded the Soviet Union, its troops rapidly overran the rich coal fields around Donetsk in Ukraine. Stalin's government, in desperate need of fuel, charged the prisoners with laying rails across the tundra to Inta – founded in 1942 – and to Vorkuta. The rails laid, the prisoners that survived worked in the mines to produce the coal to keep the factories churning out bombs and guns.

The soldiers and the factory workers are honoured now. Surviving veterans are greeted by the president every Victory Day, afforded special privileges, given medals. Its triumph in World War Two has, if anything, become ever more sacred to the country as the years have passed. The role of the prisoners in forging that victory has been all but forgotten, however, even though many of them had committed no crime at all and worked harder than anyone. They were guilty only of being slightly richer than their neighbours, or of failing to join a collective farm, or of telling a joke. Their torment is largely unacknowledged in Russia today.

Although Vladimir Putin in 2010, during his spell as prime minister between his two stints as president, made *The Gulag Archipelago* compulsory reading for schoolchildren in their eleventh year, he does not encourage modern historians to delve into the past. The KGB's files are closed to all but a chosen few, and there has been little acknowledgement of the oppressors' guilt from Russia's new supposedly democratic government.

As the train rattled along, I had a strange feeling that the suffering of every one of those forgotten victims had, because it was unacknowledged, hung around in the air like the spirits of unburied children. The haze would be purple, I thought, and so dense that no breeze could disperse it. As fresh prisoners came to replace those who died at work, the suffering built up into a great pulsing tube. The tube followed the railway line, until it became an artery linking the cancerous organs of the camp system. To the north it flowed round the bump of Inta, before ending in the coal fields of Vorkuta. To the south, it converged with dozens of other tubes at the great beating heart of the KGB headquarters on Lubyanka Square. From there, arteries spread in all directions. Some stretched east and north through Siberia to the camps of Norilsk; others went beyond that to the far east and over the sea – where the purple congealed on the waves in a loathsome slick – to the nightmares that were Magadan and Kolyma.

As I lay sweating on my damp bunk, the hallucination became real for a second, and I could see the purple outside the windows, filtering the sunlight pouring into our carriage. My neighbours did not notice it. Perhaps they were used to it. Almost everyone in the north is a prisoner, or the child of a prisoner, or the wife of a prisoner, or the friend of a prisoner, or the jailer of a prisoner. The purple miasma clings to them all, and affects how they speak and behave. It makes them cautious and unfriendly and distrustful. It was only me, the visitor, who could see it.

Most of my neighbours on the train were returning from holiday, still wearing T-shirts bearing the names of Russia's seaside resorts in the Caucasus: Sochi, Anapa, Tuapse. In the two bunks beneath me was a middle-aged couple – he had a moustache, she had tight shorts. They kept themselves to themselves, and rebuffed my occasional attempts to chat. In fairness, my overtures were self-serving. If I had made friends with them, I could have occasionally sat on their bunks. As it was, I not only had no one to talk with to pass the time, but had to pass the time lying on my bunk looking at the trees and checking my speed calculation.

Our station stops were entirely random. We would pull into what looked like a decent-sized town and chug out again after a couple of minutes. Then we would wait for half an hour at a platform carved out of the forest, where there were no shops and no one got on or off.

My two neighbours alighted at the stop for Syktyvkar and were replaced by two muscled lads in their twenties. Much to my delight, they invited me down to sit with them, meaning I could get off my sweaty mattress for the first time that day. They regaled me with tales of working on the North Stream gas pipeline, which will pump gas to Western Europe.

We drank beer and they swapped tales of industrial accidents. A comrade had slipped off the top of the pipe and broken his leg. A foreman had stepped back to check a weld, fallen off the scaffolding and broken his back. The other one laughed at that. It was far worse, he said, working for foreign contractors, since they make you check your welds until there are no leaks at all, and that takes hours.

One of them, Sergei, came from Inta and had nothing to say in its favour.

'It's a dying town,' he said, and asked where I would be staying. I mentioned the name of the hotel, and he just laughed. 'If you can call it a hotel.'

My heart sank a little as I climbed back to my bunk for the night.

When I awoke – it was hard to call it morning, since it never gets dark in summer this far north – the black humps of the Ural Mountains had heaved themselves over the horizon to the east. They were streaked with snow, and looked menacing and old.

The man who drove me from the station to town pointed out the last working coal mine. Otherwise, the town was sinking back into the swamp it was born of.

'I used to work in that one,' he said, as we passed another shuttered working.

Father Dmitry, like most of the prisoners who came through here, worked in the mines. The pressing need for coal of the war years had passed by the late 1940s. Coal was far more accessible and of better quality in Ukraine. But the logic of power in the gulag meant that the bosses' empires were untouchable. To close the mines here would have deprived someone of influence, so the coal was hewn out of the ground, loaded on to trucks and sent south to feed the Soviet machine, whether it was needed or not.

One story Father Dmitry liked to tell was how, in the coal mine, he asked the lift operator to hold the controls while he spoke to people on the level below. He lay on the ground, with his head over the shaft and shouted down to them. He focused on the conversation and did not notice when a comrade screamed for him to get back, that the lift was coming. The lift operator had forgotten his promise, and the cage was speeding down towards the back of his head. At that point, a Moldovan called Stan screamed 'in a voice', Father Dmitry wrote, 'of the kind used at the front'.

He looked back, and the cage passed within inches of his face. 'Everyone was terribly worked up, but I was calm, I somehow did not sense the danger. I still don't.'

Father Dmitry arrived in the camps in 1948, the year the government cracked down in earnest on the freedoms Soviet citizens had come to enjoy during the chaos of World War Two. To show how alien this was to what was happening elsewhere in the world, 1948 was the year when Britain founded the National Health Service, when the United States gifted Marshall Aid to Western Europe, and when the United Nations adopted the Universal Declaration of Human Rights.

In 1948, the Soviet government divided the inmates in two. The prisoners called 'criminals' – those guilty of murder, rape and other ordinary crimes – were now housed separately from those convicted of political crimes. The number of 'politicals', who now got a tougher routine, had increased. Among the camp inmates were hundreds of thousands of returning prisoners of war – traitors for having surrendered in battle. There were also unruly elements from all the lands – Latvia, Estonia, Lithuania, East Prussia, Bessarabia, Karelia, Poland and so on – that had been added to the Soviet empire after the war. They were all put to work.

Father Dmitry, a half-educated peasant boy, was locked up as a political prisoner and thrown together with professors and officers and priests from all over Eastern Europe. The camps were full of Poles, Balts and Germans, and even the occasional Westerner marooned here by bureaucracy.

It was a university, and many of the lessons were brutal. One professor, Father Dmitry wrote, complained about his treatment and was locked in the punishment cell immediately. The punishment cell was four walls and no roof – in winter. The professor came out chastened and never spoke up again. They were called by number – Father Dmitry was K-956 – not by name, and worked fourteen-hour days until they were skeletal and exhausted.

One Lithuanian became so emaciated that he gained extra rations, but he did not eat them. Something inside his brain had snapped. He squirrelled them away in his suitcase, until he was sent to the hospital wing and died.

Prisoners could receive one letter a year. They had ten minutes to eat lunch.

'From this hard life a lot of people became grasses, informers, so as to somehow ease their lives: many of them were killed. One Lithuanian informer was killed when he had just a month until his release.'

From the earliest days of the camps, prisoners had found solace in religion. The violence between different groups of prisoners, and from guards, encouraged individuals to form groups, to seek out like-minded inmates to share their troubles with. The rituals of Christianity helped many of them find comfort, and helped encourage them to believe in a world outside the fences and tundra that surrounded them.

'I stayed joyous and optimistic for a long time, and then I too suffered these bleak thoughts, that I would never get out of there ... My only release was that there was another life, there was God. He sees all our sufferings. When I told the prisoners that our sufferings would end, they looked at me like I was a baby who doesn't understand life. And when I told them I had been at the front – so as to say that I wasn't a baby – they didn't believe me.'

When Father Dmitry was in Inta the prisoners lived in long wooden barracks. Those are all but gone now, having rotted into the muck like many of the buildings that replaced them. The conditions in the Russian Arctic are so severe that the weather will find the smallest weakness in a building, squeeze its way in like an infection and reduce it to a hump of masonry and wood in just a few years.

My car dropped me off outside the Northern Girl hotel, identified by a sign above a doorway in a block of flats near the central square. The lobby housed a cosmetics kiosk. At the reception window was a blonde woman who clearly spent much of her spare time trying out the kiosk's products.

I had not reserved a room, but that was fine. The price was 1,800 roubles – about £36. That seemed steep, but it was manageable. I handed over my passport. That was when she realized I was a foreigner, and I needed to pay a 'coefficient' of three. She consulted her calculator.

'That means 5,400 roubles,' she said with finality.

Many Soviet institutions once had a double price scale, with foreigners made to pay vastly higher prices than locals, but it is now supposed to be illegal. I told her so. I told her I would not pay over £100 for a hotel in Moscow, even if it had a spa, pool and sauna, and refused to pay her charge. She rang her administrator, who came down and tried to ring the manager. He was not there, so she rang the former manager, who expressed surprise that he was being consulted on a business he had nothing to do with, and rang off. She then, inexplicably, rang the Federal Migration Service, who also could not help. I would still, they told me, have to pay the 5,400 roubles. I refused.

At this point, and seemingly randomly, the administrator offered me a revised coefficient of 1.2, which allowed them to save face and me to save money. We had a deal.

It was only when I was sat on the chair in my bedroom, which had a single bed, a chair and a kettle and was on the ground floor facing a yard, that I realized that – in half an hour of haggling – neither of the women had expressed any interest at all in my visit to Inta. This was a small town, in a wilderness, an overnight train journey from the nearest airport, with no tourist amenities or business opportunities. And yet, they were acting as if foreigners swanned in and out all the time. This was a blow, since hotel receptionists tend to be a key source of help in a new town. On my way out, I tried to engage the heavily made-up woman in conversation. The few miners left, she said, earn 20,000 roubles a month sometimes but normally around 14,000.

The town's coal is no longer in demand, and the shafts are largely worked out. The population peaked above 60,000 in 1989. Now only half that many people are registered as living in Inta, and many of those really work somewhere else. The trend is repeated in Komi as a whole. At the end of the Soviet period, one and a quarter million people lived in this region. Now there are 950,000 – a population decline of 25 per cent in twenty years.

I hoped the receptionist might ask about me about what I was doing in her crumbling town. But she showed no more interest in me than she had the first time round.

My fallback plan was Inta Museum, which would I hoped be full of information on the gulag. After all, the town had no other history, and the exhibits would have to include something. Here too my foreign nationality cost me extra, though I got my money's worth, since they had no 50-rouble tickets. The woman behind the cash desk had to tear out separately five 10-rouble tickets along the edge of her ruler. Another woman was ready to take my coat but I was not wearing one. It was far too hot for anyone to be wearing anything more than a shirt, and I was the only visitor, so she was presumably not having a very busy day.

The museum's first room was devoted to the Soviet Union's Victory in World War Two, under the slogan 'The victory was forged in the gulag too'. There was a photo of the order signed on 22 July 1941 which had kept all prisoners locked up for the duration. That order kept Father Dmitry's father in the camps for an extra five years on top of his four-year sentence. The exhibit did not mention the two million gulag prisoners who had died forging the victory.

The room devoted to coal had a roundabout way of showing the drop in the workforce. Coal production had dropped from 9,099,000 tonnes in 1989 to 4,851 tonnes in 2001. During that period each worker had become almost twice as efficient. I did not need to do the sums to realize the heart had been ripped out of the town.

An old woman walked the museum with me. She turned on the lights in each room; sat down to check I examined all the exhibits; turned off the lights after me. I trudged round, then asked if the direc- tor was in her office and whether I might speak to her. She was not. And no one else would have anything to tell me, apparently.

The director's secretary gave off the air of someone who received so many requests for access that she would rather corral all the visitors into one group before allowing them past. I would have to come back. It was to be another two days before I finally made it into the direc- tor's presence.

The day stretched before me, so I set out to explore. Every building looked tired. The one bit of fresh paint I saw – bright orange used to smarten up an arch leading into an otherwise ordinary courtyard – had been defaced with the single scrawled word 'cock', and a crude sketch of male genitalia. Walking on, I headed for two factory chim- neys that dominated the town. Built of dark brick, one bore the date 1952 and a red star. Father Dmitry must have seen this being built. Perhaps he had helped build it. The factory – a power station – was not working, and I briefly wondered if the only thing more depressing than a belching factory chimney was a non-belching factory chimney, before ordering myself to cheer up.

A minibus slowed down enticingly so I climbed on board and rode to the end of the line on a whim. Here the apartment blocks were invisible, and the Great Inta River surged past, muscles flexing beneath its khaki surface. This had once been a region of wooden houses and gardens on the bluff above the river. They were rotten and collapsed now, the gardens choked with stagnant grass. The entrance gates to the Kapital coal mine gaped, and the mine's lift tower stood a hundred metres away. Thickly lagged pipes rose up over the gates into a square-sided arch. The pipes were lifted high to allow trucks to pass safely underneath, but no trucks had come this way for years.

At the end of a long track was a cemetery, filled with Lithuanian names and birch trees. The mosquitoes poured out of the damp grass, covering my arms and clustering at my ankles. They were stupid and easy to kill, not like the streetwise ones in Moscow that know how to hide on dark patches so you cannot spot them against the background. But here they swarmed in such numbers that I could not keep up with them and I was bitten a dozen times in a minute. A path led through the wood, between the graves, to a monument of a woman in Lithuanian national dress bearing a ball in her left hand. On the back, in several languages, it said, 'To those who did not return'.

Although the gulag is generally imagined to have been unbearably cold, for many prisoners it was the blood-sucking parasites during the summers that caused the most torment. The writer Oleg Volkov, on lying down to sleep on his first night on Solovki, was appalled to see bedbugs dropping on to him from the ceiling. There were so many he could not sleep, and went outside. There the clouds of mosquitoes were equally intolerable.

Guards used the mosquitoes as a punishment, stripping off recalcitrant prisoners and tying them to posts in the forest. Their whole bodies would swell up. As I fled the graveyard I had a glimpse of that torment. The mosquitoes might not blot out the sun but, given the chance, they could swell your face enough to turn you blind.

For half an hour I waited for the bus to return. Then I got tired of beating off the mosquitoes and walked.

There did not seem to be much else to do, so I retreated to the Barakuda bar and took out the thick bundle of papers that is *Two Years in Abez*, a memoir by A. A. Vaneyev, a former inmate of a camp a few dozen kilometres to the north of here, and an account of life inside. I had been carrying a few books around with me, including Father

Dmitry's various volumes of memoirs and a couple of books on the gulag. Vaneyev's manuscript was the only one I had yet to read, so I `~red a beer and settled in.

`ook is mainly a description of the writer's relations with Lev a religious philosopher who fled St Petersburg after the lution. After wanderings in Europe, he found a new home ua which, between the two world wars, was an independent learned Lithuanian and became an inspiration to a generation rthodox writers.

In 1939, Stalin and Hitler carved up Europe between them, and Stalin got Lithuania – as well as eastern Poland, Estonia, Latvia and various other places that took his fancy – while Hitler got western Poland and a free hand with France. This inglorious episode is one that modern Russia prefers to forget. The two dictators fell out a couple of years later, and their armies would chew Lithuania to pieces between them over the course of World War Two. Eventually, however, Stalin came out on top and thousands of patriotic Lithuanians ended up here: many of them, like Karsavin, for ever.

One of the strangest quirks of the gulag was that, although it took no interest in keeping prisoners alive when they were healthy, it provided hospitals to nurse them back to health when they were sick. Karsavin, born in 1882 and thus an old man when he was arrested in 1949, never left the hospital.

The memoir's main theme is how life continued in the camp. Professors of all subjects and priests of all religions were happy to discuss their disciplines with each other and anyone else who was interested. The camp was surrounded by barbed wire, bitterly cold in the winter and plagued by mosquitoes in summer, but it was a strange kind of haven from the horrors Stalin unleashed on the Soviet Union in his last paranoid years.

'When they brought us here,' Vaneyev wrote, 'all of these circumstances created a terrible impression. With time, however, they became somehow familiar and did not stop us living. And life went on in its own way, not so much independent of the circumstances, but finding its own unexpected way within them.'

The strange side-effect of the influx of educated people from all over Russia and Eastern Europe was that the camps had a freedom

absent in the Soviet Union as a whole. Stalin's last year featured crack-
downs on, among others, biologists who believed in Charles Darwin's
theory of natural selection through inherited characteristics. Stalin
favoured the non-scientific but ideologically purer Trofim Lysenko,
whose idea that you could pass on to your children characteristics
you had acquired during your lifetime squared with the communists'
desire to perfect human beings.

One of Stalin's last acts was to unleash an anti-Semitic campaign
against the Jews, marked by the arrests of Kremlin doctors who were
allegedly plotting against him. Stalin had come to believe that Jewish
nationalists were all American spies and wanted them dismissed from
their jobs and arrested.

In the gulag, however, none of this mattered since everyone shared
the same miserable conditions, Russians, and Jews, Darwinists and
charlatans alike. The bedside of the ailing Karsavin became a debating club and a university for young men like Vaneyev. In one of the
most touching exchanges, the doctor orders the debaters out of his
hospital ward when a winter evening has gone on too long.

'It is so cold, is it not time to go to your homes?' Then he paused. 'Oh
my God. What have we come to, when we call these barracks home,
where your only home is a bed and a table. Terrible, terrible. And this
is by our standards comfort, most people don't even have this.'

People, infinitely adaptable, found a way to survive even here. They
even adapted to the mosquitoes. There are stories of the insects swarm-
ing in numbers large enough to suffocate reindeer; of reindeer herds
so maddened they will drown in rivers to escape the bites. People of
Vaneyev's age called the mosquitoes Messerschmitts after the German
fighter planes, and delighted in killing them. One evening Vaneyev sat
with Karsavin in the open air, along with Nikolai Punin, husband of
the poet Anna Akhmatova, when a mosquito alighted on the professor's bald head. Karsavin did not brush it off, but allowed it to drink
his blood and fly off.

'You are like a Buddhist,' Punin remarked.

'Not in everything,' Karsavin answered. 'However, I definitely sympathize a little with the Buddhists' attitude to small living things.'

'If you love mosquitoes, you should have driven that one off before
it got too fat,' Punin replied.

At that moment, a second mosquito landed on Punin. 'You'll never make a Buddhist out of me,' he said, and killed it.

Back at the museum, the director's secretary was once more coldly obstructive to my attempts to gain access to her boss. Eventually, enough time passed and she relented, though if I thought my troubles were over, I was wrong. The director – Yevgeniya Ivanovna Kulygina – greeted me with all the warmth of a border guard. I had expected her to be friendly, to be glad someone was taking an interest in the gulag, so it came as a shock when she demanded my passport and my press accreditation, insisting that I explain myself and the nature of my journey. I told her I was trying to trace the movements of Father Dmitry, at which point she asked me what I already knew.

Cross with my reception, I then described what I knew of his life in ludicrous detail, from his birth in Berezina to his father's imprisonment, to his service in the army, his education in Moscow and finally his arrival here.

'Well then, you know more than us,' she said coldly, and told me there was nothing more she could do to help. I was spoiling for an argument, and she was swelling like a thundercloud, when the door opened and a second woman walked in, middle aged and short haired. She greeted the director as Zhenya, the diminutive of her first name, and introduced herself to me as Tanya Podrabinek.

Surprised by being greeted warmly for the first time since my arrival in Inta, I told her that I knew a man called Alexander Podrabinek in Moscow. Were they by any chance related?

He was her brother-in-law. And it was as if a switch had flicked. Yevgeniya Ivanovna's frown vanished. She sank back in her chair and smiled. Tanya put the kettle on, and suddenly it was decided that we should all go to Abez the next day together, because – apparently – Father Dmitry had spent time in the camp there. The table filled with pie and coffee, and the room with buzz. At times, there seemed to be more conversations than people, especially with the arrival of Nikolai Andreyevich, a greying man summoned for my benefit. He was renowned for his knowledge of the gulag camps and lectured everyone with good-natured persistence.

Yevgeniya Ivanovna had delighted earlier in telling me I would never make it back to Moscow, that train tickets would be unobtainable and that I was mad to have come all this way without a return berth. Now, she was on the phone reserving me a ticket.

After a couple of cups of tea, she tried to talk me out of leaving at all. I should marry a local girl, she said, and suggested a few candidates. I shrugged apologetically. I was married already.

'Ah, no problem, she can move here too and you can live like political exiles. Phone her up now and invite her,' she said, holding out the phone.

An hour earlier I had been sitting on a hard bench in the gloomy lobby failing to gain access to this very room. Three-quarters of an hour earlier, we had been on the brink of a full-scale row. Now it was like we had been friends for ever.

I had read many times about how, in the Soviet Union, access to almost anything was a function of who you knew, but I had never witnessed such a dramatic example of it. If Tanya had walked in ten minutes later, or had failed to mention her surname, I would never have achieved anything. As it was, I was having a great time. I reached for another piece of pie. It was made with berries that grew on the tundra and was delicious.

Nikolai Andreyevich was all the while piling relevant books and magazines in front of me. It became rather overwhelming. When I mentioned that I would like to talk to someone who had known Inta in the years when Father Dmitry was here, he grabbed the phone and began to make calls.

That was why an hour or two later, he and I were sat at a small table in a sixth-floor flat. David Badaryan had had little warning of our arrival, but our welcome was warm: stew, rice, cutlets, cheese, ham, tomatoes, bread and shot glasses for the vodka we had brought with us.

He was an Armenian from Tbilisi, and had been arrested in August 1942 aged seventeen and sentenced to a decade in the gulag for some non-specific anti-Soviet activity ('They accused me of being in anti-Soviet groups. I was a teenager. What groups could I have been in?'). He was in the Urals for six years before arriving in the town in the same year as Father Dmitry.

'A lot of people said it was bad and of course it was. But when they brought us here, we thought it was heaven. There were barracks to live in, and a bathhouse. When we came to the Urals we lived in a tent, in winter. Some mornings you would wake up with your hair frozen to the bed,' he said.

He wore a blue shirt and dark-blue jacket. He had a neat moustache and almost no hair on his head at all.

'My first impression of Inta was the cold, but then I saw the northern lights. You cannot imagine. They went round round round, up up up up then down. You never see them like this now, it is rare. It was so beautiful, but so cold. It was minus 50, minus 52 sometimes.'

He worked in a deep mine, 300 metres down, for four years. He showed me a photo of himself in 1949. He had been a handsome man, with thick dark hair pushed back from his brow.

He said they lived in barracks in groups of fifty or sixty, and one to a shelf. They played backgammon a lot, and clustered near their one big stove in winter. If you worked near your barracks, you could come back for lunch, but often you did not have time and only got fed at the end of your fourteen-hour day.

'Sometimes though I am thankful I came to the camps. I survived. My friends from Tbilisi who went into the army all died. They were conscripting people born in 1924 when I was arrested. I was born in 1924 as it happens, but my parents registered me in March 1925. I don't know why they did that, but that's why I didn't go to the front. But you know the camp was hard. All we got was just 600 grams of black bread, soup and porridge. In Inta, they started giving us potatoes.'

The phone rang at this point and he held a long conversation about medicine for his legs, which would cost him 3,500 roubles unless he could find someone to buy it in Moscow, where it was cheaper. His pension is 19,000 roubles a month, so the potential saving was a major issue and he took his time about discussing it.

Nikolai Andreyevich and I drank some vodka. He held out his hands to show me. They were pitted with strange marks where the flesh was sucked in between the bones. He too, it transpires, had been a miner.

'Who would go to their death in the mine for pennies?' he asked.

Badaryan nodded: 'Look at me, I have grey hair. Look at my hands. These are not from a good life. I survived by a miracle myself. If you were a miner, it meant you were somebody. This nation now is completely ruined. The future of the town is under threat even. If there was a good boss it wouldn't die, but …' He tailed off.

The two of them talked about the one coal mine that is left in Inta, and which provides fuel for the power station and the central heating plant. When that mine closes, the heating plant must close too, since it is built to burn only local coal, with its high clay content. Coal from Ukraine would burn too hot and ruin it. Without a heating plant, without a mine, the town would have to close. Without a town, the villages near by would vanish, and the tundra would return to how it was before the gulag, with just the graveyards and the humps of rotted buildings to show for the decades of human endeavour.

Nikolai Andreyevich and I walked back between the towers of the apartment blocks and he showed me where a stadium had been planned, but never built. Three stray dogs watched us as we walked past.

That evening, I sat with Father Dmitry's writings and looked up more references to his time here and how he got on in the camps. His camp's hospital became – as for Karsavin – a meeting place for the religious believers, and Father Dmitry went there often.

'The priest whom I met was a real treasure for me. He was attentive by nature and soon he got a job for another priest in the hospital. After a hard day's work, I would go to him, after roll call, and we would talk about everything.'

They celebrated Easter in the infirmary, with the service led by the priest who worked there.

'We took communion, and I sensed an extraordinary joy. We separated then, when it was already getting light, and the camp was plunged into a strong, twilight dream.'

One time he described how he and a Ukrainian nursed a Lithuanian back to life. Another time he described how a Spaniard – it is not clear what he was doing in the camp – said all Russians love slavery, and then escaped.

'They caught him, shot him and left him there on the watchtower so all the prisoners could see.'

Father Dmitry was always a compulsive writer. Despite having been imprisoned for writing poems, he kept writing them. He hid his poems in an old suitcase, but no hiding place was safe in the camps. Guards found the stash of poems during a search.

'We are arresting you,' he was told.

'What? Have I not already been under arrest for six years?'

'That's nothing, we're arresting you anyway.'

He was kept in a prison cell where a harsh light shone into his eyes at all times. Most of his fellow prisoners were there for murder or attempted murder.

'A Lithuanian who killed informers was young, eighteen years old, tall, thin, spoke with a bass voice. He knew he was not long for this world, he had tuberculosis, and he wanted to kill as many evil people as he could before he died. He was kind, he was a believer, he missed his Lithuania, and was not as evil as a murderer should be.'

The prisoners were not allowed to go out or to lie down during the day so they took turns telling each other everything they knew. They loved to talk about murder and rape, using the ferociously obscene and all-but-incomprehensible jargon of Russian prisons. Father Dmitry asked to be put in solitary confinement to escape them, but nothing came of it.

Every now and then he would be summoned for interrogation, when his investigator would also swear at him. But these insults about his poems, some of which criticized Stalin, came as a relief after the conversation of his comrades.

'How could you allow yourself to commit such slander? The name of Stalin is spoken with gratitude in China, across the whole world, he is the leader of humanity, and you call him a butcher,' his investigator shouted, according to Father Dmitry's later account. 'Just think what you look like. You're like Christ when he was on the cross. You have no blood in your face, you're a skeleton, and you will die here if you don't repent. Admit everything. Tell me you're guilty.'

Father Dmitry admitted nothing, even when they brought in new investigators to increase the pressure on him, or when they brought in friends who had been twisted into accusing him of organizing a revolt in the camp.

'What do I have to fear? I am not some criminal, these are my beliefs,' he told them.

When the court case came he expected the worst: execution or a new term of twenty-five years as a minimum. When he received a mere ten years on top of his existing sentence, he was surprised. He had already been inside for six years, now he would have another decade to learn how a Soviet citizen should behave.

Tanya, the sister-in-law of my friend in Moscow, had instructed me to bring a packed lunch for our trip to Abez the next day. So, in the minutes before they came to collect me, I made egg mayonnaise sandwiches. Lacking a kitchen I fell back on one of the cooking techniques I had learned as a student. I took the lid off the electric kettle and hoped the fuse would hold out long enough to boil some eggs.

Tanya was a pianist, and an Inta native. We sat on the train, if you can call a single carriage pulled by an engine a train, and she told me about her teacher: Olga Achkasova. Achkasova's parents moved to Germany when she was a child, and she married a German before World War Two. She survived the Nazi period without being arrested, but fell foul of Berlin's communist liberators. When she saw the first Soviet soldiers, she welcomed them in Russian. They arrested her, tried her and sent her off to the north.

We sat around a table: Tanya, Nikolai Andreyevich, a local hunter and me. Nikolai Andreyevich fetched out his map and used the opportunity to ask the hunter if he knew any gulag burial sites that were not marked. Since retiring, he has studied the gulag system and tried to create a database of the prisoners' final resting places. Most of the camps were closed after Stalin's death and their buildings have vanished into the swamps, which makes finding them now all but impossible. In a way, an alternative future for Russia is buried with them out there in the tundra. Almost all the brightest people from every industry and every town served time in the gulag, and many of them died. Those who survived learned habits of obedience the country has never shaken off, while those who were not imprisoned – and who were thus complicit either in locking them up or in profiting from their labour – prefer not to talk about it. Amnesia and sullen obedience are two of the crucial characteristics of modern Russian politics, and who can say how the country would have developed had these camps never existed?

Nikolai Andreyevich is one of a tiny number of Russians who want to reveal that shameful past, and hunters are a crucial source for him. They have often seen these old graveyards, and this man traced the line of the rivers with his finger, suggesting sites for him to check.

By 1948, the year of Father Dmitry's arrival, the railway headquarters was at Abez, where the central hospital stood and where the weaker prisoners like Karsavin were concentrated. The first prisoners to build the railway voyaged up the rivers by barge, along with the rails and sleepers. The main camps therefore sat where the line crossed a river.

Nikolai Andreyevich was one of those rare people in Inta who had not sprung from the gulag. He had come here voluntarily from Ukraine. Perhaps because the gulag's history was not personal to him, he had become fascinated by it.

'I love history. I read all the time. I worked in the Young Communist League, the party. In the army I was the political worker. And then I came to the north in 1978. Then in the 1980s, the papers started to print memoirs, there was new openness. We knew there had been camps, but you could not talk about it,' he said. 'I collected these writings like a book lover.'

His interest had become all-consuming. He now takes children on trips to hunt for graveyards, and erects crosses on the graves he finds.

'We put a cross as a memorial mark. We take two birch trees, take the bark off them, and then we chop down all other trees for 20 metres around so it is visible. In this sense the cross is a symbol. It is a symbol of the suffering these people went through. They all suffered, whether they were criminals or political prisoners,' he said.

Tanya was on a similar mission. Karsavin had inspired her to such an extent that she had decided to organize for a monument to stand on his grave. For her, this trip was both a pilgrimage and a reconnaissance.

As our train crawled through the tundra, Nikolai Andreyevich pointed out the sites of the vanished gulag world. 'There was a hospital, and where the trees are is a graveyard, you see. There was a woman's camp there, and they lived up on that rise. See there that river, there was a camp there as well.'

The tundra opened as we approached the bridge, affording us our first view since we had left Inta. Grass and weeds lined the banks. The Ural Mountains, humped and smooth and white-flecked like killer whales, rose in the distance.

'There, wait, wait, wait, there in that pier of the bridge, there's a body. The criminals cemented in a comrade of theirs, just there,' Nikolai Andreyevich said.

The trees closed around us once more. They were scrubby birches, with the spiky silhouettes of conifers on the horizon.

'Abez', Nikolai Andreyevich told me, 'is within seven kilometres of the Arctic Circle, so you can pretty much say we're now in the Arctic.'

We crossed the River Usa on a long clanking steel-framed bridge, and halted on the far side. A dozen people alighted: hunters, railway workers and us, carrying our packed lunches. A bearded man in thick glasses and camouflage greeted us. This was Alexander Merzlikin, a local with a piercing, thoughtful air, who keeps a watch over the graveyards when he is not out hunting in the wilds.

We walked over the stagnant pools of the marsh along a raised path of planks. Heather rose around us, and green scum rimmed the pools. Hundreds of mosquitoes swarmed up, nosing on to our arms and ankles, nestling in our hair.

'Wait until you get to the graveyard,' said Alexander, sardonically. He was smoking. 'This is nothing.'

We dropped off our bags of lunch at the school, and donned hats he gave us. Made of nylon with a wide brim, they were screened to keep the mosquitoes off our faces. I put on my cagoule, buttoned the sleeves tight and tucked my trousers into my socks. My only bare flesh was my hands, and I could police them with ease. I was safe from the swarm, I thought.

Abez was a neat collection of houses around the two-storey build-ings of an apartment block and the school. A gaggle of children cycled between the houses, clad only in shorts and T-shirts. I felt rather over-dressed in my mosquito armour, but the insects' hum as they hunted a weak point was constant and I was grateful for the protection.

'There were 1,500 people living here before,' said Merzlikin. I was hearing that word 'before' a lot. It means 'before the end of the Soviet

Union'. 'Now there are 400. The dairy closed eight or nine years ago. You could get milk cheaper from the south.'

He pointed to the derelict barns, empty-windowed, that had once protected the village's dairy herd from the weather. The Soviet Union had created a collective farm up here, despite the near-impossibility of carving food out of this poor soil in the three months of summer. It gave employment to the locals until the early 1990s, but could not survive the transition to a market economy.

The people who laid the bricks for the barns and houses must have thought they were creating something permanent, that they were taming nature. An electricity substation, built for the collective farm, had '1977' set into its side in lighter-coloured bricks. You only put a date on the side of a building if you intend it to outlive you and speak to future generations. Perhaps the man who laid those bricks imagined children in a hundred years mouthing the numbers and being amazed by how old it was.

If he did, he will not be getting his wish. The bricks were rotting, and the mortar had fallen out. No wires led to it, and the roof was slipping off. Before long it would be another lump in the fields like the old camp morgue which Merzlikin led us past.

We walked through the village's own cemetery with fresh graves and plastic flowers, down a slope and up into the trees. And here, the mosquitoes came in their thousands. The hum around my veil became a scream as we passed into the prisoners' graveyard. Row after row of little metal signs, and occasionally a cross, marked the graves. Some of the humps had personal monuments erected since 1991 by relatives: Ukrainian names, mostly, and Lithuanians too.

But most graves had nothing to identify them. These were Russians, and their nation did not have the desire of the Ukrainians and Lithuanians to remember the victims of the Soviet Union as martyrs.

The records noting who is buried where are not perfect. Often people seeking to reinter a body find it does not belong to the person they're looking for. A Lithuanian general – Jonas Juodišius – is buried here somewhere, having been imprisoned for being a Lithuanian general. When Lithuanians came to try to repatriate his remains, they could not find him, so they left him be and erected the monument on this foreign soil instead.

Hryhorii Lakota, a bishop from the Ukrainian Uniate Church, which is Orthodox by ritual but acknowledges the pope, was buried here too. His crime was his refusal to accept Russian Orthodoxy. He has been canonized, and his body moved to Kiev.

Moss and horsetails grew among the graves, and I traced the rows of humps, reading the few names that had been picked out for separate commemoration, while trying not to overlook the 99 per cent that had not. Here was Punin, Akhmatova's lover and the man who did not share Karsavin's warm feelings towards mosquitoes. And here was Karsavin too. Tanya stood by his grave, planning her memorial.

'It is like a debt to my father and mother,' she said. She had come a long way to repay it, and would be back next year to see it done.

We sat in the schoolroom and drank a bottle of vodka that Nikolai Andreyevich had brought. Then we ate our lunches. I was secretly pleased when Tanya asked for one of my sandwiches.

The year before, Merzlikin said, workmen had come to repair the school, which is an important building since children from remote villages have to live here as well as study. They had done a very poor job. He pointed to damp stains which had started in the corner of the room and now spread across much of the ceiling.

'It was not like this before,' he paused, for emphasis. 'Before they repaired the roof. This building won't last long now unless they come back and do it properly.'

I think we were all rather affected by our experience in the cemetery, though we had spent only an hour or so among the hundreds of graves, because Tanya and I got into a pointless squabble over whether British people or Russian people were more cultured. Perversely, we were each arguing the merits of the other's nation. Merzlikin hovered around us, his kind eyes concerned by this inexplicable disagreement.

The vodka drunk, the sandwiches eaten, we walked back to catch our evening train. Nikolai Andreyevich continued his lecture on the journey back, and Tanya and I let it wash over us, tired out by the day. Despite my mosquito armour, I had rings of bites around both ankles, where they had found the weakness of the single layer of sock. I fingered them, trying to relieve the itching without scratching. There were nineteen bites on my left ankle, and seven on my right. My scalp felt like a moonscape beneath my hair. They had bitten through the cloth of my hat so many times I could not distinguish the individual bites. I was feeling unsteady.

'You have the mosquito fever,' said Nikolai Andreyevich. 'It will pass.'

I had been in Abez for seven hours, and half of those had been inside, and I had mosquito fever and felt unsettled. Prisoners stayed up here for years.

Our carriage was hitched to the Moscow train, and I wanted to go and find my bunk and lie down and sleep, but I felt bound by politeness to sit on this hard seat for the two hours to Inta and listen to Nikolai Andreyevich.

'There, that was a camp,' he said, 'there were 30,000 people living there.' He pointed through the grimy window at an unremarkable stretch of tundra.

'Up there was an aerodrome.' He pointed to a slight rise above the track. 'See see see see see the embankment. Now you will see a bridge.' Pause. 'There was another bridge there before.'

At last, at Inta, they left me to continue my journey alone, and I picked my way down the train to my bunk.

4

The generation of change

Back in Moscow, I recognized Alexander Ogorodnikov as soon as I saw him, although I had previously no idea what he looked like. The man walking towards me – tall, slim, bearded, rimless glasses – looked like a filmmaker, a ladies' man or a Soviet dissident, and Ogorodnikov had been all three.

Mutual friends recommended Ogorodnikov to me as a man who could tell me about Moscow in the years after Father Dmitry had been released from prison, the years after Stalin's death. I wanted to know how religious believers had been treated, and how they had behaved towards each other. We shook hands and he ushered me out of the cool of the station into the flaying heat of Moscow. If anything the city was even hotter now I was back from Abez. The tar melted like chocolate and the air throbbed on streets designed for parades not shade.

We stopped off in a supermarket, where he chose herring, biscuits, tea and bread before walking me to his home: a flat near the top of a nine-storey block. His kitchen window commanded a view of other nine-storey blocks and, in the distance, a factory chimney with four horizontal stripes.

He was curious to know why I wanted to talk to him and, when I told him, he said he too was planning a book about the 1960s and 1970s. For almost all Russians who remember the Soviet Union, those decades now glow like a golden age. Most people remember them for their stability, for holidays, jobs and even a degree of access to consumer goods. For the likes of Ogorodnikov, the memories are different: those were the heyday of Soviet dissent.

All over the world, the generation that grew up after World War Two proved rebellious and iconoclastic. The Soviet Union may not have seen the kind of protests witnessed in Paris, Prague or Chicago, but young people still tried to change the world in their own way. Poets, writers and historians like Solzhenitsyn circulated their work in illicit copies. When they were arrested, their friends publicized their trials and imprisonment with fresh home-printed pamphlets.

Older dissidents like Andrei Sakharov – a nuclear physicist whose anger at unnecessary Soviet bomb tests morphed into concern about the denial of rights to Soviet citizens – acted as a focus for younger men and women. They made contact with Western journalists and diplomats who helped them smuggle their writings out of the country. Everything they did ran counter to the direction desired by their government.

Some of their actions were deliberately high profile, such as a protest on Red Square by eight people against the invasion of Czechoslovakia in 1968. They knew almost all their fellow citizens would criticize them, in the same way their fellow citizens criticized the Czechs for not being grateful for the Soviet army's help in defeating the Nazis. One participant recorded how a pleasant-looking blonde woman saw their protest and joined in the chorus of 'scum' directed towards them.

'People like you should be stamped out. Together with your children, so they don't grow up as morons,' the woman said.

But the protesters did not care. They wanted to show that not everyone in their country believed in force being used to defeat the popular uprising of the Prague Spring.

'We had already crossed over to the other side. Freedom was the dearest thing on earth to us,' a participant said, according to a book prepared later by Natalya Gorbanevskaya, one of her comrades.

Other dissidents favoured smaller actions: reading poems, collecting information on Stalin's victims, studying their nation's ancient traditions. Their discretion made little difference to the government, however, which saw them all as dangerous and used the police, the KGB, prosecutors and even psychiatrists against them.

The men who governed the country had all risen to the top under Stalin, when thousands of top officials were dragged off and shot as spies on the flimsiest of evidence. They found themselves in senior positions after the last major purges took place in 1937–8 and knew instinctively that innovation and free thought were dangerous. After all, everyone who had thought freely in the 1930s had been killed. Stability was the new spirit of the times. The rapid and bewildering changes of the 1930s and 1940s were over: the war was won, and the great new industrial cities were built.

After Stalin died in 1953, most of the gulag camps were closed. Stalin's successor Nikita Khrushchev felt able to condemn his methods, and tried to introduce a more humane form of communism, sacking incompetent and corrupt officials, altering the system, chivvying people along rather than murdering them.

In 1956, he gave what was called the Secret Speech, though its contents were known across the country and beyond in weeks. In it, he criticized Stalin's cult of personality and the great purges of 1937 and 1938. He did not admit to all the regime's crimes – perhaps because he was implicated in most of them – but it was still the first admission that the Soviet Union had done anything wrong, and it jolted communists all over the country.

Some 98 of the 139 members and candidates of the Central Committee elected at the 1934 party congress had been arrested and shot, he said. And 1,108 of 1,966 delegates at that congress had been arrested on charges of counter-revolutionary crimes.

'Many thousands of honest and innocent communists died as a result of this monstrous falsification of such "cases", as a result of the fact that all kind of slanderous "confessions" were accepted, and as a result of the practice of forcing accusations against oneself and others,' Khrushchev said, even singling out individual judges for censure. 'He is a vile person, with the brain of a bird, and morally completely degenerate. And it was this man who decided the fate of prominent party workers,' he said of one.

He urged ordinary communists and other Soviet citizens to believe that the party was now back on the right track, but the shock of finding out even a partial truth about what had happened caused many people to see the country with fresh eyes.

Leonid Plyushch, for example, was a member of a unit of the Young Communist League, targeting crime and prostitution. He was rocked by the Secret Speech, almost as much as he was when the head of his unit raped a prostitute.

'I was a very active member of the Komsomol and a communist by conviction, but when I learned of the exposure of Stalin's crimes it had a tremendous impact ... I felt the ground had moved from under me, and then the idea: it should never happen again – which stayed with me for many years.'

Khrushchev attempted to allow such disoriented citizens to speak out, and even permitted the reality of the gulag to appear in print. Alexander Solzhenitsyn's novel of an ordinary peasant in the camps, *One Day in the Life of Ivan Denisovich*, was published in November 1962. Khrushchev was mercurial, but this was concrete proof that he intended to open discussions on previously forbidden themes.

But all of this alienated the senior bureaucrats. They too had been implicated in Stalin's crimes and felt Khrushchev was going too far. Besides, they disliked the prospect of being sacked and no longer feared rebelling if they would not be killed for it. Khrushchev had promised communism would be built, more or less, by 1980. But then he was forced out in 1964, and replaced by Leonid Brezhnev, who promised stability. Under Brezhnev, change stopped altogether. Communism was postponed and replaced by the concept of 'developed socialism'. The state would not wither away, as Marx had predicted it would, for many many years. The party was needed to guide the revolution for the foreseeable future, which meant everyone got to keep their jobs. The class of 1937 dug in on the summit of the state. It would rule the Soviet Union until Mikhail Gorbachev. Young people were frustrated that their paths to promotion were blocked by increasingly old men.

Ogorodnikov was eager to start down the track of his life story but kept being derailed by the glorious confusion of his kitchen. His wife was trying to spoon soup into Andrei, their three-year-old, who had a mass of hair, no trousers and lots to say.

Then an Uzbek man arrived to discuss the reception centre for homeless men he and Ogorodnikov had set up. After a couple of minutes of that, we switched to police corruption. We all had anecdotes to tell, but the Uzbek beat us flat with a story about being randomly detained in Astrakhan and forced to work in the police chief's garden for three days until his non-existent debt to society was deemed paid.

Lunch was soup and bread, and Ogorodnikov recited a long grace. He and the Uzbek then vanished to talk business, and I made faces at Andrei whenever he peeked around the corner of the corridor.

At last I had Ogorodnikov to myself: his wife went out, the Uzbek left, and Andrei lay down for a nap. I studied Ogorodnikov while he made more tea. He had the long hair and beard of an Orthodox priest but none of their over-ripe sleekness. He was born in 1950. He looked burned by the sun, and hardened by it.

'My generation was the generation of the change. You understand,' he started.

Growing up in the 1960s, the post-war children, he and his friends were part of the global wave of protest. Like their counterparts around the world, they were living in unprecedented prosperity and peace. Obviously, their wealth did not compare to that of contemporaries in North America or Western Europe. There was no mass ownership of cars for Soviet citizens, no transistor radios or cheap fashion. But they were still considerably more prosperous than their parents or grand-parents had been. The generation before them had suffered the priva-tions caused by World War Two. The generation before that had struggled through collectivization. Ogorodnikov and his friends had food and clothes, and could be proud of their country's achievements: sputnik, Yuri Gagarin, the hydrogen bomb.

Ogorodnikov grew up in Chistopol, a little railway town on the edge of Siberia, and was not immediately a dissident. Indeed, as a child, he had no cause to complain about his life at all. He was far away from the rarefied world of Moscow intellectuals, and was a pure product of the Soviet system. If the country had a future it was in people like him: bright and committed. It took him a long time to rebel.

'We were all raised in Soviet ideology,' Ogorodnikov went on. 'I was completely devoted to the Soviet idea and Marxism. For me, I had the ideals of communism. To understand how deep this went into me, when I was sixteen a girl wrote me a note, a love letter, in which she chided me, telling me that Pavka Korchagin would not have behaved the way I had done. And for her it was a real example of how to live.'

Korchagin was the hero of Nikolai Ostrovsky's socialist realist novel *How the Steel was Forged*, which presented a glorious narrative of the Bolshevik victory in the Civil War. Young Russians were inspired by his example to dream of building the new world order just as Westerners of the same generation were dreaming of running away and heading for the horizon like Jack Kerouac. Members of the Young Communist League signed up in their thousands to work on massive construction projects like the Baikal–Amur railway line. Many young Russians at the time would have jumped at the kind of offer Ogorodnikov received when he was eighteen: to hold a senior post in a Young Communist detachment helping build a new truck factory on a tributary of the Volga at Naberezhnye Chelny.

Through mass education, which reduced illiteracy from near universal to almost non-existent, the Soviet Union succeeded in inspiring its youth to great feats of effort. Stalin called writers the 'engineers of the human soul', and he was right. Books like Ostrovsky's created a loyal army for the state, and Ogorodnikov at the time was completely unaware of how cleverly he had been indoctrinated by heroes such as Pavka Korchagin.

'For me he was a serious realistic life model, you understand. She was condemning me by saying that I was not behaving like a revolutionary hero. This was my girlfriend, in a love letter.'

Ogorodnikov was bright, driven by the desire to improve his country and rescue it from its enemies. He joined the Pioneers – where children paraded in red neckerchiefs and boasted of being 'Always Ready' just like Boy Scouts in the West were told to 'Be Prepared' – and then the Young Communist League. But that was not enough for him and, aged fifteen, he and his friends formed the Young Communists' Militant Wing. They wanted to clean up their rough railway town, where too many people drank and fought and swindled, far from Moscow's watchful eye.

'We fought with non-socialist remnants, with non-Soviet ways of life,' he said, mocking the Soviet jargon. 'There were these fops, these dandies, and we had a lot of authority. But don't laugh; this was very serious. Two of my comrades were killed by bandits. They tried to kill me too. We risked our lives.'

On 15 November 1968, *Komsomolskaya Pravda*, the daily news-paper for Soviet youth, with millions of copies printed daily, devoted the centre of its front page to one of those deaths. Sasha Votyakov, the paper wrote, had remonstrated with two 'boorish, arrogant, and drunken' men who refused to buy bus tickets. They followed him off the bus and killed him.

'Imagine what *Komsomolskaya Pravda* was, there were 60 million copies printed every day across the whole country, the youth paper. And imagine, there was an article about me on the first page with the headline "Valour Patrol".'

He might be from a small and remote town, but this was enough to qualify him as a high-flyer. In the late 1960s, he was already living the communist dream, creating his own legend. He was defending the revolution. Once he beat up a friend who had had sex with a female classmate in the Pioneers' room. They were welcome to have sex of course, that was their business, but they should never have used the Pioneers' banner as a sheet. They had fucked on the flag, and needed to be taught a lesson.

Another time, some locals were out in the middle of town in winter. It was cold and they were warming their feet on the eternal flame, which burned to commemorate those who had died defending the Soviet Union. Ogorodnikov was not having that. 'So I go up to this group of people, and they think I'm joking, and they laugh. And I then, I knock one of them so badly that I put him on his knees and make him promise that he will never come to this eternal flame again, or use bad language or anything.'

Ogorodnikov was enjoying his tale, and the effect it was having on me. I had come to meet a religious dissident and was listening to a fervent communist. His flow was broken, however, when Andrei, still not wearing any trousers, trotted into the kitchen, presented me with a toy pirate, hesitated and trotted out again. Ogorodnikov laughed, and promised to hurry his tale along.

He had been unusually committed, he said, but he insisted that he had not been totally abnormal. Cynicism had not yet set in by the late 1960s, and everyone he knew believed in communism. In that, they were not alone. Even the dissidents were communists. They might have disagreed with their government's tactics, but that did not mean they objected to its goal of establishing a society where everyone lived equally.

'I regard communism as the only goal that can be put forward by the modern mind; the West has been unable to put forward anything like it,' said dissident Andrei Sinyavsky at his trial in 1966. The government was about to jail him simply because he had written something it did not like, but he still supported its ideology.

There is purity and naivety in this kind of dissidence. Soviet officials saw CIA plots and foreign intervention in the dissident movement, but most of these young people were simply idealists who wanted everything to be better for everyone, not only for themselves. If people like Sinyavsky criticized the authorities, or people like Ogorodnikov beat up cold people for warming their feet, they did so honestly, because they wanted to improve the system, not for money or advancement. It is a crucial distinction. They saw problems and they tried to correct them, and they met their friends and debated how best to do so. It did not occur to them that the state did not want their help, and they had to be forcibly shown the error in their doctrine.

By the time Ogorodnikov went to university, a lot of officials were no doubt thinking it was time he learned to shut up. For the Soviet hierarchs, the revolution had been won. That meant Ogorodnikov was a revolutionary without a revolution, and that is a dangerous breed. The government had no need for such as him. It needed passive, non-complaining workers to run the machine that supported the top officials.

'Life was cynical. The leaders understood it was all a lie; it was money and a career. Public service was for their good, not for the good of society. The holiday homes of the Young Communist League had already become brothels, you understand,' said Ogorodnikov.

He lasted two months studying philosophy at the university in Sverdlovsk before being expelled. It was a disillusioning experience. He had got to university to find that the Young Communist League was dominated not by tireless strivers such as himself, but by mini-politicians, people using the system to climb the ladder of party and state, people who wanted wealth and power.

Bureaucrats, secure in control of their empires, began to divide up the system, to morph into mafia groups. Organized crime spread, and disillusionment with it. Ogorodnikov was out of step with the times. He was not the man to work patiently at politics behind closed doors, to swap favours and to pay bribes. He needed crowds and applause and action. He had created a discussion club at university, where they read poems by authors who were already dissidents, or who had never been rehabilitated. That was unacceptable, even for a rising star such as himself, and he was thrown out of the Young Communists as well as out of university. He was back in Chistopol, with the KGB watching him. They found unofficial literature during a search of his house, and opened a criminal case. It was looking grim.

He still wanted to go to university, however. Theoretically this should have been impossible, but there were chinks in the Soviet system's armour if you knew where to stab. It was slow and lumbering, whereas he was quick and decisive. He worked out a plan to outwit the authorities. He wanted to get into university in Siberia, which was probably far enough away for the security services to lose track of him. In order to be sure, however, he decided to distract their attention. He went to Moscow first, where he made as much noise as he could.

Playing for the highest stakes, he applied to VGIK, the Soviet Union's film school and one of its most prestigious centres of higher education. He knew he would be refused entry. He just wanted to distract the KGB from his real plan. Bizarrely, and in testament both to his charm and to the KGB's incompetence, he got in.

'It was a miracle,' he said simply, describing how he was one of the lucky people picked out of the hundreds of applicants. And his life became something wonderful. Expulsion from Sverdlovsk had been a blessing. He was a handsome student at one of the country's top universities. He had a generous stipend. Women wanted him, and their mothers encouraged them. He had so much money that he could fly off to a Black Sea resort for a break, fly home for an exam, then fly off on holiday again.

'I had a mass of girlfriends. VGIK was like a key to every door. In the Soviet Union, cinema was everything, and when you said you were at VGIK, and had good clothes, and so on, well, mothers really wanted you to marry their daughters. In hotels where there were no rooms, they would find a room for you, and so on. When there were no plane tickets, they found them for me.'

He no longer believed in the communist ideals of his teenage years. Who would after seeing the corruption, inefficiency and cynicism he had encountered? But who cared? He was young, rich and clever, living it up in the capital of a superpower.

These trainee Soviet aristocrats needed to learn how to produce high-quality films that would satisfy the ideological requirements of the old men at the top of the party. They also needed to know what the Soviet Union was up against, propaganda-wise. That meant they had special viewing rooms for Western films that the general public never saw.

One day in spring 1973, they sat down to a treat: Pier Paolo Pasolini's *The Gospel According to St Matthew*, a version of the Bible story by a gay communist Italian, and a modern classic. It is a stunning production, full of genuine landscape, and broken faces. Pasolini's Christ, played by a Spanish student, is a pretty boy, a gentle revolutionary, railing against hypocrisy, begging for a return to spiritual values and honesty.

The music alone must have been a revelation. Ogorodnikov would have already known the Prokofiev, Mozart and Bach. But Odetta's 'Motherless Child' cuts the soul like a saw, while Blind Willie Johnson's slide guitar mends the wounds. 'Gloria' by a Congolese choir adds drama to the scenes of rapture. The screening was supposed to warn Ogorodnikov, to demonstrate the West's propaganda techniques and show him how to counter them. Instead, it converted him.

Christ, as presented by Pasolini, is a young dissident, with pure revolutionary yearnings, no matter how hard the cynics around him tried to burn them out. It is hardly surprising it inspired the young man who watched it. It was a blueprint for action, and the parallels between the Holy Land and the Soviet Union were there for all to see. The Pharisees were the communists, claiming to be motivated by higher values but really stuffing their pockets. They even had the ridiculous hats.

Watching the film, Ogorodnikov decided that he too could be a man who overturned the tables of the moneylenders, who held up to them a mirror showing what a true believer looked like. He came out of the cinema a committed Christian, and his life began.

'But I was in a vacuum. I was outside the Church, I did not know what the Church was, I had no knowledge. What does it mean to be a Christian? How do I live in this totalitarian society, which is pressing on our freedoms, on our spirits?'

He smiled at the memory.

'We were the first swallows of a new spring. Before us the Church was all old people, old people, and we were the first swallows. One time, I went into a church in one of the provinces, and the old women tried to force me out of the church. "We won't let you close the church, we won't allow you, we won't let you," they said. In the understanding of these old women, a young man could go into a church with only one aim, to smash things up, to close the church. It was only when I went up at the end of the liturgy to receive communion that the old women understood. All the church was crying, they were crying. I was a new generation, you understand?'

The trouble was that he did not know how. Books on Christianity were hard to find. Khrushchev, in one of his spasmodic attempts to keep communism alive and fresh after he had denounced Stalin, closed more than half the churches in the country. Those that operated were largely a formality, where old women attended sterile services rushed through by ignorant priests.

The Orthodox hierarchy was completely subordinate to the state. Priests were answerable to local committees controlled by atheists. Bishops made no efforts to rein in the government's anti-religious campaign. In fact, they defended it if ever challenged by foreigners.

One such bishop, Metropolitan Yuvenali, during a visit to Britain in 1975, used an interview with the BBC to attack 'some circles in England' who present 'a biased and one-sided picture of Russian Orthodox Church life'. There was a 'spiritual revival', he insisted.

If there was such a revival, it was no thanks to Yuvenali and his fellows. The Church printed almost no official literature on the faith. Believers received no support from the Church hierarchy, were forced to discuss religion in their own homes, and were on their own when it came to finding texts and puzzling out their meanings.

This is alien to Orthodox tradition, which stresses hierarchy and the importance of priests in administering the sacraments. If these new young believers were to be truly Orthodox, they needed churches to attend, but where could they find one that sated their energy, their intelligence and their questing spiritual hunger?

That was when Ogorodnikov heard about a church on the edge of Moscow, in an old cemetery, where an unusual priest was actually preaching to parishioners. Russia's Orthodox Church never had much of a tradition of preaching, even in pre-revolutionary times, but there were always itinerant preachers, holy fools who rejected the world and travelled from town to town, enlightening crowds at markets and crossroads. The priest was cast from that same rebellious, truth-telling mould.

He was Father Dmitry.

'In his services, in these talks, it was like being alive,' Ogorodnikov said, the wonder still audible in his voice. 'The Church had lost so much, there were so many martyrs, but it was quiet about it. Sermons were censored and had to be as abstract as possible. Priests had to talk in an incomprehensible language in the sermons. It was like they were not addressing the people, but something they could not see. If the words entered into your soul, so you heard the meaning, so you felt Christ in your heart, then the priest would be banned, he would be sacked, and you know he would not be able to find work, feed his wife. It was a dangerous situation.'

Although Father Dmitry had been in the camps, he was rehabilitated in 1956 and his criminal record erased. That meant he was free to finish his religious training and get a job as a priest. His original church at Transfiguration Square was blown up, but he got a job in another one less than a kilometre away and there he administered to his parishioners as best he could. People of all ages, he said later, kept coming to him with questions about depression, about alcoholism, about abortion and violence.

One night, he had the radical idea of treating the questions he kept being asked not individually but collectively. Many of them were on the same themes, after all. If he could gather the afflicted people together, not only would they hear his words of comfort, but also they would feel support from each other.

On 8 December 1973, he encouraged the attendees of his regular Saturday service to write down questions – 'about what you'd most like us to talk about, about the questions you have, about your doubts, about the things that puzzle you' – that they would like him to answer. The questions covered every topic he had hoped for: from the practical ('Where can I find a Bible?') to the theological ('They've flown in spaceships but didn't see God. Where is God?'), and, increasingly, to the personal too ('Father, I'm a drunk. My family is gone, my life is shot, and yet I can't stop drinking … What should I do?').

Ogorodnikov was astonished.

'This was completely unexpected, and when Father Dmitry answered our questions publicly, it was like a mouthful of water, it was so unusual, you had a sense that it was not true, it was hard to believe that in Moscow there was suddenly a place you could freely speak out. And the most important thing is that the public came to these talks, and these were people you never saw in church, serious intellectuals, and not just intellectuals. There were a lot of Western correspondents – you could tell them by their clothing. Everyone else wore black and grey, so you could tell them immediately.'

The day after our conversation I went out to see the church he had been talking about. From the sun-blasted tarmac of Transfiguration Square, site of Father Dmitry's first church (the one that was blown up during Khrushchev's anti-religious campaign), I walked past the Mossovet cinema, along the tram tracks, and there it was, through a fine gateway. Before entering, I wandered into the attached cemetery, mainly to enjoy the shade under the trees. Although still early, the heat was building again.

From the graveyard, I walked to the church, a fine pink building, with a green roof. A plaque told visitors it had been built in 1790 and was protected by the state. Inside was cool relief from the dry furnace of the street. Old women wore headscarves tightly knotted under their jowls. Young women's heads were covered more artfully, their scarves showing the contours of their hair.

The sanctuary, and the icon-covered screen that protected it, was off in the left-hand corner of a wide, shallow room. It was an awkward arrangement, reflecting the fact that the church had been cut in half to allow Old Believers – members of an ancient Orthodox sect – to share it with the official Orthodox. I had in fact initially entered the Old Believer side of the building, and been faced with a young man in peasant garb crossing himself and bowing to the altar repeatedly. I waited for him to stop so I could ask him if I was in the right place, but he kept going for two or three minutes, so I left and found someone else.

From Father Dmitry's first days as a priest, he kept notebooks, little accounts of meetings. He mentioned no names, just described a woman, or an old woman, or a child, or a man, in encounters that provide unique flashes of insight into private life in the 1960s and 1970s.

Official literature was still full of Soviet advances in healthcare and the extensive provision of leisure facilities. Father Dmitry's notebooks tell a different story: despair. Stalin's re-engineering had failed to make the Russian soul happier. Instead it was sick. Father Dmitry's notebooks record the squalid crimes they committed and the procession of horrors that filled horrible lives.

'An old woman came to confession. She did not give her child the breast. He died. She had two abortions,' said one entry.

In another he told a drunkard not to drink.

'When you drink, you forget a little,' the drunkard replied. 'I don't see the point of not drinking.'

Father Dmitry had been preaching for more than a decade when, in the early 1970s, his sermons began to gain more attention and the likes of Ogorodnikov began to attend. He was part of a small group of believers – Gleb Yakunin, Anatoly Levitin-Krasnov and Alexander Men were the others – who wanted to revitalize the faith, to make it relevant to modern people and to reach out to the casualties of the Soviet experiment. They had a lot of work to do.

Before the 1917 revolution, the Orthodox faith was so conservative and ignorant that it was largely confined to the illiterate. Most educated Russians had abandoned the Church for Marxism and materialism. Now, in the 1960s and 1970s, the trend was reversed. It was Marxism that was sterile and corrupt. One atheist wrote, after attending Father Dmitry's church, 'the immorality of Soviet society, its inhumanity and corruption, its lack of a moral code or credible ideals, means that Christ's teaching comes through to those who it reaches as a shining contrast. It stresses the value of the individual, of humaneness, forgiveness, gentleness, love.'

Marxism was now the official ideology and it became the target of the same kind of revulsion that had once been aimed at the Church.

Father Dmitry compared the death and horror he saw and heard about every day to a war, but a war with no clear enemy.

'There are other difficulties, perhaps as great as times of war,' he said in one sermon recorded in 1972, 'pervasive sin, when vice, like rust or vermin, is corrupting our values and morally crippling the rising generation, when moral standards are disintegrating, when drunkenness, hooliganism and murder are increasing.'

Khrushchev had briefly spoken out about Stalin's crimes. His was only a partial account – he did not mention his own role, for example – but even that vanished when he fell from power. Under Brezhnev, the victims of the KGB were expected to keep their mouths shut. For Father Dmitry, that meant their wounds would fester. He believed in openness, and in talking about what no one else mentioned: his own eight and a half years in the camps, the KGB agents standing among the parishioners while he addressed them, or the police trying to block access to his services.

'What a mob of them there was, in and out of uniform, and all gathered just to prevent people from entering the church,' he said in his third question-and-answer session. This was heady stuff. No one else acknowledged publicly the way police officers abused their powers to harass ordinary Russians. 'As a priest, I must defend the faithful when they undergo persecutions of any sort. I, the shepherd, must defend my sheep from the wolves. As long as the atheists act like wolves, I'll come out against them.'

He stressed hope, and the impossibility of living without it. Why stay sober if tomorrow will be no better than today? Why have children if the future they live in will be as miserable as the present we have now? The important thing was to believe that tomorrow could be better. As he answered one alcoholic who wrote him a question: 'I ask all of you in church right now to pray for such unfortunate people. Surround them with your attention and warmth. Remember that saving such a person is the greatest of deeds.'

He realized that trust between people is what makes us happy. Any totalitarian state is based on betrayal. It needs people to inform on each other, to avoid socializing, to interact only through the state and to avoid unsanctioned meetings. This was unspoken of course. No official came out and said the communist state survived only because of suspicion, distrust and slander, but it was true. The greatest enemy of the state was its own people. If they began to trust each other, it could not command their fear and obedience.

The misery that Father Dmitry heard in confession was the symptom of the state's policy. No one trusted anyone, and that is a parlous way to live. People were living in solitary confinement in the middle of crowds, and it was killing them. Father Dmitry set out to break down the walls and tear the bars from the windows.

He launched his mass discussions in December 1973, and by the beginning of January all of Moscow seemed to know about them. Thanks to their fame, we have several different accounts. One dissident wrote, 'People spoke about them who were very far from the Church: professors and writers, believers in the transmigration of souls, and the same number of people who believed in nothing; followers of yogic philosophy and the same number of people who followed nothing. And most importantly, young people: kind Russian boys, wonderful Russian girls, fervent Jewish youths with fire in their eyes, excellent, determined and tough Jewish girls, Baptists and Zen Buddhists, Anthroposophists and Marxists.'

Ogorodnikov had told me how old women had feared him when he first entered their church, and that generation clash was the first topic tabled for discussion in that first discussion. Perhaps it was Ogorodnikov himself who asked about it. Perhaps it was an experience shared by many of the swallows of this new religious spring. The discussions were written down, typed up and passed around from hand to hand. They were hugely popular, and they confirmed Father Dmitry as the star of the religious dissidents. In one account, he is hailed as 'the bravest and one of the best men I have ever seen'. The worshippers marvelled that he should have the courage to speak up fortnight after fortnight, apparently with no fear of the consequences that surely awaited him.

'Why does he do it? I can't understand how he continues,' a friend of one chronicler remarked. 'He is quite difference from Solzhenitsyn. I have spoken to them both, Solzhenitsyn simply was afraid of nothing and nobody, but this man is afraid, all the time. Yet he carries on.'

Soon enough the records of Father Dmitry's sermons slipped under the Iron Curtain and into the West. Emigré publishers printed them, bound them and sent them back by their secret couriers. That helped cement Father Dmitry's position, especially when his name began to feature on the BBC and the Voice of America, the radio stations that dissidents listened to in private and called simply 'the Voices'.

The format Father Dmitry created was simple and brave. Again and again, he was asked to help a parishioner trapped in a pit of despair: 'I get drunk till I pass out – so I can forget. But once I sober up, the depression will be back, only stronger.' These people had been suffering alone, unable to understand why they were so miserable, unable to talk about it, and suddenly they learned that everyone else felt the same way. 'I was a wasted individual. Alcohol had destroyed me. There was no light, no joy, no rest. My soul was destroyed.'

In his answers Father Dmitry repeatedly appealed for his hearers to trust each other. The authorities, he said, were splitting the molecules and compounds of society, trying to create moral, domestic and social atoms. Many of his listeners were clearly alarmed by what sounded like a political campaign.

'What are you doing? These interviews are propaganda and agitation, and they're forbidden. They can get you for that,' said one question he read out. It gave him the opportunity to express his belief that their faith in God and each other could defeat alcoholism and despair, and to voice his defiance of anyone who tried to stop him.

'Atheism has corrupted people. Drunkenness, debauchery and the breakdown of the family have all appeared. There are many traitors betraying each other and our country. Atheism can't hold this back. Faith is what's needed … If this is so, then I must preach. If they forbid me to preach from the pulpit, I'll speak from outside the pulpit. If they throw me in jail, I'll preach even there. Preaching's my main job.'

Although he thought the Christian God was the answer to the crisis they were living through, he also argued that his lessons applied equally to non-Orthodox believers and he appealed to them too.

'A kind of unwritten brotherhood is forming. Believers and non-believers are coming, Orthodox and non-Orthodox – Roman Catholics and evangelical Christians,' he said. And he reached out across that great divide within Russian society that had provoked so much violence for so long. He talked to the Jews. It was an ambitious attempt to heal all of society, regardless of who was in it.

By the 1970s, Jewish activists were campaigning for emigration to Israel. The Soviet government, however, did not wish for many of Russia's best-trained specialists to work in a capitalist country and denied them permission, instead sacking them from their jobs and turning them into pariahs. Many of these passionate young people found a home in Father Dmitry's parish, feeling no contradiction between their own religion and his inclusive doctrine.

'I have many times heard what Russians say about Jews, that they have a conspiracy, that they are perfidious and only do evil, that these are not people, but demons,' Father Dmitry wrote. 'And I have many times heard what Jews say about Russians, that they are brutal Black Hundred nationalists, that they are ready to kill all Jews, and are scared of them, and assign some kind of power to them … Where is this misunderstanding from? Relations between Russians and Jews have become particularly strained. O Lord, open their minds and hearts, show them that they are brothers and must love each other.'

It was intoxicating. By his fifth or sixth session, the church was packed to capacity and his followers rigged up loudspeakers in the yard outside. Hundreds of people came hours early to be sure of a place.

'There is a choir, which sings a little flat and, at the back of the church, an open coffin containing the body of an old woman, from which comes a strong smell of spices. It is very hot, and the hat of the woman standing in front of me is made of some angora-like substance, which is constantly going up my nose. Somewhere in the church a mad woman is barking like a dog and pawing the ground. I wonder if I will be able to last out the service without fainting,' wrote a visitor.

It sounds like a medieval church, like a sermon in England during the Civil War. The ferment and the excitement gripped the hearers as they heard spiritual ideas discussed openly for the first time in their lives. Father Dmitry criticized the police, begged people not to drink, feud or lie, and all the time called on his parishioners to unite among themselves and trust each other.

'As the communists use the slogan "Workers of the world, unite", we must say "Believers of the world, unite". We must create the Kingdom of God here on earth,' he said. 'If you do not defend others, then you are not defending yourself, and you are leaving the field open for attack.'

It could not last. There was no way the authorities would allow this defiance to continue in their capital city. Dissidents could just about meet in flats around Moscow to whisper their heresy, but this was too much. To gather every fortnight and hear instructions to reject communist authority was close to sedition.

The authorities were in a tricky position, however. They feared criticism from the West, and could not arrest a priest for preaching the gospel, because that was his job and he was doing it in a church. Father Dmitry's appeals were rousing: 'I'm looking at all of you here. If we were all armed to do God's work, nothing would be impossible for us. So let's all help each other. Communicate Christian knowledge to each other, support each other in misfortune and temptations, and in general manifest an active love for each other.' But they were not treasonous.

In late April, he gave the authorities the opening they needed by reading out a question that accused the patriarch of 'grovelling before the authorities'. Even though Father Dmitry's answer defended the patriarch as a man surrounded by enemies, this was too much.

A fortnight later, on 4 May 1974, when the faithful crammed into the church to hear his tenth fortnightly discussion, they were disappointed. The patriarch had banned him from talking to them until he had explained himself. Two weeks later he stood before them again, with his beard and his blue eyes, but without his priest's robes, which the churchwarden refused to hand over.

He would not be silenced, however. 'The condemned man', he said, 'is allowed a last word.' He told his parishioners that the Church authorities had sent him away to a new parish in a distant village. He could keep preaching as much as he liked, but all of Moscow would not be his parish any more.

'The atheists are using the bishops' power to smother the Church, to dispose of those who don't please them,' he said, in his last words to the church of St Nicholas as its priest.

His congregation complained bitterly, sending letters to the patriarch and the bishops. They said they had found spiritual freedom in his church, that he had comforted them in a comfortless place, but to no avail.

'I am a Jewish woman,' wrote one worshipper. 'Previously I thought that Orthodoxy was Jewish pogroms and chauvinism. Having heard Father Dmitry's sermons, I understood that true Christianity and Orthodoxy preach fraternal love to all people. I understood that God is love. Father Dmitry's words opened this path to me.'

It is clear that Father Dmitry's message had got through to his parishioners if not to his superiors. The patriarch and the security services felt threatened by him, and had taken prompt action to ensure that his influence was contained. Ogorodnikov and his fellow worshippers would need to go to considerable inconvenience if they were to keep hearing his sermons out in the villages.

'A whole lifetime has gone by. It was 1973, so almost forty years have passed, but it was an important, strong thing. People gathered whom you never saw in church. Not just intellectuals, but others,' Ogorodnikov said at the end of our conversation. 'There were discussions, and conversations, and meals. There we created an independent Christian society. It is not just that we had lunch or something, we lived the life, you understand.'

5

Reds admit ban of rebel priest

I missed my train to Kabanovo, the village where Father Dmitry was exiled when he lost his church in central Moscow. The next train would not leave for another hour, but it was already waiting at the platform so I sat in my seat and felt the carriage heat up as the sun grilled the roof. I was careful to select a place on the shady side.

Other passengers were filing in. Most of the men – like me – had bought bottles of beer, to keep them going on their journeys out to their dachas. It was too early in the day for vodka, which was a relief. Vodka needs company, but beer can be drunk alone. Beer-drinking neighbours would allow me to read Father Dmitry's sermons in peace.

Russia has, of course, always been famous for drinking. One of the first mentions of the nation in all history – in the tenth century – features King Vladimir in Kiev rejecting Islam because 'drinking is the joy of the Russians. We cannot exist without that pleasure.' Books about pre-revolutionary villages describe how drinking was the major form of entertainment. If peasants had savings, they spent them on vodka. Their drinking was largely restricted by their spending power, however, so alcohol consumption became self-limiting. If peasants got rich, they got drunk, which meant they got poor, which meant they got sober.

Before 1917, duties on alcohol provided up to 40 per cent of government revenue and Lenin pledged to ban the trade, since it was blocking the nation's path to communism. That proved hard to do, however. Like the tsarist autocracy before it, the Soviet Union struggled to provide consumer goods and found alcohol a useful way to make money from its population. By 1925, alcohol was a state monopoly, and by 1940 there were more shops selling alcohol than fruit, meat and vegetables put together.

It did not stop there. Production of spirits trebled between 1940 and 1980, and the consumption of all alcoholic drinks – including wine and beer as well as vodka and brandy – increased eightfold. Most of this growth was in the Russian heartland, rather than on the traditionally Muslim fringes of the empire where drinking was less popular. Wages were rising and living standards too, as the damage caused by the war was repaired and stability allowed economic advances. Thanks to the more humane style adopted by the government after Stalin's death, it became almost impossible to get sacked, and Russians got paid whether they turned up to work drunk or sober. There was no longer a limit on how much people could drink, and alcoholism became epidemic.

The novelist Venedikt Yerofeyev, in his underground masterpiece of the late 1960s *Moscow–Petushki*, satirized the standard working week of his cable-laying gang as follows: 'We would play brag one day, drink vermouth the next, play brag again the third day, and on the fourth back to vermouth again ... Needless to say, we didn't lay a finger on the cable drum – in fact if I'd so much as mentioned touching the drum, they'd have pissed themselves laughing.'

Conspiracy theorists speculate that the state liked a drunken population, since that made the Russians easier to control. That may be true, and it is certainly the case that the government was hooked on the revenue from drinking as much as the population was hooked on the oblivion it gave. Taxes earned from alcohol were greater than the defence budget by the early 1970s.

The trouble was, of course, that the same drinking that was financing the government was destroying the population. Alcohol was blamed for a third of car accidents, and four-fifths of deaths on the roads. Almost all sexually transmitted infections were linked to alcohol consumption.

If you look at the figures for how long Russians have been expected to live, the high point to date – just under seventy years – came in the early to mid-1960s. Life expectancy spiked upwards again in the 1980s, briefly surpassing its 1960s level, through only by a couple of months, when Mikhail Gorbachev severely restricted access to alcohol, but fell back once more when the campaign was unwound. By 1994, the average Russian was predicted to live for sixty-four years, and the average Russian man for less than fifty-eight.

In 1965, the first year for which the Russian government presents statistics, 119,170 Russians died from 'external causes' (car crashes, murder, suicide, poisoning, drowning), the majority of which are connected to alcohol. By 1995, that number had almost tripled. In 1965, a total of 419,752 Russians died from problems with their cardio-vascular system, which are often caused by drinking and smoking. By 1995, that number had more than doubled.

National security was at risk too: ground crews apparently would siphon off the pure alcohol in fighter jets' de-icing fluid and replace it with water, causing the planes to crash.

And look at the army, saviour of Russia on the many occasions when foreign invaders have coveted its wealth. Russia's most sacred holiday is Victory Day. Every year, soldiers goose-step over Red Square on 9 May to mark the 1945 triumph over Adolf Hitler. Wave after wave of Red Army troops threw themselves at the German positions defending Berlin that year, clambering over the bodies of their comrades. Finally, the Germans broke and fell, allowing the Russians to wave their red flag from the Reichstag and establish the Soviet Union as a superpower.

That could not happen now. In 1990, some 1.021 million potential Russian soldiers were born. In 1999, that number had dropped to 626,000 – a fall of almost two-fifths in less than a decade. For comparison, since we were on the subject of World War Two, almost 150,000 more babies were born in Germany in 1999 than in Russia, even though there are far fewer Germans than Russians and even though Germany is itself afflicted by a shrinking population.

It is as if Russia's army had already suffered a series of major defeats before even picking up a gun. You cannot fight a war without soldiers and, to breed more troops, you need mothers to have babies. In mid-2009, Russia had 11.7 million women in their twenties. By 2015, that number will have fallen to 6.9 million – that's another two-fifths decline.

In the last sixteen years of communism, 36 million Russians were born and 24.6 million died. In the first sixteen years of capitalism, those figures were more or less reversed: 22.3 million Russians were born and 34.7 million died. If you plot a graph, in which the number of people alive is laid out according to their date of birth, with the youngest at the bottom and the oldest at the top, Russia looks like one of those rocky stacks in the North Atlantic, undermined by the waves until its huge overhang threatens to collapse altogether. The base of Russia's diagram – children – is washed away, and the consequences are almost impossible to predict.

And then there is alcohol's effect on the economy. Some estimates from the late Soviet period had a third of the workforce absent at any one time thanks to over-drinking. 'Drunks are to be found on the shop floor more and more frequently. At some enterprises, special brigades have been formed to "grab" those who have drunk too much and stop them getting to their machines, to prevent accidents. They drink during working hours, they drink after work,' one Soviet economist said in 1981. 'This is the ultimate lack of respect for work, the ultimate negative attitude to it.'

Visitors to Russia remarked on the drinking, but foreigners' travels were restricted, and few people guessed how deep rooted the problem had become. The cost to the state from drinking was estimated, by 1985, at 160 billion roubles, which was four times the revenue from alcohol, and only then did the government wake up to the problem. In Brezhnev's time, the official response was embarrassment. State statisticians stopped listing vodka as a separate item on the yearly sales digest when its sales climbed too high. They instead lumped vodka into 'other' with ice cream, coffee, cocoa and spices, which instantly made 'other' the largest item on the list. Their inaction allowed alcoholism to become epidemic, and sufferers turned elsewhere for help, including to Father Dmitry, as evidenced by the questions he read out in his sermons.

'I know that abortion is a sin … but I'm afraid with my drunk of a husband – what kind of child will I have? Do we allow abortions in such cases?'

The train was filling up, and vendors pushed past trying to interest us in their wares: an eggwhisk-shaped back massager, magazines, ice cream. A man sat down opposite me, then his wife. He was large and our knees touched. He had a two-litre bottle of homemade wine, opened it and downed a couple of inches. He offered it to me, but I gestured to the beer bottle tucked between me and the side of the carriage. He nodded, and left me alone.

Three more people joined us on our benches. There was no room for my bottle, and I put it on the floor. A sharp-angled metal ashtray jutted out in front of me and I could either wedge my knee against it or lay my thigh alongside it. Either way, it cut into my leg. I was uncomfortable before we had even set off, and my buttocks were numb by the time we reached the city limits.

The train rattled through parched fields. My plan to avoid the sun had failed. The train had swung round and I was in the full glare. The beer was beginning to make me nod, and the sun was battering the right-hand side of my scalp. Despite the discomfort and the crush, I fell asleep.

Every weekend Father Dmitry's disciples took this two-hour train journey. It was a long way to come to hear a sermon, but his was the only one on offer. I awoke before Kabanovo, and alighted with a dozen or so others on to a long platform lined with a picket fence.

I walked through the village, along the dusty shoulder of a busy road. On either side were the kinds of solid brick buildings owned as weekend houses by wealthy Muscovites. Bare-chested men were watering their gardens, visible through chinks in high metal fences. A teenager at a bus stop pointed me to the right towards the church. The dust had coated my shoes light brown by the time I got there.

I had no one to meet, and no particular plan worked out for what I would do here, so I sat down on a rock in the shade and pulled out Father Dmitry's sermons once more. This one was in the question-and-answer form that he preferred, and repeated his core message.

'How do you relate to Jews?' someone asked.

'As sacred friends,' he replied.

'And how do you relate to Russians?'

'As sacred friends,' he continued.

'And how to other ethnicities?'

'Also as sacred friends,' he concluded. But that did not satisfy his interrogator.

'You have all sorts of friends. But let's be specific. Russians say that Jews destroyed Russia, planted atheism here. Do you agree?'

'We all destroyed Russia and implanted atheism: one person did in theory, and another in practice. We are all people before God, and you should not divide us up or blame someone for it.'

Father Dmitry would not be drawn into prejudice, into the language of blame used by the state. He preached tolerance and trust. It was his weapon against the misery and distress he saw around him. The Soviet government's strategy for controlling its population – and one it inherited from its imperial predecessor and all other empires since the beginning of time – was divide and rule. The fact that he was asked such questions shows how divided Soviet citizens had become. Russians distrusted Jews, and vice versa. Armenians distrusted Azeris, and vice versa. Uzbeks distrusted Tajiks, and so on. Father Dmitry's response was the opposite: unite and resist.

When I looked up from the sermon, two puppies were observing me. They barked and scurried behind a bush. When I read on, they emerged. When I stopped again, they vanished. We played the game for a while, until I became distracted by a particularly itchy mosquito bite on my index finger which had swelled my whole left hand like a rubber glove filled with water.

A light beige Lada car pulled up outside the church. It was old but well cared for. The driver gathered his belongings. He was aged around sixty, wore thick spectacles with cheap frames and a pocketed waistcoat full of screwdrivers and tools. He was carrying a bag with a pair of aluminium valves that appeared to be part of a heating unit. I asked if he was local, and he nodded.

We chatted about the village, and life there, about jobs (none), the collective farm (closed), children (few) and old people who might remember Father Dmitry.

He shook his head: 'The people who knew him are all dead now. I was a student then so I did not know him but people still remember him, and talk about how he was investigated.'

He was going into the priest's quarters to drop off the valves, he said, and offered to show me around. Father Dmitry's room had been subdivided into two smaller rooms since he lived here, with the partition between them decorated with teddy-bear wallpaper. I tried to imagine Ogorodnikov and his friends eating their communal meals here and discussing their faith.

Father Dmitry might still have been under suspicion in Moscow, but he received a warm welcome from the locals. 'When the upper hierarchy threw me and my children to the mercy of fate and attempted to make me admit my supposed slanders, when all these rumours spread around, the people helped me. They fed me and did not let me despair, and did not condemn me. When people close to the hierarchy tried to accuse me, saying I had not obeyed them, that I had broken some law, the people sympathized. Sympathy and love, that is what you need.'

I followed the handyman out of the room, and he unlocked the door into the church itself – a simple structure of brick and tin that had been rebuilt since Father Dmitry's day – then we crossed the road to the church's schoolroom, with its garden full of potatoes.

'You should not leave land empty,' the handyman said, squinting at me for approval through his lenses.

'They appear to be doing well,' I ventured, although in truth the plants looked spindly.

'Ah, how are they doing well? Our soil is just sand.'

He offered me a lift to the station and I accepted with pleasure. It was not as hot as Moscow out here, but it would still be uncomfortable to walk far. He had, he said, previously lived in one of the more remote villages, but the bus service was cancelled and he had been forced to move into Kabanovo. He could not afford to run his car all the time, but liked to drive on occasion.

Back on the platform we stood for a while in silence, watching a crow, its hands behind its back, balancing along one of the rails, then jumping nimbly round and stepping back.

'Do you think', he asked me at last, 'someone like me, with the experience I have, could find a job in Britain?'

I said I did not know, but before he left I asked him his name. He told me: Father Nikolai. I looked after him. He was the village priest, and I had had no idea.

Father Dmitry did not last long at Kabanovo. The local authorities had no appetite for groups of bearded Muscovites turning up and perverting the locals' minds with dangerous talk of trust and community and the deficiencies of the state. All the same, he continued his single-minded campaign against alcohol, abortion, despair and degradation, noting down the talks as he had before.

A woman came to Father Dmitry to confess.

'Do you have any particular sins?'

'Yes, abortions.'

'How many?'

'Many.'

'Well, how many?'

'Thirty,' she said, and cried.

By 1991, the average Russian woman had had 3.4 abortions over the course of her life. Stalin banned abortions but, after they were legalized in 1955, they became the dominant form of birth control. There were 8.3 million in the Soviet Union in 1965. In 1992, Russian women terminated 3.3 million pregnancies. The number has fallen since then, perhaps because the contraceptive pill is now widely available, but there are still more abortions than live births in many Russian regions, including Komi (where Father Dmitry was imprisoned) and Bryansk (where he was born), and the overall rate is four times the European average.

Other dissidents did not have Father Dmitry's insight into the health concerns of ordinary Russians, since they did not really encounter them. Sakharov, although a brave and humane man, was still calling for Russians to have fewer children in the late 1960s to combat global over-population.

'Mankind can develop smoothly only if it looks upon itself in a demographic sense as a unit, a single family without divisions into nations other than in matters of history and traditions. Therefore, government policy, legislation on the family and marriage, and propaganda should not encourage an increase in the birth rates of advanced countries while demanding that it be curtailed in underdeveloped countries,' the great dissident wrote, in his typically lofty style. His calls for intellectual freedom and peaceful coexistence were very powerful, but they were also very irrelevant to the kind of people Father Dmitry was dealing with.

In 1970, Russia's homicide rate was eight times the European average, but such numbers – with their implicit rebuke to the government – were increasingly hard to find. In 1972, Brezhnev's government stopped publishing life-expectancy statistics. That same decade, infant mortality figures dropped out of the data too, having risen sharply from 22.9 per thousand in 1970 to 31.4 in 1976. The government instead boasted of having one of the highest proportions of doctors in the world, but hid how little effect they were having.

Healthcare spending dropped from 6 per cent of national wealth when Brezhnev took power to half of that by the mid-1980s. Over the same period, the number of cigarettes imported doubled to more than 73 billion a year: that means the Soviet Union imported a packet of cigarettes a month for every man, woman and child in the country. It made its own cigarettes too.

In December 1975, Father Dmitry was sacked once more. A letter from his bishop accused him of the 'systematic inclusion in his discussions and sermons of political material of an anti-social character, including tendentious criticism of the life of our state'. The bishop went on to criticize him for having used the church buildings for preaching to groups of people who had gathered to hear him preach, although it might be supposed that such was a priest's job, before attacking the Western media that had spoken out in his defence.

'I consider it unacceptable that on some internal question in Church life, including in relation to Church discipline, which is regulated by the canons, laws and traditions of our Church, anyone at all from abroad should put pressure on us, in this case in defence of Father Dmitry, in the aim of furthering their own interests,' he concluded.

That was a nod to the kind of conspiracy theorizing that was already consuming the KGB, who established a special Fifth Directorate in 1968 to crack down on intellectuals, students, nationalists, religious believers, Jews and anyone else suspected of serving foreign powers. Even before Father Dmitry came to Kabanovo, the KGB were trying to break dissidents through long interrogation and the planting of sympathetic agents in their cells as fake detainees. If they succeeded, the dissidents were paraded before Western journalists. Foreign reporters were showing increasing interest in the dissident story, and were beginning to write about Father Dmitry. His sacking from Kabanovo in December 1975 made the news in papers across the world.

'Reds admit ban of rebel priest,' said the headline in the *Baltimore Sun*. 'Soviet priest draws anger of government', read the headline on an Associated Press report picked up by other US newspapers. And he was not the only famous religious dissident. His friends Gleb Yakunin and Lev Regelson gained a splash of their own with a report to the World Christian Council on the persecution of believers.

In response, the Soviet authorities unleashed the heavy weapons of their propaganda arsenal. *Izvestia*, one of their two largest newspapers, went on the attack. In January 1976, Vladimir Kuroyedov, the government's most senior religious official, took over almost a whole page to detail how in fact Soviet religious laws were the most 'humane and democratic in the world', and that anyone saying otherwise was lying to harm the country's international prestige.

There were, he continued with sadness, a few malcontents, but religious believers themselves could be trusted to drive them out. Although, in fact, a hundred of Father Dmitry's parishioners – at considerable risk to themselves – had signed a petition protesting against his sacking, Kuroyedov insisted they had expelled him because of his 'sermons of an anti-social content'.

'For this same reason his parishioners have thrown him out of two other churches,' Kuroyedov added. That was a lie. Father Dmitry lost his first position because the church was dynamited and his second because he was sacked by the bishop – neither of them things Kuroyedov could admit without fatally undermining his own argument that believers were free and unhindered. Instead he linked Father Dmitry to the state's enemies.

'This "shepherd", previously convicted of a crime, has been declared by reactionary propaganda in the West to be a "genuine fighter for the faith, suffering for Christ",' Kuroyedov's article concluded with heavy Russian irony, naturally without mentioning the nature of Father Dmitry's criminal offence – writing a poem – or his subsequent rehabilitation.

It was a warning to his parishioners and friends to shun him, to leave him alone, but they did not heed it. Father Dmitry had taught them to trust each other, and that meant defending each other too.

'To tear a priest away from his flock is like a doctor leaving his patients, or a teacher his pupils. But these comparisons are weak. It would be nearer the truth to say it is like tearing a mother away from her children,' said Igor Shafarevich, a mathematician and prominent dissident, in a statement on Father Dmitry's dismissal.

'Father Dmitry's living, free, Christian word went into the hearts of listeners and fanned their faith; it also gripped those who were seeking, those who doubted, unbelievers. Father Dmitry attracted young people – this was his main crime,' said an appeal by Father Dmitry's friends Yakunin and Regelson to the BBC.

Not everyone agreed with them, of course. Father Dmitry's notebooks include a conversation with a fellow priest who told him he liked the sermon, but would have taken out 'the sharpness'.

'And if a sword isn't sharp, if a sabre isn't sharp, how do you fight? With a blunt blade? The sharpness is the point,' replied Father Dmitry.

The priest was not so sure: 'If we are tough, they will shut the churches. As it is we are preserving something.'

But Father Dmitry was an old campaigner, and refused to change. He said the fight to save his nation was urgent, and could not be put off for tactical reasons.

'In the camps we used to say "You should eat today what you could eat tomorrow." And I am doing today what I could do tomorrow, since otherwise tomorrow might not come,' he said. 'How many people were shot, how many were killed in the camps, how many died at the front with a meaningless scream? They died, and for what? So their children could suffer?'

6

They behaved like free men

I met Father Vladimir Sedov between the platforms of a metro station in western Moscow. Cheerful and lean in his black robes, he looked like a wolf with a sense of humour. His flat was chaotic, full of books and icons and bunk beds and living things. His cats regularly interrupted our conversation. One was bald and as friendly as a dog, one more cautious, despite its spangly collar. There was also a parrot, and several sons.

Father Vladimir is straight-backed and dignified with the bearing of a man in early middle age, but he shared his memories of Father Dmitry with the eagerness of a schoolboy rushing for lunch. He was born in Baku, but grew up in the Moscow region where his father was an engineer. He studied in the mathematics department of his university, and a distinguished career beckoned when this happened: 'There were these rumours about an unusual priest who held question-and-answer sessions. My friends had been, and I heard about him, and I wanted to go too.'

This was in 1976, just a few months after *Izvestia*'s assault on Father Dmitry and his dismissal from the church in Kabanovo. It is clear from Father Dmitry's sacking, and from the criticism of him in the national press, that the authorities considered him a significant threat by this stage. Nonetheless, in April 1976, he got a new parish. Perhaps the Church authorities calculated that he would, after having been sacked twice, not behave so unorthodoxly another time. Perhaps some individuals in the Church hierarchy secretly admired his stance. They were all believers after all, and a few bishops may deep down have been proud that one of their fellows was doing his job as they were all supposed to. Perhaps top officials were sensitive to foreign opinion, and did not want to give Westerners an opening to criticize the Soviet Union by depriving Father Dmitry of a post, no matter how irritating he was for the old men in the Kremlin.

Besides, the security organs were no doubt hoping that, after the very public warning of the *Izvestia* article, ordinary churchgoers would shun Father Dmitry's services. It was well known that association with dissidents could lead to a summons, to questioning, to unemployment and, potentially, to prison. And prison was a place to be dreaded. Dissidents like Anatoly Marchenko had written prison diaries and circulated them in typewritten and carbon-copied manuscripts, so everyone knew that the Soviet jails were brutal, diseased and cruel. At one point, Marchenko, who was jailed for illegally attempting to leave the country, described seeing a fellow inmate chop off his penis and throw it out the window at a female guard. The other prisoners barely flinched, so accustomed were they to human degradation.

But, in many ways the authorities' approach proved counterproductive. The young people coming to Father Dmitry's church knew the risk they were running. But, for many of them, that was the point.

Father Vladimir was at that time a gangly young man, barely out of his teens, and felt stultified by the official culture dished up to Soviet citizens like prison slop on a tray. He had looked at yoga, at progressive rock, at Buddhism and at all the other bits and pieces of other people's cultures that drifted through Moscow in those days. They did not appeal. He wanted something he could feel part of, something Russian.

He was intrigued therefore by the thought of a Russian priest who refused to walk the official path, so he took the train to Grebnevo, Father Dmitry's new parish. As he told me about it, he turned to his computer and called up a satellite image from the internet. He zoomed us in, click after click. First we saw the whole of Russia, then Moscow appeared, before it vanished to the left of the screen as he magnified a spot to its east. The word 'Grebnevo' appeared and the village itself filled more of the screen until we could see the church too, in a wood on the shores of a reservoir.

'He asked everyone who went to the church whether they were christened, and there were a lot of people who weren't christened. But

I told him I was christened, even though I wasn't, and he blessed me. My friends knew I was lying, and told me they knew, but I insisted that I had been christened secretly,' Father Vladimir said, smiling at the knots his younger self had tied himself into.

'I felt ashamed of having lied to them, and to him, so when I got back to university, I went to the church near Moscow State University and I got christened. I did not know the creed or anything, so the priest was cross with me, but I insisted and my happiness was so great afterwards that I ran back to the university like I was running on air.'

At that time, getting christened was a risky step. Many priests took lists of these new believers and shared them with the authorities. That meant being christened could hurt your employment prospects, or lead to attention from the security services. Father Dmitry, to avoid this, often christened people in his own home and deliberately did not write down their names. He later said he christened thousands of adults, sometimes a dozen a day. His rebel attitude captivated Father Vladimir.

'It is hard to fight a totalitarian system. People who were scared, who needed support, they went to him. There were poets, artists. They had heard of this priest that you could talk freely to. A lot of people sensed what I sensed, that Father Dmitry was the most life-loving and optimistic man we ever met, and he was a man who had lived the hardest life.'

His friends were surprised by Father Vladimir's passion. After all, they had been the believers, not him. His sudden conversion took them by surprise. He caught the train to Grebnevo the next time Father Dmitry was speaking, then the next time also. He devoured every word the priest spoke, as well as those of the older believers – Ogorodnikov was there, of course, so were his friends Yakunin and Regelson – and decided to follow the priest as a disciple: a spiritual child in the language of Russian Orthodoxy.

'I was a student, and I had a room in the halls, but after that I mainly stayed in Grebnevo. I wanted to stop university, but Father Dmitry thought people had to try not just to swim with the current, but to make something of themselves. He thought believers should not be marginalized, but should be part of society, so I stayed at university.'

Father Dmitry already had a son and daughter, but he took his spiritual children into his home as if they were new additions to the family.

'I helped him in his services. Before me there was another young man, but he had married so there was a free place. Father Dmitry was so open that I lived with him there and in his flat in Moscow. He slept on the bed, and I slept on a quilt on the floor,' Father Vladimir remembered.

He glanced back at the satellite image on the screen, fiddling around with the mouse to zoom in a little bit more on the church itself. At maximum magnification, the quality of the picture was not very good. You could see a dome, with a long shadow stretching north, and woods around the church, but very few details.

'I can remember it so clearly. It's a shame you can't see much in that picture.'

I asked when he last went back.

'Oh, I haven't been since those days,' he said.

Well then, I asked, would he be prepared to show me the church? We could go together. He paused, looking at the screen again, thought for a while, then nodded. On Thursday, he said. He would drive me out there to save us the train journey in the heat. We would visit the scene of his conversion. It was also the scene of Father Dmitry's final confrontation with the security services, and Father Vladimir would talk me through how it had happened.

That Thursday, therefore, I was sat in the front seat of Father Vladimir's little white Toyota. It had right-hand drive, like a British car, because it had been imported from Japan. Such second-hand cars have taken over most of the far east of Russia and are increasingly available in Moscow too. Since they are cheaper and more reliable than many of the other cars in Russia, it is not surprising that drivers like them. For passengers, however, they are disconcerting. I was sitting in what should have been the driver's seat. Oncoming traffic whizzed by inches from my left knee, and I felt vulnerable without a wheel to hold on to.

The Moscow ring road was, as usual, heavily congested. We crawled forward, and Father Vladimir and I discussed the Olympics, and whether the Summer Games – next hosted by Britain – or the Winter

Games – next to be hosted by Russia – was more prestigious. Retail mansions and supermarkets passed by on both sides. When we finally turned off to the right, they gave way to botched-together markets for building products. When we turned off to the left, even those vanished, giving way to the glories of the Russian countryside. With the air-conditioning on, I could appreciate its beauty without having to gasp in the heat.

'There were fewer cars back then. We used the suburban trains, or the bus,' said Father Vladimir after a while of silence. He had clearly been reminiscing to himself about his first journeys to see Father Dmitry in Grebnevo. 'There were fewer stray dogs too,' he added, as we drove past two puppies and their mother, her teats swinging in time with her legs as they walked along the verge. 'I haven't come back here, because he was not here. Without him, there was no reason. I followed him here.'

The broad horizons of Russia opened around us: birch trees, scrubby fields, little houses with lace carvings around their windows, all painted in fine blues or greens. I left him to talk as I looked at the view.

'The Soviet government was like a great wall, you know. It did not let good or bad develop. But since those days the weeds have grown fast, the wild capitalism has spread.'

We entered the town of Shchelkovo – five-storey apartment blocks, trade centres, generic restaurants, scattered trash – and Father Vladimir decided we should stop and see the church. Most Russian churches have onion-shaped domes made of silver metal or wooden shingles. In the grandest churches, the domes are golden or painted in bright colours, and cluster in clumps like tulips.

This church was, however, built of red brick and spired like a Protestant chapel. Father Vladimir told me that he had once known the priest here. There was some connection to Father Dmitry too that I did not catch as we passed inside. More than a hundred women were following the service, which was an impressive turnout for a Thursday, and the sweet harmonies of the choir were unusually well sung.

A young priest held out a gold cross for the worshippers to kiss. A grand screen was half obscured by scaffolding, but its ranks of gold icons – all the bearded faces looking to the middle, where two icons of Jesus and Mary gazed out at us – were arresting nonetheless. Several of the women noticed Father Vladimir and pushed over to him for a blessing, cupping their hands at waist height, casting their eyes down.

While they gathered, I watched the heat haze from the candles dance before the icons. It was mesmerizing to see the ancient faces of the saints come alive in the shimmering air. An elderly woman standing next to me asked me who I was. Raisa Ivanovna, she was called, and it turned out she had worshipped at Father Dmitry's church in the 1970s.

'It was amazing how young people came to his church. Normally it was just us old women. I was already old then, like I am now.' She laughed. 'I had always believed, but I believed more after I heard him, if you know what I mean. He was so kind. The security services questioned me. They asked me who, what, when, where, but I just told them I went to him as a kind shepherd, and that he was like a father to me. He was a man under surveillance, you know, and we were amazed by how many people came to him anyway. They did not care. What did they have to be scared of, what did we have to be scared of? We were not spies. We knew we were not spies.'

Father Vladimir had returned, and was preceded by a middle-aged woman: plump and handsome, with laughter around her eyes. She shook my hand. She was Zoya Semyonova, she told me, and had been another of Father Dmitry's spiritual children. We would, she said, go for lunch.

We turned our backs on the service. Another few women begged a blessing from Father Vladimir on our way out of the door. We walked over the road, around the back of a nine-storey block and into the lift. She rang the bell next to a door – steel with padding over it – and we waited. She rang the bell again, until we finally heard movement. It swung open, to reveal another Zoya – Zoya's daughter – who had clearly been asleep.

'We have come for lunch,' Zoya senior announced, with the authority of a mother, so Zoya junior stood aside and we all trooped into the kitchen. Zoya senior then summoned her husband, who was also a priest who had known Father Dmitry, and we sat down to drink tea.

Zoya's husband, Father Alexander, arrived before Zoya junior had finished her preparations. He was dressed in black shirt and trousers, but not in a robe like Father Vladimir. He had the priest's full beard,

however, and a wide-nostrilled nose that made him look almost ridic-
ulously Russian.

While Zoya junior attempted to improvise a meal for this unexpected kitchenful of guests, he launched into the story of Father
Dmitry.

Father Alexander, it transpired, had been the young man who preceded Father Vladimir as the altar boy. In fact, it was his marriage to
Zoya senior that opened up the spot that Father Vladimir then filled.
He had, like Ogorodnikov, experienced those first sermons in the
cemetery church in Moscow, when it seemed the whole city was
packed into the courtyard to be intoxicated by free speech. He was
just twenty-three then and worked as a conductor on the railways, a
job that gave him a lot of spare time to dedicate to the faith.

'He christened people at home in those days because the KGB were
following him. He had a domestic chapel where he held little services.
My brother had been christened as a child, but I had not. My parents
were scared of the KGB; my mother had been in a German concentration camp and was scared of everything. We were believers, though
of course we did not shout about it. We lit candles, painted eggs, all of
that,' he said. His eyes were dark and direct, and did not flinch while
he told his story. I would look up from my notebook and he would be
sitting in exactly the same way as he had been two minutes earlier, his
eyes focused on me whether I was looking at him or not.

When Father Dmitry was sacked, his congregation gathered in his
flat. 'It was like the earliest Christian times. People sat anywhere they
could: on windowsills, on the floor. They drank tea. It was unique.
They asked questions. It was a festival of faith. For a year the KGB
were thinking, wondering, how they could stop this. They gave him a
church to keep him under control; that was at Kabanovo. But of
course they didn't control him. Oh, it was so beautiful there.'

Zoya junior had by now, from somewhere, produced soup, fish,
salad and bread. She too was listening to her father as he evoked the
different world they had lived in just forty years before.

'People came from Moscow to him, you could not stop this.
The villagers, these collective farmers, saw how these beautiful ladies
from Moscow came. It was like a place of pilgrimage. People would
pray, eat, sleep, then stop for the night. And in the morning, they

would clean, talk, have these discussions. Then they would put up the antenna and listen to the BBC and the radio would broadcast these same words he had just spoken in Kabanovo.'

It was like a different country, the way he described it, as if they were living outside the Soviet Union.

'The local people were kind. They brought mushrooms, eggs, even chickens that would run around everywhere.' He laughed. Everyone else chuckled too. 'And there was a china factory, I remember, so we only ever drank tea from new cups. We had a big kettle, and I was the main operator of the kettle.'

The KGB were circling outside the windows, the nation was sinking into a depression, but in their little room in Kabanovo – the one I had seen that is now subdivided by teddy-bear wallpaper – they had been free. One evening the stove was burning, and it was howling winter outside.

'It is so good,' said Father Dmitry. 'And it is so scary. It cannot last long being so good in such circumstances.'

'We knew the KGB were all around,' said Father Alexander, after a mouthful of soup, 'and of course it was scary, but we were together.'

Father Dmitry wrote later of the kind of tactics the KGB used against him. Marina, one of the congregation, was repeatedly summoned and questioned about him; then her mother was summoned; then her younger brother; then the family's friends and neighbours. It was designed to drive people away from Father Dmitry, who wrote to his spiritual children to reassure them, and to raise their spirits.

'The godless have used everything: libel, forgery, traitors among the priesthood, but everything has been without result, and now they have moved to their favourite method: violence, physical force. But as was said long ago: physical force is powerlessness. In their powerless fury, they don't know what to do.'

Father Dmitry had learned about violence himself in 1975 on a trip he made with Alexander and a couple of others. They all wanted to drive to Bryansk, to Berezina, to Father Dmitry's home village, to see his brother and his relatives. The four of them squeezed into a Zaporozhets, a small, rickety, noisy Soviet car. Alexander and a doctor friend were in the back. Father Dmitry and the driver were up in front.

When they set off down the main road to Bryansk, a barrier was across the road. It looked new, as if it had just been installed, and they had to make a 400-kilometre diversion. It was a daunting prospect, but they were determined. Perhaps the driver got tired on this extended journey, or perhaps it was too dark. He did not see that a truck had been parked across the road until it was too late.

'We crashed into the back tyre. They were right in front of us. They wanted to kill us. Both of Father Dmitry's legs were broken below the knee,' said Alexander. It is impossible to know now if the crash was really an assassination attempt or just a strange accident, but they could be forgiven for thinking the worst. A black car had been following them, and a bus arrived soon after the accident, full of people who laughed at them, at how the God-botherers had got in an accident.

They were taken to a hospital intended only for workers at a nearby nuclear power station, and left untreated all night.

After lunch and back in Father Vladimir's white Toyota, we drove through Shchelkovo, the drab apartment blocks sliding past. It merged almost without a break into Fryazino, with more apartment blocks, then into Grebnevo, where at least the houses were smaller.

I could see Father Vladimir's eyes flitting around, as he looked for things he recognized. At last we mounted a small rise, and he sighed. We stopped on the edge of a beaten stretch of earth that faded into a garden. Ahead of us was a gate, and beyond was the dome of the church. He sat for a while without getting out of the car, smiling.

Zoya senior was there before us, looking up at the church. 'It's beautiful,' she said. And it was. The green dome on its white and ochre columns was proud against the blue sky. Bright summer vegetation filled in the scene. 'When Father Dmitry first came here, he was with his wife Nina and she gaped at this. She thought they had been mistaken – she told Father Dmitry to check they had come to the right place.'

Father Dmitry took up his new post here in April 1976, a time when the Cold War was getting distinctly colder. The early 1970s had been marked by détente, when the two sides wished to trade with each other and resolve their differences. Washington was losing the Vietnam War and facing massive anti-war protests at home. It did not want diplomatic trouble abroad as well. Henry Kissinger, national security advisor and later secretary of state, was not interested in ideology or in lecturing the Soviets on how to behave. He wanted good relations, and both sides wanted to spend less money on weapons.

The culmination of détente was a summit in Helsinki in August 1975, where almost all European countries, as well as Canada and the United States, signed a series of accords recognizing each other's borders, and establishing a multilateral framework for negotiations (it later became the Organization for Security and Co-operation in Europe).

This was a triumph for Moscow, which had long wanted the West to recognize the existence of a separate East Germany and its own dominance of the eastern half of the continent. Almost as an afterthought, the signatory countries tacked on an agreement to respect basic human rights. These obligations were nothing new for the Soviet Union. Its own constitution contained most of the freedoms guaranteed in a democracy, and it had signed up to the founding documents of the United Nations, with their guarantees for all human rights. Officials had never kept these old promises, however, and Brezhnev himself told journalists he had no intention of enforcing the new ones.

'No one should try to dictate to other people … the manner in which they ought to manage their internal affairs,' he said after signing the treaty. He seemed to think it would have no significance beyond the paper it was written on.

Some senior KGB officials, including KGB head Yuri Andropov, thought differently. They warned Brezhnev about the risks of signing up. They said these obligations might give the dissidents and critics in the West new tools to use against Moscow, but Brezhnev's government – intoxicated by its success in winning recognition of the borders the Soviet Union had imposed on Eastern Europe after World War Two – ignored them.

The dissidents, ever imaginative, soon proved Andropov right. In October 1975, Sakharov won a Nobel Peace Prize, giving the dissidents a morale boost. Over the next two years, they formed Helsinki Groups to monitor the Soviet Union's compliance with its obligations under the Helsinki Accords – the first in Moscow under Yuri Orlov, the others in Ukraine, Georgia, Armenia and the Baltic States. They knew these groups were illegal, but they presented them as civil initiatives to assist the government, and they could claim to be doing so under a treaty Brezhnev had himself signed up to.

Every report they wrote was written dispassionately, singling out the particular clauses of the agreement that had been violated. It was a severe embarrassment for the KGB, and Father Dmitry was in no mood to make the agents' job any easier.

If officials had hoped that, by giving him a place in this elegant church, built in the late eighteenth century, they could persuade him to shut up, they were disappointed. This was closer to Moscow than Kabanovo, just 30 kilometres away from the city, and even larger crowds of worshippers came to hear him speak, and to enjoy the freedom of true discussion.

'We discussed everything freely, not needing to look around us, expressing ourselves in our own language. It was like we lived outside the state. It was as if our country wasn't militantly atheist. This freedom amazed one schoolboy from Leningrad. He at first announced that he was an atheist, that he could not believe, but after spending three days with us, he asked to be christened, and became a militant believer,' Father Dmitry wrote later.

The state's pressure did not of course let up, no matter what Father Dmitry thought about it. The dissidents' underground newspaper – the *Chronicle of Current Events* – repeatedly detailed the police raids on his home and those of his friends, just like it recounted the arrests of Jewish activists and Ukrainian nationalists and the exiling of scientists and writers. Police officers marched through the church during services, taking photos and making recordings. Police volunteers in red armbands jostled the worshippers as they filed into the church.

But Father Dmitry and his friends were together, and they were not afraid. In the words of Andrei Amalrik, one of the founders of the Moscow Helsinki Group and a prolific writer, 'The dissidents accomplished something that was simple to the point of genius: in an unfree country they behaved like free men, thereby changing the moral atmosphere and the nation's governing traditions.'

The police might be outside, but inside the dissidents had each other, and they had their radios. They could hear about themselves on the BBC, and sometimes they could even read about themselves in the Soviet press.

In April 1977, the *Literary Gazette*, one of the Soviet Union's top publications and – KGB defectors later revealed – one that could always be relied upon to print whatever the security services wanted, launched a fresh assault on Father Dmitry, Ogorodnikov and other friends of theirs. Considering that he was supposedly just a village priest, and the others were ordinary citizens, it was a vastly disproportionate response. But the government had to do something. The repeated reports on foreign radio were in danger of turning Father Dmitry into the country's most authoritative religious figure.

The *Literary Gazette*'s story used the standard Soviet technique of heavy irony to undermine its targets, and combined it with excessive use of quotation marks to cast entirely unfair doubt on them. Father Dmitry was always called 'Father Dmitry', for example, and his friends were not described as very respectable, they were 'very respectable'.

The effect is certainly comic, and as I sat in the library reading the old yellowed pages I laughed at the memory of a story my wife once told me. She is a doctor and had a colleague who would, when bored, use the same technique employed by the Soviet propagandists and highlight random words in a patient's medical notes to amuse later medical teams (patient came in with a 'friend', complaining about a sore 'knee' and other 'symptoms'). It is not a sophisticated form of humour, more suited to an exhausted doctor on a night shift than supposedly the best propagandists in the world.

The paper quoted some of Father Dmitry's poetry, and then levelled the allegation that he had, while living under German occupation, collaborated with the Nazis by having his verses printed in an occupation newspaper. This, the article implied, was the reason he had been arrested and sentenced to the gulag.

'"Father Dmitry" does not so much preach the Ten Commandments as transgress them, and at the same time the laws of his country,' the paper said. That was a major accusation. In what was clearly a warning sanctioned from on high, Father Dmitry was being told he was breaking the law.

The article ended, however, with an admission of how the Soviet government was losing the propaganda war. It said the article was written so as to warn innocent people away from talking to these dangerous criminals – or, as it quoted an unnamed citizen as saying, to 'protect those close to us from the pernicious influence of these swindlers … let everyone know what is hidden behind their masks' – but admitted that the potential victims would not hear the warning since it would not be rebroadcast on foreign radio, which was the only source of news they followed.

Father Dmitry understood his growing celebrity and his own news value for foreign correspondents. He called a press conference in response, so as to deny the charges. He had not, he said, had poems printed in fascist newspapers, nor was he a traitor. He was just worried about the fate of the nation.

'My heart was wounded by the suffering of the people, and so I forgot my own well-being and the well-being of my family and made a decision: no matter what may happen, I will bring my mite, however small, to the treasure-house of human salvation, and with this mite I will appear before God saying, look, Lord, that is all that I could do,' he told the assembled journalists. 'They can imprison me again, they can contrive catastrophes, they can execute me, I shall know what I am suffering for.'

It was almost like he was taunting the authorities, laughing at their inability to halt his growing fame and influence. In August 1977, he gave an interview to a journalist from the *New York Times*. He denied that he was involved in politics, but still delved into the politics of his country, and into its unfolding demographic catastrophe.

'Our nation has become corrupted, the family has fallen apart, the nation has got drunk, traitors have betrayed each other, or, as we call them now, stool-pigeons – in huge numbers. We say: a third person could be a traitor, so we try to speak one on one. People say the walls are listening, and we are starting to lie to each other, we do not trust each other,' he said. 'The poor Russian people. What a diabolic storm has broken upon it.'

In Grebnevo, we walked through the gate into the churchyard, a shady wooded area, where the church's cross rose up to catch the afternoon sun. Zoya senior and Father Vladimir were looking around in delight, while Zoya junior and I were smiling at every comment they made and every memory that burst out of them. To the left of the gate had been Father Dmitry's living quarters, and the hall where the believers had gathered for their Sunday discussions.

Zoya senior walked around the side of the building and was trying to get her bearings. 'This was where the room was, it's gone now,' she said, standing on a patch of lawn. 'This is where the ambassadors came. All the great people sat here, French people, English people, Americans, they all sat here.'

Father Vladimir was closely examining the door. 'This was where they arrested me,' he said at last, with a broad smile. 'They broke the second door.' Father Vladimir was arrested in Grebnevo in November 1978. 'It is so strange to be here,' he said. 'It is like it is all living in front of my eyes. I brought some people here after work on Friday, then on Saturday some police cars came from over there. This was in November. Father Dmitry came and told us to stay in bed, that he had a plan to confuse the police, but I was worried they would kill him. So I barricaded the door. All of us were holding the door shut and the police started to smash it down with a log.'

Zoya senior had joined us now: 'I had come up by then, so I was outside with the police, and someone said there were terrorists or bandits inside the building.'

Father Vladimir: 'They finally came in and I tried to hang on to the table, but they took me away.'

Zoya senior, laughing: 'They were saying he's a terrorist, he's a bandit, and I was saying it's just Vladimir, he's a student.'

Father Vladimir was dragged away barefoot, in his underwear, and held for ten days of detention. His arrest was the culmination of three months of police harassment. Uniformed officers regularly pushed into the rooms where Father Dmitry lived and insisted on checking the number of beds, the number of chairs, the number of people. In December, Father Vladimir was detained again and his friend Georgy Fedotov was taken off for psychiatric assessment, in what could have been the prelude to the forced treatment that so many dissidents had to undergo.

Soviet officials began having dissidents diagnosed as insane back in the 1960s, and came to appreciate the value of psychiatric drugs in social control. These chemicals could sedate or torture anyone who refused to obey orders, or who acted differently.

Pyotr Grigorenko, a general who disagreed with the policies followed by Nikita Khrushchev's government, was among the first to be treated this way. The Serbsky Institute in Moscow, supposedly the country's leading centre of psychiatric medicine, proved more than willing to co-operate with the KGB in restraining people such as him. In April 1964, it diagnosed him as suffering from 'paranoid development of the personality, with reformist ideas arising in the personality, with psychopathic features of the character and the presence of symptoms of arteriosclerosis of the brain'.

The report went on:

> Reformist ideas have taken on an obstinate character and determined the conduct of the patient; in addition, the intensity of these ideas is increasing in connection with various external circumstances which have no direct relation to him, and is accompanied by an uncritical attitude to his own utterances and acts ... Because of his mental condition Grigorenko requires compulsory treatment in a special psychiatric hospital, as the paranoid reformist ideas described above are of obstinate character and determine the conduct of the patient.

When his wife Zinaida, genuinely concerned, asked when he had gone mad, a KGB official responded: 'The illness is a subtle one, not everyone would notice it ... but his ideas are socially dangerous.'

Soviet psychiatrists came up with new diagnoses, such as 'creeping schizophrenia', that only they were able to diagnose. Criminal investigators were allowed to request a psychological evaluation, in which doctors could almost always be guaranteed to give the diagnosis the KGB required.

Gennady Shimanov, a Christian, wrote of his own experiences attempting to persuade a doctor that he was just like everyone else.

'No, Gennady Mikhailovich,' the doctor had replied. 'If you were like everyone else, we wouldn't keep you here. How many days have you been here now? Have you seen a single normal person here? There you are. Well, all right. Now tell me please about your "conversion to God" as you call it.'

When Shimanov tried to find out what his symptoms were, the doctor was clear.

'Your symptoms are a one-sided fascination with religion. You have cut yourself off from life. After all, how do healthy believers behave? An old dear drops into church, crosses herself, goes out and carries on with her affairs, having forgotten God already. We still have such people, but in time there will be fewer and fewer. But it is quite different with you. That is what worries us.'

And it was not just the religious who were targeted. Zhores Medvedev, a respected scientist, had become obsessed with disproving the theories of Trofim Lysenko – a charlatan biologist whose ideas had convinced Stalin and thus replaced orthodox genetics as official scientific doctrine. This was not just a subject of academic interest. Scientists who backed the Mendelian and Darwinian views of genetics and natural selection had been sacked and jailed. After Stalin's death, the ideas of Lysenko had been gradually allowed to fall into disrepute, but Medvedev wanted acknowledgement that they were wrong. He wrote up a history of the affair and published it abroad.

'I read it recently – it's a polemical work,' said the doctor who arrived to examine him. 'By now people have forgotten about Lysenko – the struggle in genetics is over. And instead of forgetting about it like everybody else and getting on with your work, you recently published this book abroad. Why?'

The book is a passionate attack on Lysenko, well sourced and intelligently argued. For the doctors, however, the fact that Medvedev was combining scientific work with historical research was a sign of mental illness.

'As a matter of fact I have observed that your brother suffers from a split personality,' a doctor told Medvedev's twin, Roy, a historian. 'He is a biologist, but is also involved with many things that bear little relation to his immediate responsibilities. Besides, he is always dissatisfied about something, always fighting against something.'

The Soviet state in some ways existed like a country in the Middle Ages, when people were punished for any deviation from the pure religious line. Officials saw Marxism as the revealed truth, while the Soviet Union was the perfect society, and only insanity or dishonesty could explain any deviation from that way of thinking.

Leonid Plyushch, a Ukrainian dissident and one of the most famous victims of psychiatric abuse, said the doctors would explain to him that, since he had risked his own freedom and his family's happiness by his actions, he must be mad. He would respond by saying that the early communists had done exactly the same thing. They had risked imprisonment for something they believed in. The doctors would then respond by saying he was having delusions of grandeur, since he had compared himself to Lenin. They always had an answer.

'Since all dictatorships proclaim heaven on earth, all who refuse to live in that paradise must be crazy – or have been bought by agents of foreign intelligence,' Plyushch wrote.

During that time, he was treated with haloperidol, a powerful anti-psychotic drug that also has strong sedative properties. It was one of the few such drugs produced in the Soviet Union, explaining its popu-larity with Soviet doctors. He was also given insulin shots, specifically to suck up the sugar in his blood and plunge him into artificial comas.

Medvedev was fortunate in having a twin who believed in his san-ity. Roy mobilized support, including from Sakharov, and won release for his brother. Not all dissidents were so lucky in their friends and relations, however, and some spent months inside, enduring regular injections of sulphazin. That was a suspension of sulphur in peach oil, which had no medical use beyond causing pain and inducing fever. Plyushch saw a fellow inmate nearly killed by an injection of sulph-azin.

For now, Father Dmitry's friend Fedotov avoided all that. He was released after a few days, as was Father Vladimir, but it was the kind of harassment intended to make them rethink their behaviour.

It did not work, of course.

Father Vladimir: 'When the police volunteers came in their red arm-bands and were supposed to keep order, we wore white armbands and said we would keep our own order.'

Zoya senior: 'They asked us if we were expecting a high-up boss or someone, and Father Dmitry said we were expecting the highest boss of all. It was Easter, you see.'

Father Vladimir mused on Father Dmitry.

'He was not scared to sacrifice himself, you know. In a totalitarian state, if someone gets in trouble, then they are avoided. This is how the state creates order. It was not just those who were under investigation who were avoided, but people who knew them as well. There was no severe repression, like there had been in the 1940s, but it was not necessary because the fear survived. That was how the state controlled the people, by making them fear each other. Father Dmitry did not have this fear.

'When I ended up in Father Dmitry's big family, I felt I was with people I could trust. He did not aim to create this separate society, it just happened. He created a free society. He was not God, but he was holy. What I experienced then, it was so bright and sharp for me. What I had with him I remember like it was yesterday, I remember that brightness more than', he waved his hand around to indicate the modern world, 'more than this even.'

As we walked out of the church and back into the trees, he described how they had lived in Grebnevo. They ate in shifts, since there were always at least sixty people there, and only seventeen could fit at the table.

'While we ate, someone read out a religious book while Father Dmitry rested. Then he would come out and the discussions started. I used to collect the questions. That was one of my jobs. Some people were happy to ask the questions themselves, but others preferred to write them down, they were still scared of what might happen. This lasted all day, several hours anyway. If the service ended at twelve or one, then we would not leave until six or seven in the evening. If we came on Saturday, we would remove the table and take these screens down off the windows, put mattresses on them and sleep. One morning Father Dmitry came out and laughed, there were so many of us. You could not even turn over in bed.'

We walked along the uneven ground, and through a gap in the crumbling perimeter wall. Here apparently was a palace complex, which had been done up since Father Vladimir was last here. It had been ruinous in his day, and he was keen to see it in its proper glory.

The first herald of the complex was not promising. Someone had defecated in the middle of the path, and it lay stinking and covered in flies, next to a smeared wedge of toilet paper. We stepped over that towards a tent erected by a film crew in the courtyard. They would not be filming an aristocrats' drama, however, because the palace complex that Father Vladimir was so keen to see was in ruins, the bricks exposed and the plaster peeling off in chunks.

Father Vladimir was shocked. It turned out that the complex had indeed been renovated, but had then burned down just before the opening ceremony. He looked around at the mess, the piles of filth and the collapsing glory of the complex.

'You know, say what you like about the people who were in power then, at least they were not these criminals like we have now. Yes, they arrested me, but they did not beat me, whereas now so many people have been killed just for money.'

I said, surprised, that he sounded nostalgic. He seemed to long for the days when the police took him so seriously they would smash down a door and drag him away.

'I am nostalgic. If you think of all the horrors people live through, from these criminals. All authority is from God, and in the 1990s there was no authority. Yes, they were against us in those days, in the 1970s, but at least there was authority of some kind. At least then the oppression was for ideological reasons, now it's just for the money,' he said, looking up at the buildings, and nodding at the gaping windows. 'Lacking a master destroys more than any enemy,' he said.

Trees were growing from the tops of the walls of the old palace now, and the rot looked irreversible. I was not sure whether to take it, like he did, as a metaphor for the whole country or not. I could see his point that the Soviet Union at least looked after its citizens, but I could not agree that that was justification for forcibly injecting them with anti-psychotic drugs if they held a different opinion.

The lake was ahead of us, and provided a more cheerful topic of conversation. Dozens of local kids swam and splashed in the shallows. Others were rowing out in an inflatable dinghy, their friends trying to drag them out. When they failed, they ducked under the water and heaved the whole boat over, shrieking. According to local legend, the lake was created in honour of Catherine the Great in the shape of the Russian letter 'ye', which is the first letter in Yekaterina, her first name, although it did not look much like one when I called up the satellite picture that evening.

That evening, I read some more of Father Dmitry's writings from this period. He self-published a little newspaper, which he called *In the*

Light of the Transfiguration. He stuck it up on the wall in Grebnevo so all his visitors could be instantly informed of the troubles and triumphs of his flock, and of their friends throughout the Soviet Union. A few issues of the paper were reprinted in a three-volume edition of his works published in 2004, and in them he detailed the attacks on him and his spiritual children, and taunted the authorities with his defiance.

'O Godless ones! You have everything in your hands, I have nothing but faith in God,' he wrote. 'To send out an army with weapons against a weaponless priest is shameful and embarrassing.'

He then listed his demands: a printing press of his own; the right to speak out wherever he wanted; and the right to hold services in one of the churches in the Moscow Kremlin. That, he said, would even up the forces. He was beginning to talk as if he was at war with the government.

A couple of days later, I decided to investigate the *Literary Gazette*'s allegations against Father Dmitry. Perhaps he really had published poems in a Nazi-sponsored newspaper. It was not the most terrible of crimes if he had, but the article was very specific in its information. Admittedly it had said Father Dmitry was aged twelve when his work was printed, which would have meant the Nazi occupation started a decade earlier than it actually did, but it was curiously exact in naming the newspaper as the *New Way* and saying it had been published in Klintsy. It even gave a name for Father Dmitry's poem: 'Song from a Cellar'.

'The Hitlerites didn't give a damn about the literary form, but the content was to their liking, and was entirely consistent with Goebbels's propaganda,' it said.

I felt I had a sense of Father Dmitry's character by now. His strength lay in his refusal to compromise. He held firm to his own beliefs in all circumstances, no matter what was demanded of him. If he had published a poem in a Nazi newspaper, it would reveal a flaw in his character, particularly if the poem did indeed chime with Goebbels's propaganda, since it would mean he had collaborated with the occupiers.

I had already visited the Lenin Library's store of papers printed under occupation when I looked for information on Father Dmitry's childhood, so I returned to that high-ceilinged parquet-floored room up under the library's flat roof, with its spider plants and striplights, and found the *New Way*, published in Klintsy, in the card index.

A few minutes later, the helpful librarian brought it over to me, safely enclosed in a stiff card folder. It was stamped 'restricted' – in Soviet times, only researchers approved by the KGB would have had access to this. Now, anyone could read it. After all, no one really cares any more.

The paper was bad quality, yellowed and full of holes. Its masthead said, above the words 'under the Swastika flag to freedom', that the *New Way* was published on Thursdays and Mondays. I sat and began to read. It was pretty crude.

'The German army is bringing freedom to the whole Russian people, together we will defeat communism and secure the dawn of personal well-being,' said one issue in huge letters. And there were collaborators among the Russians who helped set the tone.

'Yid-Bolshevism has not killed the spirit of the Russian people,' said an article by a Russian Orthodox priest published on 11 April 1943, which listed fifty-five churches restored and twenty-nine priests appointed. In June, an article announced a training course for would-be priests.

By 19 August, in the last copy in the archive, fifty-eight churches were open and thirty-five priests operating. However, if Father Dmitry was tempted to celebrate that fact with a poem, he did not do it here. There was no poem or article under his name that I could find, nor a poem called 'Song from a Cellar' published anonymously or otherwise.

The Nazis also issued another newspaper with the title the *New Way*. It was published in Riga, Latvia, but I thought I might as well scan through it anyway. Its first edition had a map of Europe, featuring an enormous Germany stretching from Romania to the North Sea. Photos showed happy Russians surrendering, and Russian youths cleaning German boots with smiles on their faces. There were no poems by Father Dmitry here either, nor in another paper called the *New Times* published in Vyazma, nor in *New Life*, or any of the other forgotten publications issued under the Nazis on the thin and fragile wartime paper.

'It was probably just a libellous article,' the helpful librarian told me. She had become quite involved in my search, and shuttled back and forth with piles of these strange old newspapers.

I returned to my Formica desk and sat with the long drawer from the card index in front of me. I was tempted to agree with her that the *Literary Gazette*'s accusation was a crude lie. It was a strange lie, since if you are going to libel someone and try to blacken their name, it would seem more sensible to make up a really dreadful crime for them to have committed.

According to people quoted in one of Father Dmitry's books, for example, at one point in the 1970s the police alleged during private conversations that he had murdered children on the Nazis' orders. That was proper defamation, which could really damage someone. I mused on why they had not made that allegation public. My imagination started to get tied in knots.

Maybe it was the irrelevance of the poetry offence that meant I should doubt its veracity. Perhaps the KGB were acting in the knowledge that since people know big lies are supposedly more believable than small lies, then small lies are actually more effective as libel. Could it be an advanced double bluff? Or a triple bluff? They had after all had decades of experience in deception. This, I imagined, is the kind of paranoia that must have swirled in everyone's mind in the 1970s. In trying to keep one logical step ahead of the opposition, you began to see shapes in a fog of suspicion that gets thicker the further you go.

I willed myself to snap out of it, and wrote down a conclusion. From the evidence available, I wrote, the allegation that he wrote poems for the Nazis looks like a lie. There, I could leave and get on with other things. I breathed out, and gathered up my notebooks. But then I doubted myself again, pulled out the long drawer full of the dog-eared index cards and scanned through them one last time, checking off all the names of the Nazi papers to make sure I had missed nothing.

In doing so, I accidentally flicked past the cream-coloured divider marking off the next section of the index. Before I had time to rectify my error, my eyes automatically read the index card my clumsiness had revealed. There, staring back at me, were the words *In the Light of the Transfiguration.* That was Father Dmitry's self-published news-paper. I forgot all about the Nazi poem and whether it existed or not. Surely they didn't have Father Dmitry's words here? In the Lenin Library? I bounded back to the issue desk, filled in a request form and handed it over to my friendly ally.

'Have you found it?' she asked.

'No, but I've found something better. It's his own newspaper, I think.'

She shook her head, chuckled at the strangeness of foreigners and walked back through the door to the restricted section. This could be truly extraordinary luck. The Lenin Library was the official reference library for academic researchers. It did not concern itself with the dis-sidents' self-published documents. I had been informed that the Lenin Library possessed no such archive, and yet here one was. I mused over how it could have ended up here at all. Perhaps it had been deposited here after some long-ago K GB investigation ended. Maybe a secret Christian archivist in this bastion of scientific communism had stashed it among the more respectable papers.

When she finally brought me the brown envelope stuffed with doc-uments, I pulled them out with trepidation. I need not have worried, however; it was the real thing. I had seen some issues of the news-paper in Father Dmitry's collected works, but they were incomplete and they lacked the immediacy of seeing a genuine hand-typed, car-bon-copied version.

This was an original. It was typed out – if not by Father Dmitry himself, then by someone who knew him well. It was clearly the work of an amateur. Misspellings were stamped over with rows of capital X X Xs, and each edition had a hand-drawn cross in the masthead. It was like taking a time machine back to the heady days of freedom at Grebnevo. After the fog of the Nazi and Soviet lies, it was a clear, crisp morning.

The threat circling around him was clear on the very first sheet of the very first paper, dated Sunday, 3 June 1979. A priest called Vasily Fonchenkov, he wrote, had joined Yakunin's Christian Committee for the Defence of Believers' Rights, whose statements Father Dmitry regularly republished. The Christian Committee had been founded in December 1976. It worked in partnership with the Helsinki Groups and tried to publicize the troubles that believers of all denominations faced in living their daily lives: arrests, sackings, harassment.

The KGB were acutely sensitive to information leaking into the West that revealed any persecution of believers, much of which came from the Christian Committee. Yakunin had kept the group small, with just three or four members, to prevent penetration, but that tactic had failed. Defectors later revealed that Fonchenkov, though a priest, had been recruited nine years earlier by the KGB's Fifth Directorate and given the codename FRIEND. They did not know it at the time but, by admitting this false friend, Yakunin had given his enemies access to the very heart of their free community, and their every move would now be reported back to the KGB.

Flicking through the pages of Father Dmitry's newspaper – each issue was three sheets of paper, stapled together, typed on just one side – was like fast-forwarding through 1979. On 17 June, there is an account of Father Vladimir being arrested again, although of course at that time he was just a student called Vladimir Sedov, not yet a priest. The police did not know how to deal with him. Officers still believed the old stereotype that only ignorant old women went to church, and had failed to learn that educated young Russians flocked to see Father Dmitry in their dozens.

'How can you be a believer if you have higher education?' he was asked by the police.

'Today it is people with higher education who believe, only dunces don't believe,' he replied with commendable cockiness, and was held for three days without charge.

On 24 June, Father Dmitry conjured up an amusing contrast in generation gaps. In the 1920s, he described a grandmother being challenged by her grandson in the act of hiding an icon under her pillow. The grandson then ripped the cross from around her neck, leaving his grandmother in tears. In his imaginary scenario for the 1970s, the roles are reversed: a communist grandfather challenged his Christian granddaughter.

'I have heard, I have been told, you have been christened,' the grandfather says. 'How could you? You don't think about your grandfather at all, what will happen to me?'

Having provoked a few chuckles with that, Father Dmitry then warned his congregation to be careful of the unknown men who were attending his services, in case they were agents sent to undermine the congregation. Then he ended with the account of a religious man who was locked up in a mental hospital for five months, and given eight of the dreaded injections of sulphazin, the 4 per cent suspension of sulphur in peach oil, which was prescribed to induce a fever and torment the patient.

He wrote about anything that concerned him: about religious festivals, about persecution and about the decline of his nation into alcoholism. A train crash was caused by the driver being drunk. 'History has not known such a number of railway catastrophes as are happening at the moment.'

And there were constant reminders of the danger that the wolves in uniform posed to his flock. In August, a spiritual daughter of his wrote about being summoned by the KGB and questioned for four hours about Father Dmitry and his sermons. The three agents told her not to tell anyone, but she wrote to her priest anyway.

'It is interesting what their aim is in summoning her. We do everything openly, anyone can come and listen. It is clear they are searching for lying witnesses. Well, whatever, let them search,' he wrote. He was confident in the loyalty of his friends.

A week later the same woman recounted a second summons, and the KGB's threat to try her under Article 70 – anti-Soviet activity – of the criminal code, if she did not testify that Father Dmitry himself was engaged in anti-Soviet acts. The threat was clear, but he ignored it. He had more important subjects, like a woman who prayed in the church every day.

'Everyone around her drinks: husband, father, even her fourteen-year-old son. She does not know what to do. Only the church gives her the strength to bear this unbearable cross.'

The impression grew upon me, as I turned the pages, of an embattled community strengthened by the pressure upon it, and of Father Dmitry as the cheerful, smiling centre, the rock on which they could all stand. He printed a letter from a prisoner being held in Vorkuta in the north, who wrote about his interrogations.

'When they ask me who my spiritual father is, I reply with respect that it is the Holy Father Dmitry Dudko ... In Dmitry Dudko I find the spiritual powers that help me serve Jesus Christ,' the letter said.

If he ever doubted himself, letters like that must have kept Father Dmitry going, for he was under no illusion that they could soon all be arrested. He regularly hid the surnames of people who wrote to him, and now used the language of war: 'I don't name surnames on the principle that at the front it is dangerous to pronounce them, since the enemy may be listening.' Together his friends and allies would be strong enough to resist anyone, however.

It was September 1979. The hot Moscow summer was over, and the leaves were turning gold and russet. The first cold nights were biting, and the geese were flying overhead, honking, heading south, reminding the people stuck on solid earth that the cold times were coming. Father Dmitry's neighbours were piling their hay into stacks in the barns and the fields, and preparing to bring the dairy herds indoors for the winter.

Father Dmitry was still pounding away at his typewriter, however. 'They ask us whether our militant mood is not recklessness. We answer that it is less reckless than compromises would be, since they would give up our positions without a fight.'

And a couple of weeks later, on 23 September, when night and day are the same length and summer is undoubtedly over, he returned to the language of war. 'In struggling against our external enemies, against their attacks and persecution, we sometimes forget about or pay too little attention to our internal enemies. If the attacks of external enemies serve to mobilize our forces, to strengthen and unify us, then internal enemies weaken our forces, disorder our ranks, disturb our unity.'

He denied repeatedly that his language was political, or that he was opposed to the Soviet Union, but his words belied him. The film student-turned-believer Ogorodnikov was in prison by now, and Father Dmitry described his hunger strikes. He criticized the Church for being controlled by the Godless. He criticized the government for doing nothing to save the nation from its despair. He criticized the murder of the Russian tsar by the Bolsheviks, and prayed for the souls of the royal family.

Then on 11 November, he wrote that his friend Yakunin, leader of the Christian Committee, had been arrested. The net around him was tightening. The stress was getting to his spiritual children too. Under the constant harassment, the believers were clearly beginning to argue among themselves. He begged them not to divide along 'ethnic' lines – Sovietese for division into Russians and Jews.

'Let the words of the apostle "in Christ there is no Greek nor Jew" be not just words, but a rule for life,' he wrote, in a quotation (actually, a misquotation) of St Paul's letter to the Galatians that he was particularly fond of. 'Free yourselves from prejudice and received opinions.'

He sensed that a decisive battle was close, that this was the calm before a downpour. Ogorodnikov and Yakunin were in prison, so he was the last major Orthodox rebel still at liberty, and the authorities were saving him for last.

Outside his little world, the whole dissident movement was under assault. The security services had been obsessed with squashing the tiresome self-publicists for a decade now. Solzhenitsyn, who was exiled in 1974, brilliantly summed up the state's increasing paranoia, with its insistence that everyone pull together because 'the enemies are listening'.

'Those eternal enemies are the basis of your existence. What would you do without your enemies? You would not be able to live without your enemies. Hate, hate no less an evil than racism, has become your sterile atmosphere,' Solzhenitsyn wrote in an open letter to the Writers' Union.

Dissident opposition to the authorities' sterile atmosphere grew despite the harassment, however, and the arrests severely damaged the Soviet Union's international image. The dissidents' allies in the West were lobbying hard to damage it further, and proved very effective.

The policy of détente pursued by Washington in the first half of the 1970s changed under the presidency of Jimmy Carter, elected in 1976. Activists in the United States, particularly from Jewish groups, had learned well how to lobby US officials and to demand that they put pressure on the Soviet Union to protect basic human rights. Carter even wrote a personal letter to Sakharov saying he would 'use our good offices to seek the release of prisoners of conscience ... I am always glad to hear from you, and I wish you well.'

For Jewish groups, the main priority was the fate of the hundreds of thousands of Soviet Jews who wanted to emigrate to Israel. American Jewish groups bombarded their representatives with demands that they take action, and sent cards and letters to their kin the other side of the Iron Curtain.

The Soviet Union did allow a certain amount of emigration but resented allowing young Jews that it had educated and trained to go and work in a capitalist country. It often demanded they refund the cost of their education before they leave, which was all but impossible. The Jewish activists maintained close contacts with Western groups and in 1977 Natan Shcharansky, the most famous of them, was charged with treason. His conviction was a foregone conclusion, and he used the trial to shame the Soviet government, saying how investigators had threatened him with execution if he did not cooperate.

'Five years ago, I submitted my application for exit to Israel. Now I'm further than ever from my dream. It would seem to be cause for regret. But it is absolutely otherwise. I am happy. I am happy that I lived honestly, in peace with my conscience. I never compromised my soul, even under the threat of death,' he said. He thanked his supporters, among them the veteran dissident Alexander Ginzburg and the Moscow Helsinki Group founder Yuri Orlov, both of whom were also on trial.

'I am proud that I knew and worked with such honest, brave and courageous people as Sakharov, Orlov, Ginzburg, who are carrying on the traditions of the Russian intelligentsia … Now I turn to you, the court, who were required to confirm a predetermined sentence: to you I have nothing to say.'

After his conviction in 1978, his face made the cover of *Time* magazine with the crumbling word 'détente' above him as a headline. He was in prison and his fate had become synonymous for many Westerners with the fate of the whole Soviet people. The government in Washington was finding it harder and harder to prevent public anger over the Soviet Union's treatment of the dissidents from destroying bilateral ties.

Other minorities had champions too. Evangelical groups campaigned on behalf of their co-religionists in the Eastern Bloc, while broader human rights groups kept the fate of the political prisoners in the headlines.

Despite opposition from the White House, Congress had passed the Jackson–Vanik Amendment in 1974, which made normal trade with Moscow contingent on it allowing Jewish and evangelical emigration. That had hurt, and Moscow was in no mood to be preached to. Under Jimmy Carter, the preaching continued.

By 1979, even before Soviet troops invaded Afghanistan, and the United States began to pour money into the saddlebags of the mujahedin, there were no relations left to salvage. The superpowers' détente had failed.

This was bad news for Father Dmitry and the remaining dissidents. While there had existed some chance that the Soviet Union could win trade concessions, the Kremlin abided by some of its international obligations to protect human rights. Now that that chance was gone, the KGB had nothing to lose from rounding up the last of the troublemakers who polluted their socialist utopia. The Moscow Helsinki Group of young dissidents that attempted to hold the Soviet Union to its international human rights obligations was crushed. Yuri Orlov, the group's founder, like Shcharansky refused to co-operate with his investigators. He got seven years in prison, plus five years in exile. The Ukrainian, Georgian and other nationalist groups were closed down. Jewish organizations were destroyed. The dissident Christians were arrested.

By late autumn 1979, who was left? The greatest of all the dissidents, the Nobel Prize winner Andrei Sakharov, was still at liberty, fighting his tireless and lonely battle, but he was all but alone now. His allies had been picked off one at a time. And Father Dmitry was almost alone too.

This, for him, was Russia's crucifixion. After the crucifixion would come the resurrection, which he yearned for, so it was time for the final fight. He appealed to all believers in the country. They must pray for the persecuted, for those who, like their friends Yakunin and Ogorodnikov, were not with them in the last redoubt.

He had an ultimatum for those who would imprison them, and a demand of his followers: 'All actions, that one way or another help the persecutors, must be stopped immediately.' He was calling on his supporters to boycott the state.

This was more than a taunt. It was revolution. It was practically suicide.

'Happily,' he wrote of his congregation, 'only a few people are scared. More new individuals are coming, praise God. A religious spring is beginning in Russia!'

Inside might be a religious spring, but outside Father Dmitry's windows it was winter, by now 25 November. Snow had been on the ground for a week or two, and the temperature was below zero. He was not deterred. As long as they remained united, they had nothing to fear.

But they did not remain united. Just the next week, some of his spiritual children – his footsoldiers, the crucial support he needed in his fight for the soul of the Russian nation – had left him. They had not, he wrote, even said goodbye. And their departure was accompanied by arguments, and arguments meant even he began to question their good faith. He had tried to banish distrust beyond the church walls, but it was back, creeping under the door like a cold draught from the winter outside.

'I start to wonder, is it not someone's provocation: to break the unity of my spiritual children? First there were arguments, ethnic differences, and now they depart. This must be to someone's benefit.'

He was getting suspicious and distrustful. He was beginning to think like the people he was fighting, and as soon as he did that he had lost. His whole battle was based on using his own methods, not theirs. The KGB were chipping away before their final assault.

He tried to shore up his position but a week later it was worse. Threats were exchanged between members of the congregation. The Sunday discussion had been full of alarm, and his distrust grew. 'Who knows, maybe someone planned this so as to disunite us,' he wrote. And the 'ethnic question' – the Jewish question, anti-Semitism, racism, everything Father Dmitry had tried to banish – reared up. The discussion ended with slammed doors, with shouting, despite his appeal that they needed to love each other, to keep everyone in their hearts.

He wrote later how it appeared.

Russians said: 'You only have Jews with you.'

And Jews asked: 'How can you keep all these anti-Semites?'

This internal division, he wrote, was not accidental. Someone had been sent to dig into the fault-line in his congregation, to use the old tactics of divide and rule. Distrust was all around him now. It was almost the end of the year, and on 16 December he prayed that 1980 and the new decade would bring his spiritual children back to him, and to each other. By now, fewer people were coming to his discussions, and he had plenty of time to think.

Eventually I began to read the last stapled-together document in the envelope. He could not sleep, he wrote, and he heard the bells strike the quarter-hours. The police were following ever more closely those who came to his church, and he recounted a conversation between an arrested man's wife and a state investigator. When she told him she wanted a big family, he scorned her.

'Only scoundrels have big families,' the investigator said, allowing Father Dmitry to end his newspaper and the year on his favourite theme: the threat to the future of the Russian people.

'That is why our families are shrinking. We will go far with these morals, until the last person eats the last person.'

That was the end. There were no more copies in the envelope. I would need to find an eyewitness to describe what happened next. For that, I would need Father Alexander.

We met, along with the two Zoyas, senior and junior, and Father Vladimir at a sushi restaurant just outside Moscow. The contrast was strange. Father Alexander's bearded face and black robe were like something from the Middle Ages. The flashy decor and plates of highly priced fish were pure twenty-first-century Russia.

He sat next to me, and told his story with enormous enthusiasm. He kept making barely comprehensible jokes, patting me on the back to make sure I understood them. He edged ever closer to me as he did so, squashing me against the wall and grabbing my left arm. Zoya junior took advantage by occasionally swooping on his sushi, so every time he turned back to his plate he looked slightly puzzled by there being fewer than there should have been.

He talked intermittently about their life in Grebnevo. About how they ate together, chatted, drank tea and read God's law. About how half of them were Jews, and half Russians, about their arguments, and about how Father Dmitry stood above them all, and took no sides.

Then on 14 January 1980, in the evening, Father Alexander was arrested. Zoya senior fled to Father Dmitry with their children. Father Dmitry went to find out what was going on. A policeman met him at the station: 'We knew you would come,' the policeman said. The police had no intention of releasing Alexander, but they knew that Father Dmitry looked out for his flock, and respected him for it.

Father Dmitry went home, and in the morning the police came for him too. They detained him directly after he had finished conducting the service, bundled him into their car and took him away. He was told he was just being taken to the city for his flat to be searched, and his wife Nina went with him. They did not take him to his flat, however, but to the Lubyanka – the KGB's granite-edged headquarters that looms over Moscow from its hilltop.

A search team was, in their absence, ripping up his flat, as well as the houses of Father Alexander and Father Alexander's mother, and the flats of their friends Ovchinnikova, Kuzmina, Glemyanov, Chapkovsky, Kapitanchuk and Nikolaev. Dozens of agents took part.

Father Dmitry's wife Nina sat all day in the lobby of the Lubyanka, waiting for her husband's release. It was only in the evening that she was told he had been arrested and taken to Lefortovo, the KGB's prison. He had vanished from sight, and would have to fight on his own now.

'They held me for fifteen days,' said Father Alexander. 'The KGB told me later they had no problem with me.' The jokes and back-patting were over while he remembered it, and how Father Dmitry vanished from their lives.

With the arrest, and the searches and the harassment, the dissidents' publicity machine barely survived. It was down to Father Vladimir and his friend Georgy Fedotov to tell the world what had happened. Fedotov told the foreign correspondents, and was then himself arrested and held in a mental hospital.

Father Dmitry's other friends at liberty were tireless in their campaign for him, nonetheless. Already on the day of his arrest, they organized dozens of signatures under an appeal to Christians of the Whole World. 'The appearance of Father Dmitry in our country and in our times cannot be understood but as a miracle to redeem Russia and the whole modern world. The mind cannot comprehend the colossal influence that Father Dmitry has had on the spiritual life of our nation,' it said. The list of signatures showed his wide appeal. Most of the names were Russian of course, but there were Jewish names too, as well as Soviet Muslims and Ukrainians.

'The worst plagues of our life: attacks on the Church, the collapse of the family, alcoholism, abortions, all of this appeared in Father Dmitry's sermons as a reflection of the battle between good and evil.'

Their appeals reached the world. The London *Times* on 23 January quoted a letter written by Father Dmitry just before his arrest, which he had clearly been expecting.

'Sound the alarm! Silence and compromise are not tactical steps, they are betrayal ... If anything happens to me, let this letter be my message.' The article went on to describe dozens of other dissidents from all over the Soviet Union who were swept up in this vast operation.

They included Tatyana Shchipkova, 'a member of an unofficial seminar on religious philosophy, who was sentenced to three years' hard labour'. There was Mikhail Solovov, 'who took part in an attempt to put up independent candidates in the last Soviet elections'. There was Malva Landa of the Moscow Helsinki Group, Rolian Kadiyev, of the exiled Crimean Tatars, and other discontented people from Lithuania to Leningrad to the Arctic.

A week later, in an article headlined 'Father Dudko: The Flower of Russia's "Religious Spring"', *The Times* praised the steadfastness of his fight to save his people. 'In almost every sermon Father Dudko refers to the key problems of Soviet society: the high divorce rates, widespread alcoholism, hooliganism and criminality among the young. His solution is a stable family life,' the paper wrote.

His arrest made headlines in newspapers across North America, from the *New York Times* to the *Ottawa Citizen*, and his name was repeatedly paired with that of Sakharov, the most famous of all the dissidents, who was now exiled to Gorky. His exile and Father Dmitry's arrest were the clearest possible signs of the regime's confidence. The KGB could now get rid of anyone they wanted, the papers said, even those previously deemed 'untouchable'.

The Olympics was scheduled for Moscow that summer and, in the wake of the invasion of Afghanistan, many Western countries were under pressure to boycott the Games. Campaigners added the fates of Sakharov and Father Dmitry to the charge sheet against Moscow and indeed a US-led boycott went ahead, ruining the Soviet Union's party, in what was supposed to be its triumphant ascent to the pinnacle as host of the world's biggest festival.

All of this, of course, was unknown to Father Dmitry. While his spiritual children fought and prayed for him, while KGB agents gathered evidence and while Western journalists kept his name in the headlines, he was in a cell in the KGB's prison of Lefortovo waiting for interrogation.

7

Ideological sabotage

The Lubyanka building, to which Father Dmitry had been taken, then dominated and still dominates north-central Moscow. If the democratic Russian government that took power after 1991 had wanted to change the country and to commemorate the victims of the previous regime it might have opened this building to the public or turned it into a museum. I have often thought how wonderful it would be to see groups of children running in and out of the forbidding front gate, exorcizing the ghosts of the past with their laughter.

The post-1991 government did not turn it into a museum, of course, or throw open its doors. Instead, it left it as it was. It is still the headquarters of Russia's security agency and is still off limits to ordinary citizens.

When I lived in Moscow, I walked past it every day on my way to and from the office. If I was talking on the phone when I did so, I would lose the signal as I approached the towering façade. It would only return when I was a good 50 metres beyond. The FSB, as the KGB's main successor agency is now known, takes no chances.

The Lubyanka's first two storeys are granite, made of sharp-edged blocks. Above them are six rows of windows poking out of an ochre façade, with a broad cornice along the top. A grand entrance pierces the front, while smaller doors give access to the sides. At the back is a towering entrance for trucks, blocked by high barred gates and guarded at all times by policemen. Presumably, this entrance was busy during the KGB's heyday.

The front windows face towards the Kremlin. They previously overlooked a statue of Felix Dzerzhinsky, founder of the Soviet security service, but he was toppled in 1991. Officials occasionally mutter about putting him back.

To the right of the Lubyanka's front elevation as you look at it, there is a large rock on a low plinth. This was brought from Solovki, the first island in the gulag's archipelago, and erected as a memorial to the KGB's victims. You reach it through the underground walkways that honeycomb the space underneath Lubyanka Square. They are full of kiosks selling cheap lingerie, pirate DVDs, baked goods and electrical components. The rock does not get as much passing trade as the kiosks. It is large and grey and smooth.

I have been inside the Lubyanka on two occasions, both times for off-the-record briefings with members of the FSB. The chats yielded nothing of interest from a news perspective, but were fascinating nonetheless. This had after all been the inner sanctum of the KGB, then, as the FSB is now, second only to the Kremlin as a source of power in Russia. On both occasions I entered through a small side entrance, was scrutinized by a security guard through thick glass and was left sitting on a chair for five or ten minutes until my escort arrived. Then my documents were checked and I was given leave to pass through a turnstile and climb a grand staircase to a first-floor corridor lined with doors. We turned towards the front of the building and entered a large office. It had a huge desk at the far end. That desk was, one guide told me, just how Andropov had left it. This was in fact Yuri Andropov's office.

Yuri Andropov was head of the KGB from 1967 to 1982, and thus ran almost the entire campaign against the dissident movement. Next to the phone was a switchboard, two metres wide and covered in different coloured buttons that could connect him to any of his subordinates anywhere in the country. From this desk he co-ordinated the exile of Sakharov to Gorky; the arrest of Jewish nationalists who wished to go to Israel; the harassment of Father Dmitry and his friends in their church community in Grebnevo.

Even before he headed the KGB, he had been ambassador to Hungary, and thus responsible for crushing the Hungarians' attempt to loosen the Soviet embrace in 1956. He helped send the tanks and soldiers into Budapest and cowed the nation for a generation. As chairman of the KGB, he did the same to Czechoslovakia in 1968, when the Prague Spring attempted to create a more flexible kind of socialism. These two experiences of uppity satellites showing worrying degrees of independence convinced him that the Soviet Union was engaged in a death struggle with imperialism, in which the fight against dissidents was a key front.

Not everyone in the Politburo – the leading organ in the state – shared the full extent of Andropov's paranoia. Many thought the government's critics could be won over by generous treatment and benefits. Andropov disagreed, and his KGB were merciless. They kept up surveillance and harassment of anyone they suspected of 'thinking otherwise', as the dissidents themselves termed their activities.

His aim was to extract confessions from the KGB's opponents, to make them admit that they were not honest strivers after truth and justice, but foreign spies bent on undermining their homeland. His agents were highly skilled. They were allowed to detain suspects without charge for months, and could use those long spells of inactivity to undermine the dissidents' resolve. The dissidents in response drew up precise guidelines of their own for how to engage with interrogators, approaching the conversations in full knowledge of how dangerous they were. Natan Shcharansky, the Jewish activist, was a highly skilled chess player and plotted his approach in the same way he would plot a match.

Yuri Orlov, founder of the Moscow Helsinki Group, outlasted his interrogators, and was honourably defiant to the last. 'I rely on my own inner conviction, on my experience and on my thoughts,' he said. It did not save him from a seven-year sentence, but it meant he kept true to himself and inspired fellow dissidents to do the same.

Not all dissidents were as stern and unyielding as him. In 1973, KGB agents managed to extract confessions from Pyotr Yakir and Viktor Krasin, who had been compiling the underground human rights journal the *Chronicle of Current Events*. Although Krasin had written the handbook for arrested dissidents, telling them to admit nothing, he was finally broken over months of detention. They grilled him repeatedly, extracting tiny concessions from him, holding out the chance of meetings with his wife and family. They were ably assisted by an informer sent in as a cellmate. Eventually, tiny step by tiny step, they overcame both Krasin's and Yakir's resistance and sent them back to their old friends as changed men.

'We forgot the basic truth that we are citizens of the USSR and are bound to respect and keep the laws of the state,' said an appeal that Krasin wrote from inside prison.

According to KGB records, fifty-seven dissidents were summoned for interrogation as a result of evidence given by the two men. Confronted by Krasin and Yakir, forty-two of them also capitulated.

The amount of resources put into the case – thousands of hours of agents' work, hundreds of books, rolls and rolls of tape for recordings – was enormous, but it was fully justified from Andropov's point of view. When senior dissidents such as these recanted their views, the demoralization among their friends was deep. And Krasin's recantation was so total that some of his former comrades wondered if he had been a KGB plant all along.

This did not always work. Solzhenitsyn never broke, despite near-constant surveillance – the results of which Andropov reported to the Politburo regularly. Neither did Sakharov, and nor did the religious dissidents like Ogorodnikov.

For Andropov, any act of freethinking was dangerous, as he himself laid out in a speech in 1979, less than a year before Father Dmitry's arrest. He said that Westerners often asked why, if the Soviet Union had built socialism, and was strong and prosperous, it felt so threatened by people who did nothing more than hold prayer meetings, write letters or draw pictures. Did this not suggest the government was actually rather weak? Not at all, Andropov replied. The secret of the Soviet Union's survival was constant vigilance.

'We simply do not have the right to permit even the smallest miscalculation here, for in the political sphere any kind of ideological sabotage is directly or indirectly intended to create an opposition which is hostile to our system – to create an underground, to encourage a transition to terrorism and other extreme forms of struggle, and, in the final analysis, to create the conditions of the overthrow of socialism.'

That meant that, although Father Dmitry saw himself as a simple priest, the KGB saw him as an existential threat. Today's religious believer was tomorrow's terrorist. Was he aware of how seriously the KGB took him when he passed through the doors of the Lubyanka that day in January 1980?

This was not the first time he had been picked up by the KGB and brought here. Back in 1948, when he was a student and had written an unwise poem about Stalin, this was the scene of the interrogation that sent him to the gulag.

Sitting on a low wall and looking at the Lubyanka building, I contemplated Father Dmitry's state of mind in those first hours. He had been picked up at his church. He had thought he was being taken to his flat. He was instead taken to the Lubyanka, and on to Lefortovo. Everything was being done to keep him off balance.

Did his own personal experience of the horrors he would face if he were sentenced to prison help his resolve or undermine it? I thought back to Abez, to the dying village in the Arctic where the mosquitoes whined around my head and bit through my socks.

And I thought about Alexander Merzlikin, our bearded guide to the graveyard where Karsavin and the others were buried, and a conversation we had had as we waited on the platform for the train back south. A dozen or so local people stood patiently, making no movement, while Tanya and I waved madly around our heads, trying to keep the mosquitoes off.

'I don't know how they can stand the mosquitoes,' I had said to Merzlikin, gesturing at the others. 'I don't know how you can stand them.'

He smiled and shrugged. He was not a man of many words.

'And I can't imagine what it's like in winter,' I added, slightly lamely.

He nodded: 'Unless you've been here, you can't.'

That was the problem, I realized. Father Dmitry knew what he was up against. He knew what a Russian prison was like in winter. But I did not. I could not appreciate the horrors he had lived through, nor the events that had shaped his mind. I needed to go back to the north, to see what it had been like for him in the cold and dark.

WINTER

8

It's like a plague

A Russian train in winter is a far better place than the same train in summer. With snow and the long dark night outside, inside was snug and warm. In summer, a top bunk is torment, but now I was happy to wrap myself in my blanket and, if I felt a little too hot, to hold my fingers against the ice on the windowpane. I could melt through it and leave little clear circles, then watch the crystals crawl over them once more.

The platform of the Yaroslavl station in Moscow had been hard-pressed snow and dirt. A man stood selling power tools. He had a heap of drills around his feet, and a cattle prod in his hand that he crackled at me as I walked past. On the opposite platform stood a train with destination boards proclaiming Ulan Bator and Beijing in three languages. It pulled out five minutes before us. In a few days' time, we would be thousands of miles apart.

Just before our departure, a man came swinging down the train flogging knock-off phones. A woman, one of my neighbours, asked what he had.

'Are you going to buy,' he asked aggressively. She hesitated. 'Then what's the sense in showing them to you?'

The woman looked around at us in surprise at his sales technique, and we shrugged and grunted and introduced ourselves. On the top bunk opposite me was Andrei, a snub-nosed woodsman in a vest – 'I am a driver, a sawyer and a boss. See, that's four jobs' – with strong opinions, particularly about people from Chechnya – 'They should all be killed, they don't work and see how much money we give them.' Just a couple of weeks before, a suicide bomber had attacked one of Moscow's main international airports, killing thirty-seven people. His sister had passed through the airport ten minutes previously, he said, so that may have been the source of his strong feelings, although the suicide bomber had not in fact been from Chechnya.

Beneath Andrei was a sulky-looking girl who spoke on the phone for most of the first evening, and slept for most of the next day. Opposite her, and directly beneath me, was Yekaterina, a pretty girl from Vorkuta who listened to everyone's conversations and smiled without saying much.

Most of the conversation over the next day was driven by our neighbours on the other side of the aisle. They were a mother and daughter from Ukhta. The mother – her name was Angelina – had learned English a long time ago and was delighted to show off to the carriage by holding exclusive conversations with me about Prince Charles. I spoke to her in Welsh for a while when she asked me what this place Wales was that he was prince of. She then happily explained to our neighbours that she had not understood a word. They had not understood a word of the exchange that led up to it, so probably did not realize I had been speaking in a different language at all, but she did not let this undermine her triumph.

Angelina's grandfather was in the gulag in the early days. He was a Ukrainian convicted in the 1930s, during the wave of collectivization that submerged Father Dmitry's family along with millions of others. He was released after the war but not given permission to return home. His daughter – Angelina's mother – came to join him, aged just sixteen, in 1946 and ended up marrying a Latvian and staying in the north.

'They always wanted to leave but stayed. It's hard to leave when your house is here, your children. They say that it was fun at first because there were so many young people, so many intellectuals. It's not like that now of course,' she said.

Angelina switched back to Russian to include her daughter, Olya, and the others and for a long time they all discussed life in the north. They were relatively well off, but Olya and her husband had stopped at just one child.

'A two-room flat costs 2.5 million roubles,' she said. I did a quick calculation in my head. That is around £50,000. 'And a new-build is even more. How can you afford to have a second child? This is the problem. We would need more living space before thinking about another child.'

Angelina moved on to an account of a holiday she had taken in Jerusalem, with side pilgrimages to the Holy Places in Bethlehem and Nazareth. Olya was not listening, however. She was still mulling over living standards for young families.

'You are lucky to have been born in Britain,' she whispered while her mother was talking, so only I could hear.

Up in my bunk I lay on my side, with my hand under my head, and watched the forest rattle by. As the trees receded into the distance, the partition one and a half metres away, against which Andrei was sleeping, seemed to rush towards me at astonishing speed. It made me feel a bit sick so I rolled on to my front to look out directly into the trees. The snow closed off any view beyond the first or second trunk. Every branch was laden with snow. Every twig was laden with snow. Every crosspiece on every telegraph pole was laden with snow. The tops of the poles wore a little white wig. The houses in the abandoned villages were huddled under the weight on their roofs, their windows dark and their paths uncleared. Their fences were just a few inches of black spike sticking out of the drifts, and the mammals that had left loping tracks on the snow's crust passed over them as if they were not there. The branches of birch trees sloped up, and the branches of fir trees sloped down.

I put in the earphones of my iPod and listened to the memoirs of Keith Richards, guitarist of the Rolling Stones, which I had brought for just such a long journey as this one. With my blanket tucked around my ears, and the snow glistening outside, I drifted off to sleep while he was driving through Morocco and getting stoned with Anita Pallenberg in the sunshine.

The whole of the next day I was on the train. Without the little kilometre markers of concrete and metal to look at – they were covered in snow – the main objects of interest were the occasional station buildings which we hurtled past without stopping. The station managers – women in their late teens, mostly, swaddled in furs like fresh-faced beavers – stood outside the buildings holding up little white lollipops of plastic. Otherwise, there was forest. When night fell it looked like a negative photograph. The sky was black, and the trees were white.

The next morning a sudden worry I had missed my stop jerked me awake. I had a crick in my right shoulder and winced as I craned around to look out the window. The sun was a pure yellow, like a lemon pip, rising above the bleakest landscape and sending delicate fingers towards us, reaching between the blue shadows and under the sky. Beyond the sun were the pale lumps of the Ural Mountains. Nearer, the snow was sculpted into smooth shapes by the wind. We passed through the village of Ugolny – Coal Town – without stopping. It was all ruins, with no people and no tracks except those of a mammal of some kind, perhaps a fox.

Ahead of us, a haze in the clear sky traced back to a tall chimney spewing a dark stain of smoke for miles and miles. We pulled into Inta through blocks full of shattered buildings and empty windows. I pulled on my jumper and my down-filled jacket – of a brand recommended by a mountaineer friend because it kept him warm on top of the Andes – then my gloves, which were in two parts. The inner stayed behind if I wanted to take the outer layer off to use my camera. Last came my hat.

I was ready for the cold, I thought, but I was wrong. Minus 34 degrees centigrade caught at my throat like sandpaper and at my thighs like a bucket of iced water. Nikolai Andreyevich had come to meet me. He was smiling under a peaked cap, but I was coughing in the cold and had to wait to return his greeting.

He had a taxi waiting. The road was sheet ice where it was not beaten snow, and we roared towards town at 120 kilometres an hour. For some reason, Nikolai Andreyevich had decided we should deny I was British. Perhaps he liked the pretence, or perhaps he was concerned that my presence here would attract unwelcome questions. I was, he told the taxi driver with studied nonchalance, 'from Moscow'. I was not to speak more than I had to in case my accent betrayed the lie, but in any case the headlong journey was so terrifying I did not much want to say anything.

I had friends here now, so had no need to stay in the Northern Girl hotel and argue over how much they would overcharge me for a sagging single bed. Nikolai Andreyevich had persuaded a woman called Galya, whose hair was carefully dyed but resembled a squashed magpie, to rent me her flat. I was delighted to get into the warmth and to drink a cup of tea.

Her flat was decorated with icons and with calendars celebrating the various branches of the Russian armed forces. In the living room was a flashing picture of Jesus that I unplugged as soon as I was alone. After a shower, I approached getting dressed strategically: two pairs of socks, underpants, long underpants, trousers, T-shirt, jumper. My coat, gloves, hat and scarf would come after another cup of Galya's revolting purple tea.

As we sat in the kitchen, Nikolai Andreyevich lectured Galya about Schopenhauer, then moved on to lecturing her about coal, engineers and other topics. She initially mistook the lectures for a conversation and tried to make comments, but soon learned not to. I ate biscuits, then left to find some lunch, while Nikolai Andreyevich went off on business.

Lunch was not a success. My first attempt, in a café round the corner called Ugolyok, failed when a waitress told me it was full. I could see that only one of the dozen tables was occupied but she insisted, with the certainty of a true believer, against all available evidence, that there was not a single empty chair.

My second attempt, at the Barakuda, Inta's other café, started little better. The only dishes on offer were various wizened bits of meat. I asked the blank-eyed waitress if they could fry me some eggs. She said no. I asked about an omelette. No again. I asked about boiled eggs, suggesting I would be happy to pay 250 roubles – £5 – for two, which is a pretty reasonable price by anyone's standards. No. How about scrambled eggs?

The waitress, who had the wattled neck and initiative of a tortoise, but none of the charm, refused, pointing out that she had no way to enter 250 roubles into the cash register if it did not refer to a specific dish. None of the dishes featured eggs. In fact, she was not sure they even had any eggs. Or, she added, maliciously, any potatoes. The stand-off was beginning to look unresolvable when the cook emerged from the kitchen and told me I could have the eggs and some mushrooms too if I wanted them. Since I was the only customer, she cannot have been very busy. Perhaps she agreed simply to shut me up.

I thought, as I ate my tinned mushrooms and mopped up the egg yolks with the one triangle of bread I had been allowed, that this was probably the worst café in the world.

After lunch, I walked through the cold to the museum where Yevgeniya Ivanovna greeted me with the friendly condescension that Queen Victoria would have used on a loyal native. I would, she said, have to register my presence with the local authorities. She would, she said, accompany me. She donned her fur coat, and a thick fur hat with a dangly thing on the side, and we set off.

We took a car through town. The scrubby trees looked sparse without their leaves, and the sun was just peeking through a gap between two apartment blocks. Footprints scarred the snowfields, and thickly dressed adults – men distinguishable from women because they were thinner and taller – hurried past, keen to get out of the cold. I saw no children.

The registration office was opposite a three-storey log cabin housing a Sekond Khend – one of the shops that have sprung up in provincial towns to sell old clothes imported from Europe – and overshadowed by the two chimneys of the town's heating plant. They were pouring steam into the sky in two thick white columns.

Yevgeniya Ivanovna swept in magnificently, her fur coat brushing both sides of the door frame, enquiring who we needed to talk to, and demanding to know why the organization was no longer called the Passport Table as of old, but instead the Federal Migration Service. She had, she told everyone, spent an age looking for it in the phone book. We would, we were told, have to wait. Vladimir was not currently available and only he was permitted to deal with foreigners. Yevgeniya Ivanovna was having none of that, and pushed into his office. He was dapper in jeans and a white linen jacket and working on some papers. He ordered her out into the corridor, back among the common people. She did not take kindly to it at all.

As head of the museum, she was a significant authority in town and not accustomed to waiting in line. While I sat patiently on the folding seats alongside two other supplicants, she swept up and down the corridor, muttering insults to Vladimir and the world in general. She opened the door to his office, then slammed it behind her on seeing he was still engaged in paperwork, smouldering while she did so like a volcano in a fur coat.

After two or three more slams, Vladimir's colleague – a curvaceous woman with a lot of flesh poorly concealed by a tight dress – emerged to remonstrate. 'You have changed your name but kept your old ways,' replied Yevgeniya Ivanovna, and the curvaceous woman vanished back behind the door.

We waited another ten minutes before being ushered into Vladimir's presence. He had taken off the linen jacket. This costume change was presumably for my benefit since he now wore a brick-red nylon waistcoat bearing the English words Migration Control. I wondered what possible cause there could be for English-speaking migration control in Inta. What English-speaker would move here? Still, I handed over my passport and we went through the absurd bureaucratic rigmarole of registration.

This involved a series of pointless questions about my employment, my parents and my marital status, all apparently predicated on the assumption that I was moving to Inta for ever rather than staying here for less than a week. Vladimir copied down my details wrongly, however, putting my middle name before Oliver on his form. He therefore called me James throughout, much to the amusement of Yevgeniya Ivanovna, who giggled. The giggle was infectious, all the more so when we understood the gist of a conversation between the curvaceous woman and a mumbling old man on the other side of the desk.

The old man had apparently lost his passport, and she wanted to know why.

'It was stolen, on the train,' he replied, and she forced him to complete a long and tedious form before getting a replacement. He laboriously wrote out his name, then put a dash in the box intended for his place of birth.

'Why have you done that?'

Shrug.

'Where were you born?'

'Sosnogorsk.'

'Where's Sosnogorsk?'

Shrug.

'It's in the Komi Republic, write that. No, not like that. Komi. How do you spell Komi? Four letters. Komi. You need to do it again. If you waste another form I'll make you pay for it.'

'It's nothing,' he protested.

'Nothing? You think that wasting the resources of the Federal Migration Service is nothing?'

The curvaceous woman handed the old man a form, and turned back to her computer. He picked up the pen and immediately put a dash in the box for his place of birth. Yevgeniya Ivanovna, who had turned pink with the struggle of not laughing, had to leave the room at this point, while I took a few deep breaths and faced Vladimir once more. Eventually, he gave me back my passport, along with a slip of paper showing I was legally allowed to be in Inta.

'James,' he said solemnly. 'One last thing, if you want to eat out tonight it is better to eat at home because some of our less cultured citizens may take exception to your presence on the territory of the Komi Republic.'

I could hear Yevgeniya Ivanovna snort with laughter on the far side of the door and, not trusting myself to speak, I nodded my thanks and walked out of the door. The curvaceous woman was about to notice that the old man had spoiled another form, and I would not have survived that.

I was not, as it happened, planning to risk an encounter with Inta's less cultured citizens since Nikolai Andreyevich had arranged for me to meet another old gulag survivor. The long night had fallen on the town as I walked back to the Ukrainian cultural centre where we had arranged to meet. By the time I got there, I was shaking with cold. My thighs felt like they belonged to someone else. One pair of long underpants was not enough.

Semyon Boretsky lived a short walk away with his wife Yulia. Considering the misery that fate had heaped on them both, they looked astonishingly jovial, and teased each other in the way only an old couple can.

Boretsky was born in capitalist Poland in 1922. Poland won independence from Russia after World War One and managed to gain large tracts of territory that Moscow coveted. Stalin never forgot them and, in 1939, under a pact he reached with Germany, Moscow took them back. Stalin and Hitler extinguished Poland between them, and Boretsky's country of residence abruptly changed from Poland to the Soviet Union, without him having moved house.

It was only after World War Two was over that the Soviet security services really got to sort out the new territories they had inherited. The former bits of Poland had a population with none of the habits of obedience learned in the Soviet Union of the 1930s. Anti-Soviet guerrillas operated in western Ukraine for years after the war ended, and the civilian population suffered as a result. Thousands of young men were arrested, and sentenced to entirely arbitrary terms in the camps, and among them was Boretsky. He described standing in the prison while their terms in the gulag were announced.

'They just walked along saying twenty-five, twenty-five, twenty-five, twenty-five. That was twenty-five years, you understand, but I only got ten,' he said. I asked him why he got less.

'I don't know,' he said with a broad smile, as if a decade in the camps was a small thing. 'They needed young people in the north back then, and they didn't want us to be in Ukraine, so they sent everyone. There were not enough convicted people to fill six wagons so they filled them up with people who were still just under investigation as well.'

On arrival in Inta, 'buyers' came to pick the labourers they needed from among the new arrivals. There was no pretence that they had come as anything other than slaves. He was named V-195 and sent off to make bricks.

'This number was on my breast, and then in larger type on my back. It was on my hat and my knee as well so I could find my clothes after washing,' he said.

If you worked well, he said, you got 600 grams of bread. There were fifteen of them in his shift and they had to make 20,000 bricks. That was the minimum required from their eight-hour day, which normally lasted ten or twelve hours. If they failed to make that target, they got less food: at first 400 grams, and then 200 grams. Workers weakened on the reduced diet, and could not work harder, and lost ground fast. Then they died. It was an efficient way to make sure only worthwhile prisoners survived. Fortunately for Boretsky, he was young and tough.

They got soup made of grain, or turnips, or potatoes, with a smear of oil on the surface. Sometimes there was a scrap of reindeer, or a bit of salted fish. In summer, it was good, he said, but in winter it would be frozen before they received it from the kitchen.

And it was so cold. 'You wore two pairs of quilted trousers and the wind went through like you were wearing a tracksuit. If you worked well,' he said, with the pride of someone who clearly did, 'then every day counted as double until you were freed.'

This was a system instituted in the early 1950s to try to encourage more work from the prisoners. If they worked hard they not only got fed, but their days could count double, thus bringing the end of their sentence nearer. He had a few months chopped off as a result, but he still was in the camp even longer than Father Dmitry was.

'I left the camp in 1957, and found work. I could not go home for another five years. I had lost my rights, they called it. I had to report to the police twice a month, on the 5th and the 20th.'

He did finally go home in 1962, but did not get on with it. He had been away in the Arctic for a decade and a half, and he found his old friends' jokes about polar bears annoying. He did not have the right to live there anyway, so he came back to the north and worked until getting his pension: 30,000 roubles a month now between the two of them, and they were grateful for it.

'People leave here to go to Usinsk or Vorkuta,' said Yulia, his wife. 'It is hard to live if you are not working. A lot of people with a good education do not work. I am glad we are on our pensions now, but even so medicine is expensive. We have three grandchildren, and two great-grandchildren.'

Boretsky was rehabilitated, and had his conviction quashed in the 1980s. He won compensation, but did not remember how much, 8,000 or 9,000 roubles, he said. That was when you could get a car for 6,000 roubles so it was not as bad as it sounds, though then again it still does not sound like much.

The brick factory is closed now. There is no demand for bricks, since no houses are being built, and the clay for the bricks came from the mine, which is closed too, so even if there was demand, the factory could not operate.

'People say they will find gold round here,' Boretsky said, with a hopeful shrug. 'Then there would be work.'

Nikolai Andreyevich and I walked back through the bitter cold of the evening, our feet squeaking on the snow. He had designed this whole part of the town, he said, in the 1970s when he was working as an architect. It was one of his best ever jobs.

'There was supposed to be another school there and an enclosed stadium where that park is.' The park that he gestured at was just a blank expanse of snow, with bare saplings sticking through the crust, and beaten paths crossing it in a huge X. 'The bosses here are idiots. They only think about their own pockets. I built a model of how this region would look and everything.'

He clearly mourned the vision he had had for Inta's future, back in the 1970s when coal was rumbling out of the ground and the whole monstrous inertia of the Soviet Union was keeping the town alive. That was Inta's high point, when people like him flocked here to earn the hardship wages that would set them up as aristocrats in the workers' state. In 1970, fewer than one in a hundred of Komi's population died every year. Now, the figure is twice that. For villagers, the figure now is triple what it was forty years ago. Over the same time period, the birth rate has fallen by more than 50 per cent.

Before catching the train north, I needed to buy a ticket to Moscow, since one would not be for sale in Abez itself. That meant a half-hour queue in the ticket office on the ground floor of one of the rotting concrete-slab apartment blocks that dominate Inta's second-largest square. The office had a map of the old Soviet railway network on the wall behind the cashiers, and while I stood in line I traced the route I had taken to get here. North-east out of Moscow, the rails threaded the old gulag towns, until they sank under the weight of their own illogicality somewhere to the east of Vorkuta, just shy of the Arctic Ocean.

Stalin's government had dreamed of building a spur parallel to Russia's north coast, through the Urals, over the River Ob and on to a port on the River Yenisei. That would have connected the coal fields both to the Arctic Ocean and, via the rivers, to Siberia's biggest cities. Thousands of prisoners died on the project, but the tundra was too unstable and the supply routes were too stretched. It was too much even for the 1940s. If it could not be done in the last years of Stalin's life, it probably cannot be done at all.

Turning away from the map, I realized that the man directly behind me was a priest, and I struck up a conversation. Father Mikhail was twenty-nine – it seemed strange to call a man younger than me 'father', but that is what he called himself – and from Pechora, one of those gulag towns threaded by the railway. He had a narrow, suspicious face but was happy to talk when he learned I was researching the life of a fellow priest, even though he had never heard of Father Dmitry.

His chapel, which we visited when I had my ticket to Moscow and he had his to Syktyvkar, was in the Southern District, the only part of Inta with a still-functioning coal mine, and thus the only district that might have a medium-term economic future. Named in honour of St Nikolai the miracle-worker, his chapel shares a saint with one of the churches where Father Dmitry preached his sermons in Moscow. That struck me as a happy coincidence, and we wandered around inside.

Father Mikhail described the difficulties of building this chapel, Inta's first, in minute detail, recounting every tiny triumph as a victory of the faith. A mine had closed and given him its garage, he said with a smile, as if the closure of the mine and the hundreds of subsequent job losses had been unalloyed good news. A demolished garage provided the bricks for the chapel's walls. A well-wisher had provided the red corrugated roofing slabs. Another had given cement.

'It is good that God did not give it all to us at once because we would not have noticed such a gift. It came hard and we all prayed and at every step we were joyful. When we finished the roof, we all shouted hooray. When we put in the door, we all shouted hooray,' he said, as we stood in the roughly finished interior.

'People think they have difficulties, but remember that when God went into the desert for forty days and was offered bread he refused it. It is like that. People think they want money and they bow down before it, but God said that man cannot live by bread alone. Now people say there is an economic crisis, but it is actually a call from God, telling us to throw away external things. The future of this town is in a return to faith, to trust in miracles.'

To demonstrate his point, Father Mikhail reached into the little booth where the faithful could buy candles and religious trinkets and, after a few seconds of studied concentration, selected a small icon of St Nikolai. Printed on 5mm board inside a gold rim, the icon showed

Nikolai flanked on either side by tiny floating figures of Jesus and the Virgin Mary. It was a gift, he said, for me to remember our conversation by. Perhaps it would help me come to the faith, he added. He held it out to me, waited for me to take it and, when I did, folded his hands together in front of his groin.

He kept my gaze with a slight smile of sweet forgiveness without speaking for a few seconds. He held my eyes in fact, until I understood what he wanted. Of course: I should make a donation in exchange for the gift. It had taken me a little while to realize, and I was embarrassed by my own obtuseness. I reached into my pocket in a fret, dug out my wallet from under the layers of jumper and coat and pulled out a banknote. I noticed too late it was for 5,000 roubles, Russia's largest denomination and almost half the cash I had with me. That is about £100. Indeed, it is more than a week's wages for the miners who live round here. I could hardly put it back in my pocket though and fish out a smaller one, so I handed it over. He maintained his sweet look.

A taxi driver called Sasha drove me to pick up my bag and to catch my train. I had an hour to kill so, with grisly relish, he gave me a guided tour of the ruins of his town.

'See there,' he said, gesturing to some snow-covered humps. 'There were houses there, but they're gone. And there, on that flat patch, there was a school. That's gone too. This town is dying.'

He said he wanted to move away, to give his six-year-old daughter the chance of a better future, but was struggling to find work anywhere else. A large thermometer on the main square announced that the temperature was minus 37. With delight, Sasha told me that Abez would be even colder.

At the train station, a single wagon waited for passengers, unattached to any engine. A man was smashing at repugnant icicles hanging from the hole that channels toilet waste out on to the rails, while boiling water gushed past him. A woman stuck her head out of the door, holding an empty kettle, and asked if it was defrosted yet.

'Fuck no,' the man said without emotion.

The carriage windows were filthy, and I could see only the vaguest outlines of the station buildings from inside. After twenty minutes or so, a few jolts suggested an engine had coupled on to our carriage.

Another ten minutes, and the carriage moved off, complaining. My fellow passengers were mostly railway workers, even more heavily clothed than me in their thick, stiff, dark-blue jackets. I huddled over. With my gloved hands in my pockets, and my chin sunk into my chest, I could cherish a core of warmth that felt delicious and drowsy.

The fuzzy silhouette through the windows was now the jagged fringe of fir trees, and then the approximation of a weak sunset far off to the south. I persuaded the guard to open the door so I could photograph it, and the cold draught of the evening ripped through my coat and attacked the core of warmth I had so carefully built up. The sun finally slipped beneath the tundra to the south-west. It was 2.36 in the afternoon, and the long night was ahead.

A perfect crescent moon shone over Abez, close enough to touch but a million miles away. It was paired like in a Muslim flag with a single bright star, which swam in a pure black sky. A herd of snow-mobiles had gathered at the station to welcome the two dozen passengers that alighted into the moonlight. Among them, his beard dusted with ice, and his eyes smiling behind his thick glasses, was Alexander Merzlikin, my guide of the summer.

He had a trailer behind his snowmobile, which he ushered me on to, sitting me on a reindeer skin and insisting that I wrap a fur-lined blanket around my legs. He asked if I was warm in my red down-filled jacket. I told him about my mountaineer friend and the Andes. This coat, I said, was the best Britain had to offer. He looked sceptical and muttered something about me needing to borrow a real coat. And we set off.

The single headlight cut into the dark, illuminating the cloud of powder snow thrown up by the two or three snowmobiles that had roared off before us. Alexander twisted the throttle and the wind cut into my face and tore at my arms. I began to wonder if he might be right about the jacket. The cold was intense – down to minus 40 and due to fall still further in the clear conditions – and physically painful.

The wooden houses of the village flicked past as I tried to shield my cheeks from the wind. By the time we arrived at Alexander's single-storey home, I was rubbing my face to get a bit of warmth back into it. Alexander looked at me in confusion.

'Why didn't you just face backwards?' he asked. I felt like an idiot, since that had not even occurred to me, and tried to create a convincing lie for my stupidity.

'I wanted to see where we were going,' I tried, hesitatingly. That did not even convince me, and Alexander laughed. He pointed me at the door and went to put away the snowmobile.

I entered a porch filled with firewood. The doors were lined with blankets, both for insulation and to ensure a good fit in their frames. I pulled off my boots, which were tight against my three pairs of socks. I wondered, when I realized how cold my toes were, if my boots might not be inadequate for these conditions as well. When I passed into the warmth of the house, a smiling handsome woman was waiting for me, Alexander's wife.

'I'm Natasha, but call me Auntie, everyone else does,' she said, and we walked into the kitchen and she put the kettle on. The main feature of the room was a huge brick oven, as large as Alexander's snowmobile, which gave off a pleasant heat. Three cats and a kitten were perched on top of it, among assorted pots and pans. They watched me with unblinking eyes as I sat at the corner of the table and drank my tea.

Alexander finally bustled in, his glasses iced over. He sat on a stool by the stove and lit one of his rough cigarettes. He scooped up a couple of shovels full of dusty coal and threw them into the fire. Then he sat back and looked at me. Why, he asked, had I come?

I explained that I wanted to experience the conditions that Father Dmitry had lived in. I wanted to feel, if only for a short time, the kind of conditions that he had endured and the kind of torments suffered by prisoners who refused to offer due homage to the Soviet state. We talked about that for a while, our conversation then wandering on to the conditions Alexander and his family lived in. His youngest daughter Dasha had now joined us. He told me about hunting and fishing, and the two women chipped in with comments and suggestions.

'I used to hunt bears, but what do you kill them for? I don't see the need to do this any more, it's for young men,' he said.

The next morning dawned pale. Lying in the warmth of the blankets, I could hear the wind moaning around the house, and I pulled on my two pairs of long underpants, three pairs of socks, vest, two

T-shirts and trousers before getting out of bed. A pale orange stain on the sky was the sun poking its head over the horizon to see if the Arctic was warm enough for it. Before my window was a rolling unbroken, unscarred sweep of snow. To the right was a small stand of birch trees. Beyond was a tractor, its contours smoothed by a drift that made it almost unrecognizable as a man-made object. A little outhouse was off to the left, with snow pushed up its walls in an elegant sweep. When the sun finally persuaded itself to get out of bed, it was so weak I could watch it with the naked eye, and the bright patches it left on the snow seemed to emphasize the cold rather than alleviate it.

Alexander, when I walked into the kitchen, welcomed me with a cup of tea. He was sitting on his stool by the stove, smoking.

'I don't know how to tell you this but it's warm, it's only minus 27. But the wind is 15 metres a second and it bites,' he said. The little black kitten was scratching in the coal by his feet, and I saw that the coal doubled as their litter tray. It seemed an elegant solution to burn the cats' toilet waste, since they could hardly go outside.

Before we ventured out, Alexander examined the mountaineering jacket, and pronounced it inadequate. I would have bridled at the slur but, to be honest, after the cold of the previous evening, I had my doubts about it. He handed me a stiff blue coat as used by the railway workers, then, on seeing my boots, silently handed me a fur-lined pair. Before I put them on, he made me wear padded dungarees too. Fully dressed – with a jumper, scarf and hat as well as the collection of undergarments I'd donned in bed – I could barely bend in the middle. I felt like a knight in squishy armour.

Outside in the bright morning, the cold was still startling. My cheeks tingled, and I tucked my fingers into the palms of my gloves.

Boretsky, the old man in Inta, had said that the prisoners in the gulag wore two pairs of quilted trousers to work outside, with a daily ration of just 600 grams of bread. Here I was, full of a substantial breakfast, in two pairs of long underpants, trousers and padded dungarees, and I was already cold. It suddenly seemed a miracle any of them survived at all.

In a memoir published in 2011, Fyodor Mochulsky, a Soviet diplomat, recorded the early part of his career when he oversaw a convict-labour railway-building camp near Abez. This was before the railway was finished, so they had to take a steamer from Arkhangelsk on the White Sea to Naryan-Mar, then a smaller ship up the River Pechora, then a smaller ship still up the Usa. The boat, with its cargo of building materials and food and prisoners, froze into the ice before they reached Abez, and they had to walk the rest of the way, sixteen days, over the icy crust that had formed upon the freezing mud. Mochulsky's horse plunged through the crust.

'The horse was thrashing around, and sinking even deeper into the marsh,' he wrote. 'We all shared a very worrisome thought: how will we explain that our horse disappeared when we arrive at the Gulag Camp Administration? ... This crime, we all knew, had a corresponding legal statute: ten years' imprisonment in the camps. By now, we had worked so hard to get that horse out of the quagmire that we were losing our strength. We were in total despair.'

That thought seems to encapsulate the bureaucratic insanity of the gulag. The horse was not pitied as a terrified living thing, but protected only to avoid punishment. Perhaps more terrible is that he, a free man, should accept a ten-year prison term as an appropriate punishment for losing a horse through no fault of his own. The guards were hardly more at liberty than the prisoners. The habit of giving and receiving orders was so engrained in both that it formed an internal prison they struggled to escape from.

When Mochulsky reached his final destination, a logging camp far in the wilds, the convicts had no houses or shelter of any kind. 'They had scraped the snow off of several metres of frozen ground in the shape of squares, and had placed crudely cut branches down as makeshift beds. On top of these branches lay the prisoners, dressed in their greatcoats and army boots, "resting" after their twelve-hour workday.'

Mochulsky, who appears to have written the memoir to excuse his own role as a cog in the world's largest-ever killing machine, recounted how he had mobilized the prisoners to build barracks for themselves and made them warm over the winter, and that they were grateful to him. That was the winter of 1940–1, when hundreds of thousands of prisoners died.

Perhaps more telling is an encounter he had later in Abez, with a teenage girl. A cashier, she had received a three-year sentence for an accounting irregularity, and had been raped for the first time before she even reached prison. In her first night in prison she was gang-raped, and was repeatedly assaulted by fellow inmates in transit camps and the camp barracks.

'How could I help her? In the context of the camp, other than feeling bad for her, I could do nothing.'

The prisoners here were units to be worked to death. They died in their thousands, and were not remembered. That morning, as Alexander folded the fur blanket over me on the snowmobile's trailer, he told me we would go to see the remains of such unfortunates: graves we had not seen in the summer, which had not won even the slight recognition of those in what is called the 'memorial cemetery', where Karsavin and the others were remembered as individuals, rather than ignored as random lumps in the tundra.

We set off along the bluff above the river, stopping to admire a recently finished church, which was built in memory of a young man who had died on a fishing trip. A little further on, towards the railway and the great bridge that had tamed the River Usa, we stopped and Alexander pointed to our right. He said something, but I could not hear, my ears being tightly swaddled in my woolly hat and my coat's great hood.

I looked in the direction of his outstretched index finger and could see an obelisk against a clump of birches. It looked like a grave, so I stepped off the trailer to get a better look. I instantly vanished into the snow up to the tops of my thighs. I pushed back with my left foot, but just sank deeper. My heavy clothing blocked me from turning round, and I was forced to lie full length on the snow's crust, heave myself round, then pull myself back on to the trailer with my gloved hands.

'What did I tell you?' Alexander shouted, and I realized that the unheard words had been a warning to stay on the trailer.

The obelisk, he told me, marked the grave of a boss's daughter. I asked why it was all on its own, away from the main graveyard. He laughed, and coughed on the smoke of his cigarette.

'It's not all on its own, there are dozens of graves over there but the rest are for prisoners so they're unmarked. They're disappearing back into the ground. In a few years, you'd never know they were there.'

We swooped down the bluff, past the site where the North Stream gas pipeline will ford the river, and out on to the ice. In my attempt to reach the obelisk, snow had pushed down into my boots and was beginning to melt. We zoomed under the bridge, and Alexander pointed out the sticks that mark where fishermen have set their nets under the ice. He himself preferred a site 15 kilometres upstream, he said. It might be further away but the fish were better, and there was less competition. Fortunately, the cold winter water preserved any fish he caught, he said, and he only had to check the nets every three or four days.

I wiggled my toes. My feet were cold and stiff, and my camera was beginning to misbehave as well. The little screen that tells me the aperture and shutter speed, as well as all the various focus points and ISO information, was fading out. I turned it on and off again, but it did not return to life. I tucked it inside my coat in the hope that the warmth would revive it, but to no effect.

While we watched, a passenger train of nine carriages passed over the bridge. It was the first train I had heard since being here.

'They used to pass every fifteen minutes, but that was before,' said Alexander. 'Now, you're lucky if you get one an hour.'

We turned back for home and into the wind. The air hit me in the face like sandpaper. I had not realized that previously my back had been against the wind, and my face had been protected. I tugged my hat down as far as possible, and pulled my scarf up over my face. Just my eyes were exposed now, but the cold cut at my eyebrow ridge. It was sharp and inescapable. We were driving into both sun and wind, and it was weird to feel such cold and no heat at all from the sunlight.

By the time we were back inside, my face was extremely sore. I checked the thermometer on the way in; it was indeed just minus 27. Father Dmitry had experienced temperatures colder by 20 degrees or more, for longer, with a fraction of the clothing and far less food. Still, I was not prepared to stay out any longer no matter how much I wanted to know what he had lived through.

In the days of Mochulsky, the gulag boss, Abez was the centre of this part of the camp system. From here, the security chiefs co-ordinated construction at dozens of small camps up and down the railway, communicating by a primitive telephone and setting nearly impossible targets.

Mochulsky was told to build an embankment for a bridge over the River Pechora. 'If you pull this off, you will get an award; if you don't, we will shoot you,' his supervisor told him bluntly. With such management techniques, it is hardly surprising that the bosses worked their labourers to death.

Alexander, however, came here much later. He was born in 1953 in the town of Uzlovaya, in the Tula region, which is just south of Moscow and is now close to being ground zero in Russia's demographic catastrophe.

'I left my homeland thirty years ago,' he said. 'I went back five years ago and it was like nothing had changed, nothing had improved: the same holes in the road, the same destruction; no one does anything to make it better. Our rulers say the correct words about democracy, about the market, about creating the right conditions but nothing gets done. We are the richest country in the world by natural resources, but look at us. This snowmobile we went out on this morning costs the same as a car – 160,000 roubles – but people were using machines just like this fifty years ago, there is nothing new here. All the technology you see is Western now, nothing gets made in Russia any more.'

For a hunter, of course, a badly made snowmobile or a poor-quality outboard motor can be lethal. Get stranded in the tundra without transport and you die, summer or winter. He had a brochure for snowmobiles from Germany and Japan, which he had picked up on a recent visit to town. We pored over it together, gazing at the shiny smooth bellies of these gorgeous machines. He lamented the shoddy quality of what he could afford.

'This is the problem of Russia itself,' Natasha said.

She was an Abez girl, born and brought up here. Her mother had worked as a teacher in a village on the far side of the river and, during the thaw, would walk across the river on the moving ice. It was that kind of self-reliance and edge that Alexander had fallen in love with when he first came north.

'This was like a zoo, mushrooms, berries, everything,' he said. 'You could see the Urals on a clear day and I went out in the boat, sometimes for fish, but normally just for an adventure.' His trips had made him an expert in the geography of the gulag. 'It is not like what is said in the books. They say there was a camp here or a camp there, but it is not like that. There were camps everywhere. Last year I went up the River Lemva for 200 kilometres. There is a swamp there where the prisoners cut the trees and sent them down the river. There was prisoner labour everywhere and it was used for everything.'

After he has set his nets, he said, there is not much to do, so he explores the tundra a little, looks at what is around him.

'In this place on the Lemva there's only marsh, but we looked about and found the camp. Time hides everything but the first years I lived here I often saw barbed wire in the tundra, which must have been guarding something.'

Now we – or rather I – were warmed up, we saddled up the snowmobile again. I wanted to see again the memorial cemetery that we had visited in the summer, and to photograph the village. My camera had revived in the warmth, and this time I took the spare battery too. With a battery keeping warm in my pocket, to replace the one in the camera as soon as it died of cold, I hoped I could keep it on life support long enough to get the shots I wanted.

As we set off down the hill once more, Alexander's two dogs tentatively followed us. They were thick-furred mongrels, shaggy as wolves, and were clearly not sure if they could accompany us on our trip. When Alexander did not stop them, however, they gained confidence and trotted up alongside the trailer. When we roared out on to the ice, they gambolled and danced like dolphins round a ship. They leaped and bounded with joy, sometimes running their noses along in the snow to cool down. They were mother and son, and the male – still puppyish though full grown – shoulder-barged his mother again and again, urging her to play. Sometimes, he would crash through the crust on the snow and come bouncing up again, grinning foolishly. Their tongues lolled, and they were the image of joy.

In reading books on the gulag, I always imagined the guard dogs as grim, oppressive beasts, but perhaps they were like these two, and their play would have been a comfort in the surroundings. It is hard to imagine how grins like these, or a nudge on the hand like the one I felt as we slowed to drive back up into the village, would not have cheered even the most downhearted of men. We headed off to the right, through the ruined farm buildings, to the cemetery. The path was impassable, however. No snowmobile had gone up there this winter, and without a compacted track to follow we ran the risk of crashing through the crust ourselves, and facing a struggle to extricate the heavy machine.

Frustrated in that plan, therefore, I turned to look at the village graves, hoping to see headstones with the names of gulag bosses and their families. The cemetery was too recent for that, however, so I idly scanned the names that were there. These graves were far more recent than I had imagined, most if not all of them post-Soviet. But there seemed an impossible number for such a small village. It was then that it dawned on me, as I looked from name to name, that here was the death of Russia, in hard dates, in front of my eyes. These graves were not of pensioners, but of young men and young women, dying before their prime. What chance did a village have to support itself, or to reproduce itself, if its new adults die before they can achieve anything? And if the villages are dying, then the country is too.

This was the alcoholic apocalypse that Father Dmitry saw starting in the 1960s, and fought against with his sermons. I wrote down the birth and death dates in a column in my notebook: 1988–93, 1990–2007, 1983–2007, 1962–1994, 1972–1992, 1986–2008, 1985–2005, 1975–2001. I saw a man born in 1949 who had lived to 1997, and smiled briefly. At least here was someone who had lived a full life, I thought, until I worked out that he had died aged forty-eight. His life was cut short by any standards I was used to, but it looked age-long compared to his young neighbours: 1971–2006, 1986–2006, 1970–2004, 1980–2005. That is not all the graves. Some I could not reach through the snow, and on others the drifts obscured the dates and names of the people buried beneath, but it was enough to show why Abez has shrunk like a slug sprinkled with salt.

Right by the path was the grave of Veniamin Arteyev, born May 1980, died October 2007. His little sister Zoya was next to him. She had been born three years after him, but died six months earlier, on 20 April 2007. And between them was their mother. Her birth date was obscured by snow, but she died on 7 September 2003. I looked at Alexander for an explanation of this family tragedy.

'Their father sold moonshine. He wanted to be rich, and look what happened. The two kids died in the same year,' he said with a grimace.

And a little further along was Andrei Kulikov, born March 1983; died, two months after his twentieth birthday, in May 2003.

'He was my pupil, he died of this too,' said Alexander, flicking his jaw-line in the Russian sign for getting drunk. 'He shot himself in the end. They are all kids of twenty, twenty-four, twenty-five, they all died of this,' he said, with another flick.

'It's like a plague,' I said, at last.

'Ah no, it's worse,' he replied.

A grey stone grave for a young man, 29 August 1981 to 28 October 2006, dredged up another memory for Alexander: 'That one died on his snowmobile falling through the ice. They didn't find his body for a year.'

There is apparently a disco sometimes in Old Abez, the little village the other side of the river where Natasha's mother used to teach. Drunk and exuberant, the lads race each other back over the frozen Usa, heedless of the streams of ice-cold water that run on top of the ice, concealed by a thin crust of snow. One time there were six snow-mobiles stuck in mid-river where they had crashed into water flowing under the snow and been abandoned.

Even the two dogs seemed subdued by the graves, and they sat in the snow by the snowmobile, waiting for us to move away.

The mood hung with us back to the house, and the conversation continued with Natasha in the kitchen.

'If someone comes back from working on the railway, he's cold, he'll sit and watch television and drink vodka,' she said. 'People are lazier than they used to be. Or else now they are wiser, because they do not do what we used to do.'

She reminisced about the colder winters of her youth, and the heroic amounts of work people did to stay alive.

'When I was small this was big, the biggest village of the north, 2,000 people at least in the village itself, and more in the hamlets around. Now there's no one there,' she said, leaving their fate hanging in the air, to be filled in by Alexander.

'Last year eleven people drowned, falling out of their boats,' he said.

Natasha took over again: 'They weren't all found. There was a lot of water this year and strong winds, and then there is this as well.' She tapped her jaw-line.

Do the women – I tapped my jaw-line – as well, I asked?

'They also. Everyone in Russia drinks now.'

The mood was bleak, as the conversation rolled on towards the fate of the country.

'I was like you once,' said Alexander. 'I believed in improvement and the future. I condemned this and that and everything, but I started to change. Look at your son. He is small now like a toy but he will become big and you will care more about how he will do at school, what he thinks and so on, and this will become your main concern. Your own successes will be less important.'

Young people, he said, had no concern for the victims of the gulag, and no interest in the work he does to try to keep the graveyard respectable.

'The younger generation collects berries on the graves, they light fires. Yes it happened, they say, these people died, but it has nothing to do with us. In March there will be a new mayor in Inta and he will come to the memorial cemetery. They always do. But he will only come once and never again. That's what they do,' he said.

Did that mean that officials, the state, had no interest in the graves?

'The state has no relation to any of this. They cannot afford to provide us with gas, but they can build themselves offices. Everything is done through the arse, to screw things up,' he said, with an unexpected profanity, the only one I heard him use. 'The state makes you pay. If you don't have to pay for the railway, they will make you pay for the mosquitoes that bite you. They find a way to make you pay.' And that was why the collective farm had closed, and with it had gone all work but on the railway. 'There was no point in keeping the animals, you have to make money. You have to be able to pay for processing and transport.'

There had been a geological survey base in Soviet times but it was found to be unprofitable, so it was closed and all the equipment sold off. Now it has been reopened.

'We realized that in Russia all we can do is drink vodka and sell oil, so we need to find more oil. If we run out we won't even be able to buy vodka, so these geologists are back,' he said.

I asked him whether he was depressed about being a Russian.

'I haven't called myself that for thirty years. I don't think about that. As soon as you think about being a Russian, you think about not being a Jew,' he said. 'I remember Zinoviev, the leader of the revolution, had a Jewish name because people began to talk about it after 1991, and to wash all this dirty washing and to talk about how the Jews were to blame for everything, how all the Jews were bad and all the Russians were good and so on.'

He shrugged. He had escaped to the pure clean north. He wanted nothing to do with all that dirtiness.

At four the next morning, I was a dumpy figure in the cold waiting for the train south, towards the sun. The thick clothes and darkness made all of us on the platform look the same, men or women, misshapen like clay dolls.

Alexander told me as we waited on the platform that 'before' 300 children had studied at the village school. Now there were just ninety. I thought about that word 'before'. Before, there was order. Before, there were children. Before, there was work. Before, people drank less. Before, people lived beyond their twenties.

In Two Years in Abez, Nikolai Punin looked out at the grim view of Abez. 'If you asked me what hell looked like, I would describe it just like that: the total rule of the straight line and the right angle. No free spirit was left alive by their obsession with tidiness, fences and orderly footpaths, all neatly maintained and swept constantly. Who said that hell is packed with good intentions? Quite the opposite, there were no good intentions, only meaningless ones and that made inmates lose all hope.'

A crowd of railway workers boarded the train and, although I had a ticket, it seemed I had to sit in the cheapest compartment until I got to Inta, where I could be assigned bed linen. Hunched in my coat, hat and scarf almost touching across my face, I dozed.

The train's approach to Inta was heralded by the phone of a teenage girl on the bench opposite me. There had been no reception for the two-hour journey through the forest, but we were now within range of a mobile tower in the town. Her ring tone was a repeated English-language chorus: 'I am a sexy girl. I like you fuck me well. I am a sexy girl. I like you fuck me well. I am a sexy girl.' She grappled under her coat to find it, pressed the green button and began a muttered conversation with her mother. I wondered if she knew what the words of her ringtone meant.

The prevalence of such trashy English-language culture is, I supposed, another sign of the collapse of Russian confidence. The dregs of Anglo-America had been dumped on places like Inta, and been taken up for want of anything else vaguely vibrant. As I waited for us to pull into the platform, I remembered other examples I had seen up here. One taxi driver had affixed a semi-transparent sunshade across the top of his windscreen with the English words: 'Guns don't kill people, I kill people' (I have corrected his spelling).

Most startling of all, however, had been a T-shirt – it must have come from a Sekond Khend – I had seen worn by a middle-aged man. Below a picture of a grinning male face, it bore the boast that 'Five billion potential grandchildren died on your daughter's face last night.' What path did that take to get to its final owner?

When, after Inta, I finally got my bunk and snuggled down in the warm, I mused over how it was that English-language trash culture had penetrated so far into Russia. After World War Two, Western writers feared that Russia's totalitarian state would conquer them all, but in fact the reverse happened. Russia today is like the opposite of *A Clockwork Orange*, the dystopian novel by Anthony Burgess. At that time the Soviet Union seemed so powerful that he imagined a future when Western teenagers spoke a slang peppered with Russian words: *moloko* for milk; *droog* for friend; *horrorshow* for good. But that is not how it turned out. It is not Western hooligans using pidgin Russian as slang, but out-of-control young Russians speaking pidgin English. You see it in the graffiti along the railway lines: White Pride, Skinheads, Hooligans.

This penetration began in the 1960s, when the West pioneered mass fashion and the Beatles. Russians old enough to remember talk about listening to foreign pop music on home-made LPs fashioned from X-ray film, which was solid enough to keep the groove, although it did not hold it for long. But Western culture still had to sneak through the chinks in the Iron Curtain. That meant a random selection of Western bands and writers, protected by the communist state from more vigorous competitors, flourished in the Soviet Union when they withered and died at home. Like flightless birds on an inaccessible island, bands like King Crimson, Jethro Tull and Judas Priest became hugely popular, expanding to fill evolutionary niches they had no access to in the West. Minor band members still play solo concerts in major Moscow venues when they might struggle to fill the back room of a pub in London.

Meanwhile, bands like the Rolling Stones are all but unknown. Their records for some reason failed to penetrate the Soviet counter-culture at the right time. As the train rattled along, I plugged in the spoken version of Stones guitarist Keith Richards's autobiography, and his words helped the thought process along.

'We were not destroying the virtue of the nation but they think we are so eventually we're drawn into a war,' said Keith at one point as he described his arrest and conviction on drugs charges.

If Keith thought that his one night in Wormwood Scrubs was a declaration of war by the authorities, he should have looked at what was happening in the Soviet Union. His same post-war generation, his Soviet contemporaries, full of fiery optimism, attempted to do what he and his friends did and revitalize culture, inject it with a bit of dynamism. The first post-Stalin dissidents were young people who gathered at a statue of Vladimir Mayakovsky in Moscow to read their poems in the late 1950s and early 1960s. They were the equivalent of the bohemians meeting in coffee shops in Chelsea or in Greenwich Village.

The Soviet state at first was not quite sure how to respond. Boris Pasternak was criticized for his Western-style novel *Dr Zhivago*, but he was not arrested, nor did he lose his country home in Peredelkino, a village where houses were reserved for artists and writers.

Two of his disciples – Andrei Sinyavsky and Yuli Daniel – however, were to be made examples of. And it was their arrest and prosecution for the publication of work abroad that diverted the Soviet youth movement on to a new track.

'The lack of opportunity to struggle for the Cause discouraged the most ardent Communists among the young,' wrote one friend of Sin-yavsky's. 'Can a thirty-year-old writer be expected to wait like a good boy for the censor to show a little magnanimity in ten or twenty years' time, if then? Sinyavsky had not that degree of patience.'

It is noteworthy how many of the Soviet dissidents did not begin as rebels. Sakharov was a physicist. Zhores Medvedev was a biologist. Father Dmitry was a priest. In an ordinary society, they would have continued their activities unhindered. However, the state's ideology kept intruding into their lives in ways they could not tolerate.

Sinyavsky and Daniel's trial was publicized by four of their friends, who were then themselves arrested and prosecuted. Alexander Ginzburg only wrote up a transcript of a legal hearing and passed it to journalists, but that was enough to earn him five years in a labour camp. When he came out, he was of course a committed opponent of the regime.

Whereas young Germans and Frenchmen waved the red flag and demanded a general improvement of the world, starting now, young Russians fought for the most basic of human rights. The state's oppression distorted the cultural movement. It started with poetry and writing, but it could not develop into the mass-market rebellion of the Western baby-boomers, because it never got out of the basements.

It was as if the police in Britain and America had arrested Buddy Holly and Cliff Richard, given them six years of hard labour and then kept arresting any of their friends who spoke out in their defence. It is hard to imagine how Bob Dylan's protest songs or the Rolling Stones' poseur rebelliousness would have then made it to number one.

In 1968, when Jean-Luc Godard filmed Keith and the rest of the Rolling Stones and intercut them with staged footage of actors pretending to be Black Panthers, eight real rebels showed astonishing bravery by gathering on Red Square to protest against the Soviet invasion of Czechoslovakia. Assaulted by the crowd, who shouted 'scum', 'dirty Yids' and – to Natalya Gorbanevskaya who had come with her baby – 'The tart's got herself a child, now she comes to Red Square' – they were arrested.

Gorbanevskaya, because of the baby, was released, and she told Western journalists about the protest. The Western papers and radio stations splashed with it. It was rare to see any kind of crack in the monolith of the Soviet Union. But their protest simply heightened the division between dissidents and mainstream society, which mostly approved of the invasion of Czechoslovakia and thought the Czechs should be more grateful for the Soviet Union's defeat of Nazi Germany.

'It was very strange,' Gorbanevskaya told me. 'My name became famous and there was this big noise about me, and it was like they could send troops into Czechoslovakia but they could not arrest me.'

At that time, the Kremlin was still embarrassed by unfavourable media coverage. That kept Gorbanevskaya safe, although she was eventually thrown out of the country. Dissidents like Sakharov became skilled at using the Western radio stations and newspapers to their own advantage, and a group of brave activists kept the protest movement alive for a decade. It was under cover of that embarrassment that Father Dmitry's free community developed. The Soviet government no longer had the heart to kill thousands, tens of thousands, of people to squash an idea, and any other technique was less effective.

It took the KGB more than a decade to penetrate and demoralize and finally crush the dissidents, culminating of course with the arrests of Sakharov and Father Dmitry.

As I sat and listened to Keith describing Swinging London, a long line of snow along a telephone wire slipped and fell. At first, it dropped as one long cylinder, but it broke up as it accelerated, so, by the time it hit the snow beneath, it was just a cloud of powder. Mammal footprints trotted through the forest beneath the wire. A little later we mounted a bluff, and I could see for kilometres over the snow and trees. No one lived there.

Father Dmitry was not sent to the camps in 1980. Instead, they kept him in the relative comfort of a cell in Moscow's Lefortovo prison. Within its high walls, he was free to contemplate his future during the days of inactivity, interrupted only by occasional interrogation. He knew, as he lay there, that his fate was in his own hands. He must have dwelled on the potential misery of a fresh term in the camps, back in the cold, stripped of the church where he served and the love of his children. In 1980, he would turn fifty-eight. Imprisonment would be a heavy burden for him to bear. He had no idea when he would see his friends again.

9

The unworthy priest

Every one of Father Dmitry's friends remembered the next time they saw him, however. Father Vladimir's shoulders fell slightly when he told the story. He looked down at his hands on his lap.

'Yes, I saw him on television,' he said. 'Someone rang to say they were showing him on television, so I turned it on. There were a few of us and we watched. It was a shock.'

It was an experience he shared with citizens of the whole Soviet Union. Moscow at that time only had three television channels. Other regions had fewer. That meant tens of millions of people would have seen *Time*, the most popular daily television programme in the country, on 20 June 1980. Most of them probably heard of Father Dmitry for the first time that evening. Although he was famous among dissidents, and among religious believers, this was his first appearance on a national media channel. The vast majority of Soviet citizens would have had no idea who he was.

They would have seen a plump man with a beard, a stereotypical Russian priest, happily reading out a prepared statement, then answering questions from a man off-camera called Sergei Dmitryievich. What Father Dmitry said would have satisfied the most hawkish Soviet Cold War warrior, because he rejected everything he had ever stood for. He admitted the 'systematic fabrication and dissemination abroad of anti-Soviet materials'. He admitted being a tool of the West working to destroy the Soviet state. This was not like the show trials of the 1930s. He did not look traumatized, thin, pale or disoriented. On the contrary, the most shocking thing was that he looked himself.

Throughout the conversation, he smiled and appeared entirely content with what he had done. He looked well fed. Dissidents watching said it would have been better if he had been bloodied and bruised. At least it would have made sense. He was admitting to crimes that could bear a prison sentence of seven years, yet he seemed happy. His appearance was so at variance with what he was saying that observers wondered if he had been given a euphoria-producing drug.

The *Washington Post*'s reporter, trying to explain what he had seen, called this 'one of the heaviest blows to be struck in recent years against the struggling Soviet human rights movement'. 'Dudko occupied a unique and important place in the spectrum of influential dissidents who have risked jail to speak out for individual freedoms within this author-itarian system,' the article said. 'Unlike the wooden and forced perform-ances given by other dissidents who have recanted in recent years, Dudko looked and sounded both eager and intent upon recanting his crimes.'

Keston College, a UK-based organization researching the oppres-sion of Soviet believers, refused to draw any conclusions from the appearance, apparently reluctant to confront the possibility that he might have been speaking voluntarily. Keston had been at the fore-front of keeping Father Dmitry's fate in the world's eye, and its publi-city had helped have him praised in Britain's House of Commons by a Foreign Office minister, as well as in the United States and elsewhere.

'Father Dmitry's "confession" is, perhaps, the greatest body-blow suffered by the Orthodox Church since ... 1971,' Keston said.

> The propaganda advantages to the Soviet authorities are obvious. A trial in court would have only reinforced Father Dmitry's unique posi-tion among believers. There is also considerable mileage to be gained in the international relations sphere. The 'confession', whether genuine or not, is a slap in the face to the West, which has been vocal in protesting the arrest of Father Dmitry. It is also a direct blow at Father Dmitry's individual supporters in the Soviet Union and the Christian Committee for the Defence of Believers' Rights in the USSR, who have stressed that Father Dmitry's activities were of a purely spiritual, and not politi-cal nature. Prometheus has been bound, and his terrible punishment appears to be just beginning.

And that night, while *Time* was showing him rejecting his life's work, printing presses all over the Soviet Union were churning out copies of *Izvestia*, the country's second newspaper after *Pravda*. The article he wrote for that only took up a quarter of a page, but it resonated around the world. It was proof of Father Dmitry's surrender.

Under the banner headline 'The West Wants Sensations', Father Dmitry calmly and methodically destroyed himself. 'In January 1980 I was arrested by the organs of state security for anti-Soviet activity. At first I denied my guilt, and announced that I had not spoken against the Soviet government, and that as a priest I am fighting against Godlessness. But then I understood, I was arrested not for my faith in God, but for a crime.' He acknowledged that he had done harm to his country, and thanked the government for the patience it had shown towards him over the years. He should, he now realized, have been working with the state and not against it.

He wrote that he had told himself, 'You are fighting against all criminality: drunkenness, hooliganism, moral decay, for the strengthening of the family ... but you are not being blamed for this, the Soviet government is fighting this too.' He had always said the reason he did not work with the state was because it was spreading distrust, profiting from the sales of alcohol, encouraging abortion. Now, he had changed his mind.

And he apologized to the bishops too. He said he had been wrong to lecture them when he should have been listening and obeying. By publishing books abroad, he had given ammunition to the state's enemies. 'Do you really think that in the West they understand us better than we understand ourselves? Even the ethnic Russians who live there, they long ago lost touch with their homeland and what is happening here.'

He rejected his self-published newspaper. He rejected the books he had written. He named specific foreigners – a journalist from the *New York Times*, an American professor, a Belgian bishop – who had helped him, at significant risk to themselves, by smuggling his writings out the country. He named foreigners who had tried to bring foreign-published works into the country and who campaigned for believers' rights. And he rejected them all. 'I now understand that foreigners who interfere in our internal affairs will bring us nothing but harm.' He banned the further publication of his books. He wanted to make a clean break with the past, and to start again with a new message. There would be no more talk of boycotts, of resistance.

'We live on Soviet land,' he wrote in conclusion.

And we must obey the laws of our country. Disobedience to its laws will above all bring harm to our country, disperse our internal strength, and bring unnecessary suffering. We must think not just of ourselves, but of our families, of those who travel with us ... now, when there is an external danger, we need all to unite and work together with our government and our people, which were given us by God and before whom we are all responsible.

On my return from the Arctic, I visited Tanya Podrabinek, the Muscovite I had befriended in the north the previous summer, at her home in the Moscow suburb of Elektrostal. There her husband Kirill told me how Father Dmitry's *Izvestia* article sped through the camps system, and was used by prison guards to assault dissidents' morale. By summer 1980, Kirill was close to the end of a three-year sentence he had received after he and his brother Alexander refused to abandon their investigations into military hazing and punitive psychiatry.

'It was three weeks before the end of my term, and the prosecutor came to talk to me. This was in 1980, in June, and he brought me that copy of *Izvestia*, the newspaper,' Kirill said.

I had a spare photocopy of the article and handed one to Kirill, and we sat and read it through together. It was the first time Kirill had seen it since that June day in 1980 when he was anticipating his imminent release. He finished and handed it back. He seemed keen to get rid of it as quickly as he could.

'The prosecutor gave it to me, and he said: "Look, what your friends are saying,"' Kirill said. 'I told this prosecutor that Dudko was a priest and not a fighter. Perhaps I was not fair because among those priests there were tough ones too, but I think the prosecutor understood.'

It is obvious why the prosecutor showed the article to Kirill. This was a propaganda coup for the government of almost unparalleled magnitude. A senior dissident was calling on anyone who opposed the government to give up the struggle and obey its orders. All over the country, political prisoners were being shown the article and offered a deal: surrender and be released. Kirill refused to surrender, however, and retribution was swift. A new court case was quickly arranged, and he received three more years under the law that criminalized any comments deemed to be anti-Soviet. He had been careless in whom he spoke to.

Although Father Dmitry's betrayal of his ideals did not work on Kirill, the Soviet government expected it to have a major effect on society at large. It was better even than a show trial, with the staged humiliation and then execution of an opponent. By breaking a dissident, parading them and releasing them, you showed that the reward for submission was a new life, rather than death. Previously, in the 1930s, the state had just wielded its power to crush opponents. Now, it had learned finesse.

Father Dmitry also addressed a letter to the patriarch, dated the same day as the *Izvestia* article, which was published with presumably deliberate understatement on page 40 of the Patriarchate's official journal. 'My first words are: forgive me,' Father Dmitry wrote. He signed off with the words: 'the humble novice of Your Holiness, who is not worthy of calling himself a priest but, if you will allow it, I will dare to sign myself, the unworthy priest D. Dudko'.

Patriarch Pimen, the man before whom he abased himself and whom he was asking for forgiveness, was someone who had praised the 'lofty spiritual qualities' of Andropov, the KGB chairman who locked Christians in mental hospitals. Patriarch Pimen had singled out the 'titanic work in the cause of international peace' done by Brezhnev, under whom the Soviet Union invaded both Czechoslovakia and Afghanistan. He had won the Order of the Red Banner for his 'great patriotic activities', at a time when his priests were being arrested. If anyone needed forgiveness it was the patriarch, but it was Father Dmitry who was asking for it.

On 21 June, the day after his television appearance, he was released from prison. He had been inside just over six months. His wife Nina told foreign journalists that he was tired and turned them away when they tried to talk to him. A couple of days later he released a statement for them: 'Leave me in peace, stop trying to pull me into some kind of politics, I am just an Orthodox priest, and one on Russian soil.'

Tanya's husband Kirill refused to judge Father Dmitry for what he had done, but was ruthless in his assessment.

'I just think he was weak. There are several different elements here. If you are weak, do not invite attack. That is the first thing. Secondly, it is one thing if you just answer for yourself, it is another if you answer for others. Around Dudko was a group of young people that he had gathered around himself, and his recantation was a heavy blow to them.

'He showed weakness, and that was far from harmless to those around him. The prosecutor came with this statement to me, for example. And the third element, which is the most important, is that if you show weakness, you should retire from public life afterwards. You should not shout out again, but he did live a public life afterwards and that is not good.'

Father Vladimir's assessment at the time was far harsher. When Father Dmitry, his spiritual father, had been in detention, he had battled to keep his plight noticed in the world's media at considerable risk to himself. It had, it seemed, all been for nothing.

'I would not say they fooled him, rather they broke him. I stopped going to see him then. A lot of people left and did not come back, they all said he had been broken. And if he was broken, then he was not from God because a martyr should not be broken,' he said, still with his head lowered.

10

The KGB did their business

Inside Father Dmitry's flat, behind the door closed against the journalists, he faced his family. His wife, ever understanding, was just pleased to have him back. But his son – who would grow up to be a priest himself, but at the time was a student who had faced harassment of his own for his Christian beliefs – was angry, red in the face. Even his eyes were red, Father Dmitry wrote later.

'What is wrong with you? Have you gone mad?' his son demanded.

'What? Well, you're still young. And how would you survive without me? I haven't rejected God and the Church,' Father Dmitry replied.

'I don't know what I will do now at college. I would like to vanish off the face of the earth.'

One of Father Dmitry's spiritual children expressed the shock and concern of them all in an open letter: 'I, Marina Lepeshinskaya, accuse the organs of the KGB of the murder of my spiritual father.' The Western journalists kept coming to the door, asking to see him, just to see what he looked like, just to talk to him, to ask him to explain himself, but Father Dmitry stayed in his room.

On the second day, he wrote, he hid away and cried, as he began to see quite how enormous a step he had taken. His wife's sister, walking home, was grabbed by a terrified woman who said that his former disciples wanted to kill him because he had sold them out. His sister-in-law rushed home. He told her that there was nothing to worry about, but they still went outside to check, and he decided never to sleep alone in case the threat was real.

Perhaps, while he stayed inside, he re-read the statement he had written for *Izvestia*, and saw the names of the people, people who had previously considered themselves to be his friends, whom he had accused of wanting to undermine the state and wanting to harm the Russian people.

Desperate in his guilt, he wrote to one of them, Archbishop Vasily of Brussels. 'If you had told me that I would behave like this, then I would have considered it as slander. But it appears that I overestimated my powers, I have fallen so low, like no one before me,' he wrote. 'I have never suffered such torments as now. I now know from my own experience what hell is. I am ready to do anything to correct the situation, but I don't know how.'

He did not want to see journalists, and he did not want to see accusing faces around him, so he fled to the countryside, where he issued a statement for his spiritual children. He tried to summon up the old fire, the old arguments, as if nothing had happened. 'The first thing I beg of you is don't separate, have love for each other. Forget your personal grievances, forget your ethnicity. Now we need to unite like never before in the face of this danger,' he wrote, in words that he could have written a year earlier.

But how could they trust him, let alone unite around him, when he had named their closest foreign allies in print? The obvious question they would all be asking would be: who else did he betray? He had had months of interrogations and plenty of time to list every single one of his friends for the KGB files. Then, the second thought would have been even more worrying still. If the group's leader could crumble, then so could anyone. And if anyone could collapse and give their secrets away, then how could anyone trust anyone at all? The group of friends had held together in his absence by campaigning for his release, and by keeping his plight in the headlines. Now, they did not even have that to unite them.

They were stunned by one still more enormous question: why did he do it? How had a man who had been so brave for so long surrender so willingly? It is a question that still divides his old friends.

Alexander, Zoya junior's father, was possibly the only one of his spiritual children who did not desert him and he refused to admit that Father Dmitry had done anything wrong: 'I was not sad, I was pleased. He showed he was a true son of his homeland and his Church. It was not a fall, it was a confirmation. By shaming himself before pagans and non-believers he told the whole world he was a believer.'

But he was speaking three decades after the event. In Lefortovo itself, Father Dmitry had been subject to the whole range of KGB tricks to make him change his mind. He had a cellmate accused of currency speculation. This was one of the KGB's favourite ploys. Currency speculation was a crime, but one that no one had moral qualms about. That meant anyone would happily chat to a black-market moneychanger. The man played on Father Dmitry's fears of imprisonment, and urged him to co-operate. What harm could co-operation do?

He also had an extremely convincing interrogator called Vladimir Sorokin. Once the cellmate had persuaded Father Dmitry to at least talk to his interrogator, which took six weeks or so, then Sorokin enlarged the chink to gain access to his soul.

Sorokin produced writings by a theologian called Yevgeny Divnich, who had been imprisoned first by the Gestapo and then by the KGB. He had been a friend of Father Dmitry's in the camps, but had not been released after Stalin died. Divnich held out against the KGB for more than two decades. He once told Father Dmitry that if a day went by without him somehow harming the Soviet state, then he considered the day wasted.

But he too surrendered in the end, ground down by the system and by decades in the camps. 'My Christ supports the Soviet government,' Divnich wrote in words that Father Dmitry later quoted approvingly. 'It is impossible to defeat the Soviet government with one's own primitive powers. Opposition is a primitive power, and obliges you to unite with foreigners and that is treachery, you must betray your homeland.'

That was the choice that Father Dmitry was given. As a Russian, he wanted to support Russia. As a Christian, he wanted to oppose the Soviet Union. But, if he opposed the Soviet Union, he was allying with foreigners and thus fighting against Russia. He had to choose, therefore, between his religion and his country and he chose his country. That was how he himself justified his choice.

'I am all the same a patriot' was one of the things that the television showed him as saying. But his resolve collapsed on the outside, when he understood what he had done.

On fleeing Moscow, he was stuck miserable in the village of Baydino in the Tula region, where he had a house. I went to find it.

The Tula bus station was bitterly cold. Minibuses stood in ranks in a yard of compacted snow, more grey than white. Bus information was hard to get hold of. I could get to Arsenevo, which was most of the way to Baydino. From there, the woman at the enquiries window told me, there might be a bus or I might have to make my own way. It was minus 32 when I left the hotel. I had donned two sets of long under-pants, as well as my usual vest/T-shirt/jumper/jacket combination on top. As I waited for the Arsenevo bus to edge out of line and come forward for passengers, I mused on the strange disconnect between my face, which was pinched and sharp with cold, and my legs, which were slightly too warm.

I had reading material in my bag. Father Dmitry, when he hid away in Baydino, wanted to reach out to his disciples. So he started publish-ing his newspaper once more. He would have to send it out by the mail, which meant it could be intercepted and would have little effect, but it was important to his self-respect that he did something. So, on 9 November 1980, after almost a year's gap in publication, his *In the Light of the Transfiguration* came hammering off his typewriter again. And I had it with me.

The minibus finally admitted the handful of us heading for Arse-nevo. I arranged myself carefully, wedged up against the wall of the cabin, coat zipped up to the top, hat pulled down, scarf tightened. Both gloves – the thin inner and the padded outer – were on my left hand, but only the thin inner one was on my right, so I could hold the pen and take notes.

I blackened everything honest, direct and brave. I provoked irritation in people's souls, maybe even curses. I have cut off my own support, the bough I was sitting on, as the popular saying goes. I have opened the door wide to all illegality, to the spread of Godlessness in our land. By the example of my failure, I have as a priest blessed the existence of Godlessness in our land, and I have refused Christ. That is how it is, and I need to address it directly. You can serve only Christ, it is impos-sible to serve anyone else in any way [Father Dmitry wrote in a 'confession']. I am a priest, I answer not only for myself, but I answer above all for my spiritual children, I answer for my fellow countrymen, I answer for the whole world, since God gave me the right to speak to the whole world.

But no one was listening.

'Those who were around me, they are all gone,' he wrote in the first edition of his newspaper. 'Now, when I am summoned, only my wife goes with me. And one other, who they say doesn't understand anything anyway.'

The language of crucifixion that he used before to describe the fate of his country, that was now used for himself. He was on the cross, as Jesus was. This was his personal Golgotha, the site of Jesus' crucifixion.

Is it not Golgotha in your opinion, when people throw words at me like stones, and say 'tell him that I now have a different spiritual father'? At least they could come and say it themselves, they could at least say goodbye.

Is it not Golgotha when I hear on the telephone 'I don't want to talk to you, forget my number'?

I huddled tighter into my coat. As we drove south-west out of the city, the sun rose off to our left, casting orange tendrils over the snowfields. A woman stopped the bus to get off, letting a gust of cold into our warmer cabin, and the four other passengers pulled their scarves tighter around their faces. My clumsy fingers, made thicker by cold and gloves, struggled to turn the pages. As we drove towards Arsenevo, Father Dmitry's torment deepened.

'Spiritual children, my friends, where are you? Answer me. Let us unite to do God's work around Christ. If you think I fell then, when we unite, you can raise me. Surely you will not trample on me with your feet when I lie at the foot of Golgotha?'

It is clear from his words in the next week's edition that no one replied. He keeps admitting his guilt, saying that everyone is guilty, admitting his own guilt again. 'I begin to understand how people, unable to withstand disgrace, end their own lives. This was how Judas, presumably, could not withstand his disgrace. And people feel sorry for Judas. How unhappy he was, who could be unhappier than him?'

We pulled into a little village and stopped to fill up with diesel. As the fumes crept into the cabin, I began to feel sick. I do not normally get travel sick, but this seemed to be an exception, so, as we drove out, I looked at the road. We crept up a hill, and rounded a roundabout adorned with a large globe. The sun was a glowing orange hub in the sky, but so low I could still look at it without my eyes hurting.

The sickness faded, but returned as soon as I plunged back into Father Dmitry's world. I realized then that this was not travel sickness at all, but intense shame. His guilt was so huge that it seeped off the page. It was the feeling you had as a child when you had done something wrong and felt dreadful. You want your mother to hug you and make everything better, but you know that is impossible because it is you that is to blame. It was the torment described by Father Dmitry, and his knowledge that he had betrayed everyone and everything he loved, that was making me feel sick in sympathy.

'I have stopped getting letters. It's true, at the beginning I received a few letters, but they have stopped. Have I been forgotten or are my letters being intercepted?'

The fingers of my right hand, the hand with only the thin inner glove on it, were stiff with cold and would barely unbend. I tried to massage them and dropped my pen, which evaded my clumsy attempt to catch it. It fell on to the floor of the cabin and into the slight gap left by the sliding door. I felt still sicker as I tried and failed to coax it out. Without a pen to take notes, I sat and watched the road. The sunlight was less orange now, more buttery, as we drove on a bleak empty road through a forest, the colours stripped out of the landscape.

We crept to the top of a hill and met a huge view: white and khaki, forest and fields stretching far away.

Father Dmitry was desperate to confess, and to rid himself of his feeling of guilt, but there was no one to confess to. He tried issuing a few statements, reaffirming his pre-arrest convictions, but that just tied him in knots with the KGB, who then threatened him with rearrest. Each twist in his position rendered him less believable anyway.

Without friends to talk to, or the debates he loved so much, he was thrown back on to his newspaper, into which he poured his anguish. His family – his son Mikhail, his daughter Natalya, his wife Nina –

was still around him, but they did not provide the debate he wanted. That had come from his spiritual children.

'Has no one called?' I ask Natalya, my angel of a daughter, who had circled around Lefortovo prison when I was inside, protecting me from troubles and misfortunes.

'No, papa, no one has called.'

Left alone, his guilt chewed away at him.

'The telephone is quiet. No calls and no one comes. They just judge me. They judge. They judge.'

In his newspaper, he tried to explain the choice he had made, how he had tried to reconcile the biblical instruction to 'render unto Caesar' while also remaining true to God. This is a difficult issue to square for any theologian, but particularly so in the Orthodox tradition, which developed in the Byzantine Empire where the emperor was the protector of the Church. There was no theological defence against an atheist government, since the government was assumed to be the shield of the Church. Priests had no tradition of rebellion, of asserting the Church's authority against the government, as the Catholic and Protestant clerics in the West did.

He was faced with two different instructions – obey the government, and obey God's law – but could not obey both of them. He was, as a law-abiding man and an Orthodox Christian, torn between them. In the 1970s, he had raised God's laws above human laws. Now, however, the KGB had reminded him forcefully of the power of human laws, and he was pulled in two directions.

'You are violating the rules of the fight. Instead of ideological methods, you are using administrative, legal, punitive measures,' he wrote in an imaginary dialogue with the KGB that he composed around this time.

Before his arrest, his newspaper had described the collapse of a community in real time. Now, it was describing the collapse of an individual. I could not – despite the lack of pen to take notes, despite feeling sick – stop reading. The sun flickered in my eyes through the trees and the cabin window, and the words were brutal, like a long, sliding car crash lasting hours.

We stopped in a small village, where a red-brick church with a cross was the centrepiece of a row of houses. I took the opportunity to retrieve my pen, and read on.

'We all need confession. But who will confess first? Everyone is called to confession, but let someone else confess. And no one even wants to understand my confession. Everyone is leaving, I am left almost alone, just with my family, and even Mikhail wants to go to Moscow.'

Mikhail, his son, was angry and told him what everyone was saying.

'What they are saying is that your books should be burned, that no one should come to you, that you cannot be a spiritual father,' Mikhail said. Father Dmitry replied that he did not believe it, but his son insisted: 'They are sparing you, a lot tougher things were said as well.'

And Father Dmitry began to get angry. His friends would not forgive him. No one was coming to see him, and he could not believe this was out of choice. Someone must be stopping his old friends from coming.

'I don't understand, what is this? Revenge? And for what? Are they fulfilling someone's orders, or just inspired by the spirit of evil? Are they stripping their father bare to laugh at their father?'

It was a beautiful day now. The roads were almost empty, and nothing moved in the wide flat landscape ahead of us, just the puff of exhaust from a car a couple of hundred metres in front. It was hard to reconcile the beauty around me with the pain on the page.

'Christians are leaving another Christian in sorrow. I understand that my sorrow is a bit different, that it's not the kind to inspire sympathy. And anyway I'm not talking about sympathy, but do you really not understand that they are dividing us, to drive in a wedge, to play on our mistakes?' he wrote. But he himself was as much to blame as any of them, accusing his old friends of abandoning him, of obeying orders, of anything he could think of.

His community was truly shattered. The lesson was clear: totalitarianism does not allow independence. It cannot. Even the smallest attempt to assert autonomy is a threat to the whole. Father Dmitry had understood this in the 1970s, which is why he encouraged hope and trust. Those are the only weapons that can be used against a state determined to destroy society.

Father Dmitry had thought he had been serving his nation by spreading trust, and fighting abortion and despair, but, in doing so, he was defying the state. And that was not allowed. That was why he had to be crushed. His fate parallels the fate of his whole nation. Through the twentieth century, the government in Moscow taught the Russians that hope and trust are dangerous, inimical and treacherous. That is the root of the social breakdown that has caused the epidemic of alcoholism, the collapsing birth rate, the crime and the misery.

Father Dmitry understood quickly, on emerging from detention, what had happened to him. He understood that he had been a danger to the state, and why the state had to isolate him or destroy him. The concepts of trust, hope and faith were too dangerous to be allowed to flourish. Most Russians caught in the national decline did not have his awareness. They drank or fought without knowing why life was so miserable. Father Dmitry tried to rebuild the old community, to get working again. He appealed in what was left of his newspaper for unity, for his spiritual children to come back, and for them to try again. But who would come back to him now? It was too late.

On 22 February 1981, he typed his last issue. He said he had to stop publication so as to keep his secrets to himself from now on, but I think he was just depressed that no one read his paper. He had certainly shown no desire to hide secrets in the past. I finished the page. It was incredibly cold.

In Arsenevo, it turned out that buses to Baydino did exist, but that they would not do me much good. There was one in the morning, which I had missed by more than an hour, and one back in the evening, for which I would have to wait six hours. If I were to wait for the evening one, I would still have no way of getting back again unless I was prepared to spend the night there. The temperature was if anything even lower out here in the countryside, and my breath was a thick cloud in the waiting room, so sitting around was not an attractive option. I walked out into the cold and looked for a taxi. There was no shortage. Half a dozen men were waiting in their cars for non-existent customers, and I hired the first: a stocky driver with a moustache in a white Zhiguli.

It was eerie outside the little town. The cold was so intense that the upper branches of the birch trees were covered in hoar frost, as delicate as the first leaves of spring but white and sparkling. Sometimes the low sun caught a tree just so, and then every crystal would light up and the whole glowing tree was transformed into something more magical than any neon display. Sometimes the birches were a dark screen along the road, and then I could see between them to the vast featureless fields, their snowy crust unscarred. At other times the road ran through a dense wood, threatening in black and white.

There were no other cars on the road, which stretched ahead of us in a straight, desolate line. A black figure appeared on the horizon after a while and trudged onwards without stopping as we drove past. He was the only sign of life we saw for the whole half-hour it took to reach the village.

We turned right, following the sign for Baydino, then crossed a small iced-over river and stopped on the far side. The driver gestured to a line of houses that paralleled the road. That was it, Father Dmitry's refuge when the storm broke over him.

'Quiet, monotony, fresh air, the absence of a mass of people, two or three women walk by, a boy runs past, sometimes a drunkard passes, totally inoffensive, just swaying slightly: after the city's din and fuss, it was unusual,' he wrote later, before going on to describe their first evening. 'Some young voices unexpectedly began to sing, and they played on the balalaika. They sang for a long time, and then were quiet. Calm, quiet, and nothing else. For my children it was boring, my wife was also dissatisfied, but I felt like I was in heaven.'

I had specific instructions to help me find the house he had lived in. I knew which way its door pointed, how many fir trees were in its garden and what colour it was painted.

I did not anticipate the search would take me long, so I asked the driver to wait and stepped into the cold. The field was knee deep in snow, but villagers had beaten a path across the field towards the nearest house. I could tell from the footprints that the path was regularly used by a woman (or by a man with small feet), but I could not see her anywhere in the yard of the house, where the only sign of life was a dog who barked frantically from a locked shed. The yard also contained a huge log pile, next to a shed that had until recently contained rabbits. Their hutch was empty. Perhaps the woman had taken them to market on the morning bus.

My instructions said Father Dmitry's house was the one with conifers in the garden, but there appeared to be pines all along the track that formed the backbone of the village. Finding his place was going to be slightly harder than I had anticipated. The shovelled path ended after the rabbit woman's yard, and I followed the tracks of an animal, which turned out to be a cat, since four of the creatures were looking at me from the locked yard of a house. A car in the yard was piled with so much snow you could hardly tell it was a car. Apart from the cats, there were no other signs of life. By the time I reached the top of the village, mine were the only human footprints.

The village contained about thirty houses, of which three were habitable. The rabbit house was the only one permanently lived in though, and the other two were clearly only used at the weekend, probably as country retreats for Muscovites. Of the rest, some were rotting, their walls buckling and window frames stolen for fuel. Others were still weather-proof, but forlorn, with trackless snow piled to the window sills. There would be no balalaika music here now, not even any drunkards such as the one Father Dmitry had described. Baydino was another one of the villages in the statistics, and was all but dead.

In fact, the Tula region is the core of the cancer that is eating away at the Russian population. It has just 2.2 people of working age for every one pensioner, which is the worst figure in all of Russia, but one that the country as a whole will exceed in just a few years. The number of pensioners compared to working adults is increasing all over the industrialized world, but nothing like to this extent. As a comparison, in 2010, Great Britain had 3.6 people of working age for each pensioner, while the United States had 4.5 – more than twice as many as the Tula region. Only the Pskov region has a population that is contracting faster than Tula's. It has the highest ratio of deaths to births in the country, and the second lowest fertility level. It is, in a word, dying.

Tracing my own footprints back through the village, I tried to decipher the directions I had been given. Father Dmitry's house was clearly one of three adjacent buildings that formed a line on the side of the village nearest the road, so I waded into the snow in one of the gardens, to look more closely. By this stage, I had lost all feeling in my toes, and I had my padded hood cinched tight over my face to hold my scarf over my mouth. Just my eyes were exposed to the cold. I ploughed forward. The snow was waist deep here, and I realized the best way to make progress was almost to lie on it, walking on my knees rather than my feet and supporting my weight on my stomach. I did not even to try to lift my legs clear at every step. If I walked on my feet, sometimes the crust would support me, but I would invariably crash through halfway into the next step, which made extricating myself far more difficult than if I just ploughed forwards like a cow.

The first house fitted all the requirements except that the porch pointed the wrong way. Just a few small panes of glass were missing from a decorative window, but that had been enough to let the weather in. The floorboards of the porch were rotten, and trash had blown through. This house was still together, but would not be for long.

I pushed on to the next house. Really, I should have gone round back by the road, but it was taking a long time – five minutes to go 20 metres – to get anywhere, so I just dived through the hedge that separated their gardens, and floundered round to its front door. It was hard work, and I began to sweat under my coat. I released the hood a little, and suffered as my feet warmed and the blood flowed back into my toes. Some snow had pushed down into my boots and was melting, which made me feel all the colder.

This second house was definitely not the one, being the wrong shape, so I repeated my hedge dive to get to the third. They all three looked more or less the same: cream-painted walls, single storey, porch, two rooms. But this last house was the most damaged of the three. A whole window was missing, so I heaved myself over the sill and inside, where there was only a light dusting of snow. It was a relief to be able to walk without wading. In the bedroom, two old wire bedsteads lacked mattresses. A wardrobe still held some cheap summer dresses, and a row of their matching belts hung from a rail. A Formica-laminated cupboard stood up against a wall, its doors open. Here were toothpaste tubes, and bottles of iodine, and a glass full of toothbrushes. A magazine from 1981 – the same year as the last edition of Father Dmitry's newspaper – was piled on top of some schoolbooks. A girl called Galina had done her Russian homework here.

On the wall behind the cupboard was a swallow's nest.

As I prepared to hoist myself back into the snow, I noticed, among the wreckage of dozens of dead butterflies on the windowsill, an empty bottle of vodka and a half-used bubble packet of hypodermic needles.

I retraced my way back through my trench to the house of the cats, and started again. At the end furthest from the river the houses were even more damaged, without roofs, full inside and out with snow, and with no chance of any traces remaining of their previous owners. I gave up, walked back out to the road and down to the car. In a brief panic, I worried that the driver might have got bored and left me in the cold, but he was still sitting there patiently with a cigarette. Just as I was about to get in, I noticed that smoke was now blooming from the chimney of the first house I had passed: the one with the rabbits and the barking dog. There had been no smoke before, so this could only mean someone was home. The driver said no one had passed him, and I had seen no one, but smoke was smoke. Excited to find a human at last I strode back down the beaten path, and knocked on the door. There was no answer, so I tried another door. There was still no answer.

Puzzled, I walked back to the car, unable to understand how the fire had lit itself without a person being at home. It was only that evening that I guessed the owner had probably been in all the time, but had not wanted to open their door to someone mad enough to spend two hours wading through waist-deep snow and breaking into derelict houses.

On our drive back to Arsenevo, my driver told me that he had worked for seventeen years as a coal miner near Tula, and now had a monthly pension of 8,000 roubles. That is around £160 and, as a comparison of how far out of whack the local economy is, my grim hotel room in Tula cost me 6,200 roubles for my two nights' stay. When he dropped me off back at the bus station, I gave him two 500-rouble notes, and realized as I did so that that was half a week's pension. My driver told me there was no other work, all the farms were closed, and the sausage factory that used to exist had gone with them. Food is imported now, he said.

While waited for the bus back, a three-year-old girl in a pink jacket so puffed up that she could barely move her arms commanded the little bus station. She talked incessantly to her father, delighting in the sound of the Russian words 'to Tula, to Tula'. Her father, keen for a break, phoned his wife and handed his daughter the phone. She then became silent and refused to say a word until he took the phone away. He finally did so, and ended the call, at which point she nattered away again as before. Her father's eyes met mine in a mute shrug, and then the bus came.

She was the only child I had seen all day. I made a point of looking out for more, but did not see any.

The bus back to Tula was not the modern sleek model of the morning, but an old doddery Soviet-era Icarus. The temperature inside was the same as that outside – minus 32 – and, if it warmed up during the journey, it did not warm up by much. It was far too cold to read or to take notes, so I sat with my double-gloved hands pushed up into my sleeves and nurtured the ember of warmth into a steady glow.

I could not help but muse on Father Dmitry as our bus retraced our morning route back from the bleak fields. The evening light had none of the mellow warmth of the morning. The fields were flat and greyish. The trees were gloomy, and there was no colour or warmth anywhere in the world.

My mind kept piecing together little snippets from the newspaper I had been reading that morning. I had been so mesmerized by the misery that Father Dmitry was pouring on to the page that I had allowed the actual events of his life to wash over me: the summonses to the prosecutors, the insults from his friends, the abusive letters.

Now, though, I had time, and I began to see a picture emerge of a second narrative contained in the newspaper besides the misery. The story gradually formed itself on the long bumpy journey, but was still an amorphous shape when the Icarus made a heroic effort to crest the slight rise into Tula's bus station.

Back in Tula, I walked the road from the bus station to the centre of town, partly because I had not realized how long it was, and partly because I wanted to think some more. At the end, I turned right and found a bar in a shopping centre. I occupied a table in the corner, as far as possible from a group of rowdy Armenians playing billiards. I spread out my papers, ordered a beer and began to read.

I went back to that moment just after his release from detention, when a woman came screaming that his former disciples wanted to kill him. The next day he had a meeting with a senior figure in the KGB, at his own request. Worried about his safety, and about a threat to his life from people who had been his friends, he turned for help to the authorities.

'I said to them, that I am being threatened, they want to kill me,' he wrote later.

The KGB man did not appear to believe the threat, but did offer to take him back into detention for his own protection, and that was a crucial moment. Before his arrest, Father Dmitry was urging a boycott of the state. Now he was turning to it for help against his own friends.

It is clear from Father Dmitry's own account that the KGB used a disorienting good cop/good cop approach, which worked better than they could have imagined on a priest who was alone and friendless and desperate and guilty. They spoke to him kindly and politely as if he was their old chum. They discussed the disagreements he had had with the state, and how he disliked its atheistic policies.

'Yes, we are guilty before you,' a senior KGB official told Father Dmitry. 'And not only that, the state is guilty before the Church.'

How could he resist these entreaties, when he had no other friends? He wrote that he had asked for forgiveness but that his friends would not even talk to him. And here were KGB agents admitting all of the crimes that he had been accusing the state of committing for so long. Perhaps he had been wrong about them? And, if he was wrong about them, who else was he wrong about?

Distrusted by his friends, after his release from detention he began to sympathize with his persecutors. It was a coup for Sorokin – the investigator – who shared the first name and patronymic of Father Dmitry's brother. Father Dmitry later wrote that he came to regard Sorokin as his second brother.

The KGB could control who came to see him at Baydino. They knew the community he had lived in, and they recognized its fault-line between Jews and Russians, that there had always been mutual distrust no matter how Father Dmitry tried to contain it and, without him realizing it, they exploited that.

'At last the Jews came to me. At first a young man from Kiev. He said that people are still reading my books, and he asked nothing, he just looked at me. I came to life a bit. The Russians just pester me all the time, but the Jews sympathize,' Father Dmitry wrote.

Who was this mysterious Jew from Kiev? And who were the others who came later and showed him documents printed in his defence? He was glad that they had come and grateful for their sympathy. When they brought statements for him to sign, he signed them 'mechanically', he wrote later, hardly reading them.

Father Dmitry was turning back and forth, grateful first to his KGB friends, then to his anti-Soviet Jewish friends, and he wanted to please them all. His attempt to excuse himself to the foreign bishop he had incriminated in his *Izvestia* article, and then the statements he gave to the Jews – which were inevitably found in a raid on a flat in Moscow, although he had not intended them to be published – angered the security services, who called him in once more. Although they had released him, they had not closed his case. He was still at risk of prosecution.

'We have made a mistake, we thought about closing the case, but now these new statements,' his investigator Sorokin said. 'But well, how can you write this? Who will believe you anyway? One day he's like that, another day, he's different. And anyway we don't mean you any harm, why did you write this?'

Lacking the mechanical process of serving in church to fill his time, or the discussions with the faithful that he had enjoyed so much, his hours were empty. There were only so many statements he could write, and his newspaper only came round once a week. He wanted to work, to chant the holy mysteries of Russian Orthodoxy, to light the incense, to process behind the icon screen and to dispense the ritual bread and wine.

This was the KGB's trump card, and they did not wait long to play it. Sorokin and another senior agent drove out to Baydino to see him.

'I'm going to take a holiday and come here to relax, it's so good here,' said the other agent, Anatoly Trofimov.

'You're welcome, we'll holiday together,' said Father Dmitry. They took chairs and went to sit under an apple tree. That was in late summer, a time unimaginable as I sat in frozen Tula, and the trees I had seen as skeletons that morning would have been heavy with fruit.

'We have already seen the church in which you will serve, we have photos,' Trofimov said. The conversation moved on, but the dart went straight to Father Dmitry's heart. The KGB were the gatekeepers to a future for him, a chance to escape the unchanging misery he was in.

The misery worsened because, while he was sitting under apple trees in Baydino, his old friend and fellow priest Gleb Yakunin was on trial in Moscow. He expected to be called as a witness, and worried and worried about how he would speak. Would he admit to meeting foreigners? Or would he defend his comrade? Then the trial ended. Yakunin got five years. Father Dmitry had not been summoned, and the worrying had been for nothing. And he did not come out of the contrast well. Yakunin had not appeared on television to recant his views, but had endured his ordeal and stayed true to his ideals. That was almost worse for Father Dmitry than having to speak against him in court.

Rumours churned in Moscow. People said that he had refused to go to the court to defend Yakunin, and he could hardly bear it. He and his wife decided to go to see Ira, Yakunin's wife, to sympathize and to explain. But on the way he changed his mind.

'Go on your own,' he told his wife.

'What, are you scared?' she asked.

'No, but go alone anyway.'

He was summoned to the KGB once more to talk to Sorokin. He had asked for books at Baydino, and they had sent him a pile of atheist brochures, books about Rasputin, the mad monk who advised the last tsar and his family, books by priests who had given up the faith and turned atheist. He was angry, accusing them of promising him a church and not giving it to him.

'How long have I been at liberty? And you don't let me serve for a single day, and you said you would give me a church straight away,' he said. 'I am ready to do anything. Prison is as scary to me now as my situation. Being shot would be better.'

It was the KGB's moment. Sorokin took him aside and they went to Trofimov, the big boss. Trofimov shook his head over all these statement he had signed and given to the Jews who came to see him. Those had complicated the case. Without them, everything would be fine. Nonetheless, Trofimov was prepared to take him into his confidence.

'Do you really not understand that the Jews want to put you in prison, but with our hands? And we don't want to imprison you. God grant that you reconsider,' he said.

'It's interesting that an atheist KGB man should say "God grant",' said Father Dmitry.

'God grant,' repeated Trofimov, the clever man. 'Go and reconsider.'

Sorokin left him to stew on that for a while. Father Dmitry was still trying to make up with his spiritual children. Eight of the ethnic Russians among them came to tell him their complaints. Their complaints were about Jews, and the weakened Father Dmitry was less able to rein in their prejudice.

'You cannot even stand next to a Jew,' one of his disciples spat out.

'I don't know much about theology,' said another, 'but what upset me the most is that you tried to make us embrace the Jews.'

The next morning he felt so weak that he could not get up, and he had to say his morning prayers in bed.

A while later, the KGB summoned him back. He was to speak to Trofimov again. This was a conversation so secret even Sorokin was not allowed in on it. The KGB were finally taking Father Dmitry completely into their hearts, and here was an even higher boss, Sergei Sokolov, to do it. A young woman brought tea and cake, and the two agents appeared to sit patiently while Father Dmitry said grace, then to business.

In the novel *Nineteen Eighty-Four*, George Orwell created Room 101, which contains the 'worst thing in the world'. The room's contents were different for every individual and, when they were unleashed, that individual's resistance finally crumbled away and they became a pliable servant of the state. Father Dmitry's Room 101 contained anti-Semitism. He had tried for decades to banish hatred of the Jews from his mind, but the KGB summoned it back and, in conversation after conversation, they destroyed him with it.

'You are surrounded by Jews, and they have no love for Russia. And, you know, we would never have interfered with you if you had not had around you people who then go abroad and raise anti-Soviet hysteria,' said Sokolov. He was talking about Jews who were emigrating to Israel, Europe and America and buttressing the increasingly hardline political stance being taken by Ronald Reagan in Washington and the likes of Margaret Thatcher in Europe. He was telling Father Dmitry that it was the Jews, not the KGB, who were to blame for his suffering.

Father Dmitry tried to oppose this logic, saying that among those who left the country were patriots. He mentioned Vladimir Maximov, a dissident writer who was forced to emigrate after spending time in a psychiatric hospital, saying that he had written good poems full of love for Russia. Vladimir Maximov, it should be noted, could hardly have had a more ethnically Russian name.

'Did you know Maximov was a Jew?' Sokolov shot back.

Father Dmitry said that, no, Maximov was a Russian, that he was one of his spiritual children.

'He's a Jew,' said Sokolov. 'I knew his mother well.'

Father Dmitry was near the end of his resistance now. He had resisted the anti-Semitism and hate he had been brought up with, the hate under Stalin, the hate under Hitler, and the prejudice from his spiritual children. But this was too much. He had already been lured into humiliating himself on television by an appeal to his patriotism. Once he had given in to that, it was a short step to join the KGB's paranoia and start seeing the plots they saw.

Father Dmitry mused. 'Yes, we all need to unite now to defend the honour of Russia. We have many enemies.' One of the KGB men asked him what united them, what they had in common. He thought about it and replied: 'We are all Russian.'

In the Russian language there are two words that we translate as 'Russian'. One is *rossiyanin* or, its adjective, *rossiisskiy*, which means 'someone from Russia' or 'of the Russian state'. The other is *russkiy*, which is used as both a noun and an adjective, meaning 'ethnic Russian', or 'of the Russian language'. He used *russkiy*. A Russian Jew is a *rossiyanin*, while Father Dmitry was *russkiy*. This was what Father Dmitry decided he had in common with the KGB men.

They brought up the possibility of him finally getting a new church again, and what he would do if he got one. He said he would fight alcoholism, he would uphold the spirit of the people. In short, he was saying he would act just as he had done before his arrest. But then he tailed off. He realized that was not the answer they were looking for.

'Well, you will see yourselves. Facts will show. If it's not to your liking, I'll be there,' he said, defeated at last. He wrote about this conversation many times in later years, as if unable to forget about it. The fight to save the Russian people was off. He would go along with the KGB, do their bidding, anything to get out of the hole he had dug for himself. The state could encourage abortion, spread alcoholism, sow distrust at the heart of family life, and he would not object.

'That is correct,' said Sokolov. 'But look out, don't even think about fooling us.'

The next day came the telegram from the bishop. He had a church, just outside Moscow, at Vinogradovo. It was, he wrote, a miracle. But he must have known it was not. And he knew whom to thank for it. He owed his new life to the KGB. He overlooked the fact that it was the KGB who had destroyed his old life. That had been a thousand years before. He was their creature now. It had taken them a while, but they had dug out the vein of defiance that had crossed his character, and created yet another compliant servant for the state.

In *Nineteen Eighty-Four* Winston Smith, the central character, is subjected to Room 101 and has his defiance broken, just as Father Dmitry was subjected and broken. After countless sessions of torture, his interrogator tells him: 'We are not content with negative obedience, nor even with the most abject submission. When finally you surrender to us, it must be of your own free will. We do not destroy the heretic because he resists us: so long as he resists us we never destroy him. We convert him, we capture his inner mind, we reshape him.'

That could have been written about Father Dmitry, and so perhaps could a later passage, when Winston Smith finally breaks: 'two and two could have been three as easily as five, if that were what was needed'. If two and two cease to add up to four, then everything stops having to make sense. All you have to do is stop thinking and you are free.

'How easy it all was! Only surrender, and everything else followed. It was like swimming against a current that swept you backwards however hard you struggled, and then suddenly deciding to turn round and go with the current instead of opposing it,' was how Orwell imagined it.

He wrote in *Nineteen Eighty-Four* that the future could be imagined as a boot stamping on a human face for ever, and that was what the KGB promised. They had endless power and could torment people for as long as they wanted. They could torment people until they realized for themselves that resistance was not just futile but wrong. It is a terrifying image, and Orwell's description of the destruction of Winston Smith's character is remarkably similar to what happened to Father Dmitry, but here he went too far. Humans are not machines. You cannot stamp on their faces for ever. If you deny people hope and trust and friendship, then they sicken and despair. People will not breed in captivity.

After his destruction, Winston Smith went to a bar and drank – 'It was his life, his death, and his resurrection. It was gin that sank him into a stupor every night, and gin that revived him in the morning' – alone and avoided. In the Russian case: for gin, read vodka.

Father Dmitry now had none of the young intellectuals around him with whom he had so loved to debate. They had abandoned him, or been imprisoned, or emigrated to Israel. He still wrote, but there was no one to read what he produced or to argue with his conclusions, so he held debates with himself. He wrote the questions and then provided the answers: 'There is only God. My hope in my friends has fallen to a minimum.'

'The KGB agents did their business. I was left alone, solitary. I still continue my discussions, I look for new techniques, but people don't come and the level of the discussions has fallen,' he wrote.

His writing became ever more bitter, as he lamented his abandonment. He wrote long statements to his old friends. His justification for his actions changed as the years passed. At first, he admitted his guilt and begged forgiveness. He said he was scared of imprisonment, and that he had been weak. Later, he tried to explain it away. He stopped admitting his faults. He had had no choice. He was a priest. To break with the Church would have meant damnation.

Breaking with them would mean to end up outside the hierarchy, without service, without the sacraments, like a member of a sect. They said they would expel me, that was their defence. I would have been forced to live and die without the sacraments. That scared me. That was the choice I stood before. I did not want to suffer, and so I rejected everything I had said, saying directly and strangely that it had been anti-Soviet and libellous and now I suffer all the more. My suffering could only be understood by a mother who by fate was forced to reject her own children. My children – my books – were despotically taken from me. And, like an unfortunate mother, I am scared to call those children mine.

Reading those words I felt sorry for him, but I no longer liked him. It was hard to like him. Yakunin was in prison. Ogorodnikov was in prison. Sakharov was in internal exile. Solzhenitsyn was in exile abroad. But it was Father Dmitry demanding sympathy because he had teamed up with the KGB to stay out of prison, done their work for them and undermined his friends. It did not look good, and his spiritual children did not come back because of it. And that made him angry.

'Despite everything,' he wrote, as if he had been wronged somehow, 'I love all people, I worry about them, especially about my own Russian people, about my own Russia.'

He invented a counterpart, Father Peter he called him, with whom he could hold long imaginary debates that confirmed his own viewpoint. But the debates were not like the old ones. Father Peter did not challenge his views. Before, Father Dmitry had insisted on tolerance and trust, but now he ventured further up the path of prejudice and racism the KGB had opened for him. This fictional counterpart asked him what he thought about the world, and about the faith, and about everything. Father Dmitry conflated himself and his country – 'What happened to me taught me a lot, just as what has happened to our country should teach us a lot' – and he was looking for someone to blame for the fate of both.

Before the KGB warped him, he had looked for solutions. He was not interested in finding those to blame for the demographic catastrophe, the alcoholism, the abortion. He just wanted to unite everyone, to end hatred and to build a community. Now, with his community scattered in all directions, and himself left alone, he concentrated on finding culprits.

And he had been well taught by the KGB. He blamed the Jews.

'Do you really not see that they are to blame for everything? It is not an accident that Marx was a Jew, and the creator of communism and atheism. If you try just to say that, everyone considers you an anti-Semite,' Father Dmitry said. It is hard to believe that this bigot is the same man who had so fought against prejudice and racism just a year or two before.

I I

I look at the future with pessimism

The KGB gave Father Dmitry a church in Vinogradovo, a village outside Moscow that has now been absorbed into the capital's northern suburbs. I arranged to go there with Zoya junior, the daughter of Father Alexander. She was the young woman who had been dragged from her bed by her mother, Zoya senior, and forced to cook us lunch. She is also, as it happens, Father Dmitry's goddaughter and has a letter from him in her flat.

'I congratulate you, Zoya, on the birth of your namesake Zoya. Let it be so, her name is Zoya. You will always remember yourself in her. God preserve you. I wish you strong and flourishing health. Your spiritual father Dmitry Dudko,' the letter says in his chaotic handwriting, above the date 27 February 1982. It sits on a fashionable Japanese-style sideboard.

By 1982, Father Dmitry was installed in the new church, with Alexander and Zoya senior as two of his few remaining spiritual children. When I asked Alexander why they had remained with Father Dmitry, he seemed confused by the question. Father Dmitry's televised confession, he said, had merely been proof of his spiritual worth. Father Dmitry made no mention of Alexander in his writings from the early 1980s, although he did describe that single disciple who had stayed with him because 'he doesn't understand anything anyway', and I have wondered if this was a reference to Zoya's father.

Be that as it may, it seemed appropriate to be visiting Vinogradovo with her. She looks like her father, in so far as a beautiful woman in her twenties can look like a middle-aged bushy-bearded Orthodox priest. She wears a gold cross around her neck and is an educated and sharp representative of Russia's new middle class. She works as an

interior designer, drives a smart German car, and picked me up outside a metro station at the end of the line.

She had never visited Vinogradovo before, or if she had she had no
memory of it. She programmed it into her satellite navigator, which
squawked directions at us as we drove out of Moscow towards the
great ring road that sweeps traffic around the capital. Out here on the
city perimeter are vast new developments of tower blocks and shopping complexes. The architecture, despite occasional whimsies of
towers and turrets, is joyless. You know that, while the walls may
look clean and unspotted now, in a couple of years they will be as
flaky and damp-stained as their Soviet-made predecessors.

When approaching the city, these towers meld into a solid wall,
rearing out of the virgin forest. While Russia is shrinking and its villages are dying, Moscow is booming. Here is, according to some estimates, 80 per cent of the nation's wealth. The oil and gas money is a
fountain showering Italian clothes, French wine and German cars on
the elite, and offering work to everyone else as long as they are prepared to get their hands dirty.

The total number of people living in Russia's cities shrank by 3.7
million in the decade after 2000. That is a decline of more than 3 per
cent, and in some places the collapse has been far worse. In Komi and
the Bryansk region, the urban population fell by almost a tenth, while
in the Tula region it slumped further still – by more than 13 per cent.
Moscow had none of that trouble. In the same period its population
rose from 9.9 to 10.6 million, making it by far the biggest city in Eastern Europe. And that is just the official figure. Millions of illegal immi-
grants from the former Soviet republics work here on building sites
and in the markets. They are unregistered and uncounted, but they
keep the capital moving and earn crucial roubles to send back to their
families in Tajikistan, Uzbekistan, Azerbaijan or Armenia.

It was some time before Zoya junior and I realized that her satnav
was malfunctioning. At every junction on the ring road, it directed us
to turn off, then threaded us randomly through the nearby streets
before depositing us back on the ring road again. It did this three
times before we switched it off and relied on the map.

The map was almost equally unhelpful. We drove past our destination three times without seeing it, and went down what appeared to

be every backstreet there was before finding the one we wanted. When we reached the church, I wondered what I had come for. It was just a church: yellow ochre and white, surrounded by gardens and trees that probably looked nice when not covered by a foot of snow. Inside, the church was fussy, adorned with modern icons that have for me no spiritual power, and guarded by an old woman who knew nothing of Father Dmitry and wanted nothing to do with me.

Nonetheless, looked at from outside, it was a smart and grand building. More importantly, it was near Moscow, pretty much as near as it was possible for Father Dmitry to get while remaining in the diocese that surrounds but does not include the city. It would have been a far more convenient location for his discussion group and community than Grebnevo. But the discussion group was no more by the time he was here, the community was scattered. There was nothing to see in this church, and we turned around and drove back towards the city.

Zoya junior was meeting some friends in the Sretenka monastery, a lovely building just a few hundred metres away from the Lubyanka. It was a Saturday evening and the regular prayers to welcome in the Lord's Day would be read with incense and chanting, so I happily accepted her suggestion that I should come too.

In the 1980s, just a few people would have attended services at churches anywhere, and probably fewer still so close to the KGB's headquarters. Now, however, the church was packed. President Vladimir Putin, his ministers and the country's top businessmen are all regular churchgoers, as are hundreds of thousands of ordinary Russians.

It was dark and cold that night, but the church was warm and fuggy. It was packed with worshippers, mostly women, who crossed themselves and bowed as the progress of the service demanded. Priests in hats appropriate to their clerical rank – black, with and without veils, and purple for the most senior – performed the mysteries. Back and forth the men went in the complex ballet of their faith. Two young men had the task of tending to the hundreds of candles, which were thin. They calmly and patiently straightened any candle that looked like falling over, while the heat from the flames shimmered, and the gold on the vast wall of icons flickered the light back into the room.

The gorgeous bass swell of the choir, which included several of Zoya junior's friends, tugged at my spirit and I stood and lost myself in the sound for more than an hour. Russian churchgoers do not sit down unless they absolutely have to, and that is only if they are very elderly or very sick. Services, therefore, become an exercise in endurance and eventually, despite the thrill of the ancient music, my legs were no longer prepared to tolerate it. I said goodbye to Zoya junior, and walked back into the cold.

During the 1980s, Father Dmitry worked patiently to reassemble a group of spiritual children. He never regained his position as a rebel and a media star, but he retained his passion for preaching, and a small group of young men and women eventually assembled around him once more.

Among them was Vladimir Petrovsky. He had none of the baggage of the heroic days before the televised confession, and knew a different spiritual father: quieter, more private, subdued, depressed, angry.

We met at the Botanical Garden metro station, which I know well, since it was the setting-off point for one of my favourite weekend walks when I lived in Moscow. In summer, the nearby park is a riot of wild growth, with hidden formal gardens in a vast expanse of woodland that reveals new secrets on every visit. In winter, however, it is like everywhere else: a spread of beaten dirty snow dotted with trash. The temperature was a little warmer that day, but it still bit when I stepped out of the glass and concrete metro station.

Petrovsky was slight. His grey hair was scraped over his scalp, and his eyes peered at me from behind thick spectacles. Perhaps it was just me that day, but he did not seem as open as the people I had interviewed about the 1970s, and appeared to be very suspicious of my intentions. His questions as to why I was writing about Father Dmitry at all were searching. As we walked through the edges of the park to his flat, which was up a dark flight of stairs in a concrete apartment block identical to thousands of others in Moscow, I felt myself under examination. It was not a pleasant experience, so, by the time we were in his little kitchen, where he made tea, and I sat at his oilcloth table, I was on edge.

He looked at me and waited for my questions. Perhaps the reason he looked so unenthusiastic was because he knew what kind of questions were coming. When I asked Father Dmitry's disciples about the 1970s, they could focus on arrests, and harassment, and comradeship and solidarity. The years after his humiliation had little of that, and Petrovsky probably knew I would ask about the extreme nationalism and prejudice that the KGB had kindled in Father Dmitry.

'I found out about him through my godfather,' said Petrovsky. 'I came to him in 1987. The first time I went into his flat was in July, on 1 July, after his wife was buried.'

The loss of his wife Nina after a long illness devastated Father Dmitry. She had patiently supported him through his years of triumph, then through his humiliation, and had been one of the few people who never judged him. He needed new spiritual children desperately, and Petrovsky's arrival was well timed. At first, their discussions were about literature, and Petrovsky began to go to his house regularly, or to his new church at Cherkizovo – a distant village he was assigned to after Vinogradovo.

'As a priest, he led a person's soul. He said that Dostoyevsky and Tolstoy revealed the soul more than anyone else. In this time many young people came to the faith. It is hard at first to speak of the soul so he tried to speak to them in their own language through literature,' Petrovsky told me, staring at me directly through his thick glasses. 'I became his assistant from 1987 and stayed with him to the end. I worked nowhere at first, I just helped him. I was on my own. I was given a bit of food but the first years were hard. That was before I became a priest.'

In the late 1980s, the Soviet Union was falling apart, but did not realize it yet. After Leonid Brezhnev had died, and two more geriatric general secretaries followed him to their graves in quick succession, the country finally had a leader who was prepared to try to stop the epidemic of alcoholism. Russians now claim that Mikhail Gorbachev's restrictions on alcohol, which involved grubbing up vineyards and restricting sales drastically – 90 per cent of alcohol shops in Moscow were closed, for example – were disastrous. The popular myth today is that people turned to shoe polish and anti-freeze in their desperation to get drunk, with catastrophic effects on the nation's health. But that is not true. This was, in fact, Russia's demographic zenith. In 1986–7, life expectancy bounced upwards to its highest ever level, while the birth rate zipped up too.

Had the country stuck to Gorbachev's alcohol policies, then perhaps the catastrophic post-Soviet demographic collapse might not have been so bad. If the government wanted the nation to have a future, it had to curtail alcohol consumption severely. It had no choice. Sadly, however, it could not afford to do so. Revenues collapsed without alcohol being sold in the state shops. Some money went to illegal distillers instead and thus stayed out of government coffers, some was just not spent at all and languished in savings accounts. Public support for the leadership slumped too, often because of complaints swapped in queues at the wine shops. Even supporters of the measures got bored of them. There were no consumer goods to buy with the money people saved, and what was the fun in that?

'I always hated drunkenness,' one woman from Minsk wrote to a newspaper. 'But suddenly it seems that nobody celebrates holidays any more. We used to make ourselves new dresses for the festivities. This year I didn't feel like making a single new dress. Why bother?'

That complaint was itself a sign of how, under Gorbachev's policy of openness, Russians began to be free to discuss subjects that had been taboo just a year or two before.

The huge campaign against the dissidents that culminated with Sakharov's exile and Father Dmitry's recantation was unwound. In late 1986, Sakharov had a phone installed so Gorbachev could call him and invite him back to Moscow. Yakunin and Ogorodnikov were released in 1987. Gorbachev, burnishing his image as a modernizer, told the United Nations in 1988 that there were no political prisoners left in his country, and he was close to telling the truth, although full rehabilitation did not come until the 1990s. Controversial themes were up for discussion in ways they had not been since the revolution.

Father Dmitry entered into that with enthusiasm. This was when he elaborated his theories about the Jews' responsibility for all his nation's ills.

'It is not that he went into politics, but politics came to him,' said Petrovsky. Among the people who attended his discussions at the end of the Soviet period was Vladimir Zhirinovsky, a firebrand nationalist christened by Father Dmitry, and whose misnamed Liberal Democrat Party – it is neither liberal nor democratic, rather the opposite – became the first registered opposition party in the Soviet Union.

Although this was before Zhirinovsky's more controversial remarks, such as that Russia and Germany should once again carve up Poland between them, and before his friendship with a former member of Hitler's SS, the politician was still a noxious combination of Soviet nostalgia and racism. Petrovsky attempted to explain away Father Dmitry's friendship with him – 'People asked whether he would go into a beauty contest, and he said that to save a soul he'd go anywhere' – but in truth, by the end of the Soviet Union, Dudko's views now had more in common with the extreme right than with anyone else.

By April 1992, a few months after the Soviet empire's collapse, he was appearing at demonstrations with chauvinist politicians, and was appointed spiritual adviser to a new newspaper called *Day*, which combined communism, Orthodoxy and anti-Semitism into a single package. In May 1992, *Day* reprinted *The Protocols of the Elders of Zion*, a hoax document detailing a plot (in fact invented by the tsar's secret police) by Jews to take over the world, in what was surely the *Protocols*' first publication in Russia since the Nazi-sponsored papers of wartime. A week or two later, it reprinted an interview with Hitler.

'The newspaper *Day* is showing, like no other, what is being done to the country,' Father Dmitry wrote in one of his columns. It seemed that, having lost his chance to rally people around a message of hope, he had launched a campaign of nihilism and hatred instead. Now he was even lamenting the collapse of the totalitarian state that he had once urged his followers to boycott.

> There was such a powerful strong country, the whole world respected it, and some people were even afraid, and now they just laugh at its helplessness.
>
> There was the KGB. People were scared just of the sound of it, and now no one is scared, and the KGB is seen as guilty before someone, before 'them'.
>
> There was the communist party, millions-strong, ruling, which just had to say one word to be listened to, and now not only does no one listen, but it's on trial.

I asked Petrovsky how it was that Father Dmitry could support the KGB when they had ruined not just his life, but the lives of so many of his friends. He had, after all, been imprisoned in the north for almost a decade just for writing a poem. Petrovsky shrugged, and his face set a little more. The conversation was clearly going along the path he had expected, but that did not mean he was enjoying it.

'He said that in the camp he did not die of hunger. There was always a ration, but that under this new system people were dying of hunger. The communists were better than these times, and he said that under the communists there was less temptation.'

That was nonsense, and he knew it. Millions of people died in the camps from hunger, or from deliberate neglect, or from diseases caused by their weakened conditions. Father Dmitry himself worked in a camp hospital where prisoners did just that. Petrovsky grimaced when I confronted him with the weakness of the argument. His own grandfather had died in the camps in 1937, he said, but Father Dmitry felt he had earned the right to criticize or support the communists as and how he wished.

The early 1990s got worse for Father Dmitry and for millions of other Russians. With Boris Yeltsin in the Kremlin, ill-thought-through and corrupt privatization deals were launched in an attempt to break the back of the communist system. Inflation, all but unknown in Soviet times, wiped out savings and the purchasing power of fixed incomes. Pensioners who had been assured that they would be looked after were forced to sell their belongings to buy food. Bewilderingly, unemployment appeared where previously everyone had been guaranteed a job. Often those still in employment had to wait months to get paid, while their factories' new owners used the money to fund lavish lifestyles detailed in the vibrant new press.

Where before the sardonic jokes that Russians swapped had been about their leaders, now they were about 'New Russians', the philistine, moneyed beneficiaries of the 1990s: 'How much did that tie cost?' '$500.' 'Ha, I got the same one for $700.'

An attempt by hardliners in 1993 to block this headlong progress ended with Yeltsin sending tanks to bombard parliament and imposing a new constitution in which he could rule largely unchallenged. Father Dmitry's newspaper, which had supported the attempted coup, was banned and relaunched as *Tomorrow*, but continued the same campaigns against the changes that were dramatically altering the country.

Newly rich bankers and businessmen like Boris Berezovsky, Mikhail Khodorkovsky and Vladimir Potanin flaunted their wealth, while millions of ordinary workers were paid late or not at all. By the mid-1990s, Russian men were dying on average seven years earlier than during the anti-alcohol campaign, and the birth rate dropped from an average of 1.6 children per woman to 0.8. If such a birth rate is maintained, every generation will be less than half the size of the one preceding it.

By 1996, Yeltsin's popularity rating was in single figures and he faced a strong challenge in presidential elections from Vladimir Zyuganov and his revitalized communist party. As it turned out, Yeltsin would win comfortably by brokering every deal he could, including effectively giving away Russia's most valuable assets to the big businessmen.

But while it still looked like there might be a fair fight, Father Dmitry offered his own advice to the Russian electorate. It was not now a surprise that he advised his readers to vote for the communist Zyuganov, but the reasoning he used shows how much he had changed.

He started off by defining Russia as Orthodox. He admitted that people of other faiths lived in Russia, such as Catholics and Muslims, but he denied they were Russian. 'For the Catholics,' he wrote, in reasoning that might raise eyebrows in Ireland or France, 'country makes no difference, they are citizens of the whole world. With Muslims it is a little harder, they love a particular country. But what country? That's up to them. If they live in Russia, which has been Orthodox since time immemorial, then they should dance off out of here.'

He then summarized recent history. He said that Russians love their homeland and could not conceivably have done anything to harm it, so therefore someone else must have been to blame. And who might that have been?

'Who stood in the government, in the propaganda, in the conducting of repression? Was it not people with Jewish names? There was only an insignificant percentage of Russians. There is of course nothing more to say. But the reply will come that it was people with Russian names who destroyed the churches. Yes, maybe they were destroyed with Russian hands, but not with a Russian head,' he wrote. His reasoning was exactly the same as that used by his KGB tormentors in 1980. It was the Jews, his interrogator had said, who were giving the orders that were causing his misery. And his Russian captors had no choice but to obey. It had been the Jews, they had said, who had wanted to send him to prison. And now Father Dmitry was parroting it back. The Russians had just been obeying orders.

So, to recap, he was advocating the expulsion of Russia's 20 million Muslims, almost all of whom live in their ancestral homelands, which were conquered by Russia between the sixteenth and nineteenth centuries. And he was saying that the Soviet repression of the Russians was the fault of the Jews.

Any readers wondering what this had to do with the presidential race did not have long to wait. He was analysing which of the two candidates would do the most to support Orthodoxy and oppose everything else. That, it turned out, would be Zyuganov, despite the fact that Yeltsin was the one who went to church, and the one who had given the Church its freedom, while Zyuganov was a communist, and thus a member of the party that had destroyed the Church. Why? Because Yeltsin had had dealings with the West for too long. Zyuganov would not pollute the country with foreigners.

'He is a patriot with an Orthodox style, who supports the thousand-year culture. And that is what our enemies are afraid of, that the Orthodox would make up with the communists, then it will be the only force, and then God-fearing Russia will be mighty and indivisible.'

Petrovsky was not the only new disciple attracted to Father Dmitry in the 1980s. I had heard of another one while visiting Father Dmitry's home village in the summer. He was called Father Vadim, and it was he who had reopened the church in Berezina in the mid-1990s.

Where was he now though? That I did not know. Unecha, the little railway town, does not have many hotels. The relatively convenient ones were full of railway workers coming in or passing through and so I ended up in the Amber Hotel, which was not so much a hotel as a forest base. Cut off, surrounded by trees and falling snow, it was silent and as primeval as a 1970s concrete mock-Finnish construction could conceivably be.

The hotel had several floors of rooms, a restaurant, a receptionist, a table-tennis table, and me. It was eerie. I felt like I had strayed on to the set of a horror film. Despite the cold and the snow, therefore, I cinched my coat tight around my face and walked into the forest.

The tracks of the car that had brought me here were already covered, and I followed not so much a road through the forest as an absence of trees. There was really only one direction to walk in, and so I walked in it. After a quarter of an hour of silent progress, the forest opened up to a vast empty field and, just visible through the curtains of snow, was a church.

There was something perfectly Russian about the view before me. If a Hollywood producer wanted an opening for a film, a backdrop for a fur-swaddled Anna Karenina and her troika to tell viewers that they were in Russia, that they could only be in Russia, then this sawtooth line of conifers, the bulging domes of this church, this vast empty white field and this drifting snow would have been it. This is the Real Russia, to Russians and foreigners alike. No one thinks of the giant glass-roofed malls on the edge of Moscow as being primordially Russian. They do not even think of the endless ranks of grey apartment blocks as being properly Russian. When they think of Russia, they think of flatness, and forest, and wild places, and snow and always, somewhere, on the edge of the shot, a church like this one.

The Hollywood producer might be tempted to linger on the scene for a while, but it was minus 20 and snowing hard, so I was not. I hurried towards the church. It was a Saturday evening, so a service would be due at some point and that meant a priest would be in attendance. A priest might know where I could find Father Vadim.

Two old women stood on the rough wooden boards of the church's floor. A few candles flickered before some of the icons. A pyramid screen shielded the holy core of the building, and a priest was bustling about. It was some time before I realized that a service was in progress and that I was a third of the congregation. The faithful of Unecha had clearly been deterred by the blizzard and I could not blame them. The church's radiators did not even take the edge off the cold.

After the service had stuttered to an end the priest, a suspicious-looking man with a vicious face and ginger beard, was brusque with me. He had no love, it seemed, for people with foreign accents and bright-red coats who asked questions. Father Vadim's parish was in Old Guta, he snapped, and was there anything else?

'No, nothing else, thank you.'

He turned away without a word. By that stage it was dark, and it was a long cold worrying walk through the trees before I saw the lights of my hotel in its little clearing. I was the only customer in the restaurant and thus spoiled the evening of two waitresses and a barman. They got their revenge, however, by failing to tell me that I needed to order breakfast the night before if I wanted something to eat in the morning.

Supper had not been substantial, so I was hungry even before my taxi came to pick me up the next day. It was the same driver who had driven me here in the first place and, when I told him I wanted the church in Old Guta, he said: 'Oh, you mean Father Vadim's place?' I was clearly losing my touch. Taxi drivers always know more than you expect.

He chattered away as we skirted Unecha and plunged into more forest, but I only listened enough to make polite noises. The trees here were thick and bleak, pines and birches. Some birches were dead and had fallen to make curved half-arches over the banked road. We were the only travellers that morning, and did not see another car until we arrived in Old Guta.

The village was spread out, with the church just one house among many. A cross above the door was the only sign that it was anything special. The pink-painted porch contained embroidered banners on poles like those carried by trade union marchers, except these bore the bearded faces of Jesus or Orthodox saints. I could hear the service, so I nervously pushed open the door into the interior, only to be met by the worried face of a man with rugged white hair and a jutting moustache.

'Leave it open a little, Zhanna Mikhailovna is feeling bad,' he said.

Here was a largish room, 6 metres by 3, with twenty-five or so worshippers packed in. I wormed my way to the back, and examined my surroundings. Prints of icons had been pasted on to 2mm fibreboard. A huge white peasant stove blasted out heat. The floor was plain knotty pine. It was hot: a fug of beeswax and incense and people and smoke. The screen protecting the holy place was more fibreboard and, as I looked, Father Vadim processed out, a battered face in his mid-forties above an immense tangled beard and a vast green and gold cloak.

Most of the congregation were older women, though half-a-dozen uncovered male heads stood out among the headscarves. The chants faded backwards through the room, starting loudly at the choir at the front, all the way to silent me. The hand gestures of the ritual passed out like ripples in a pond. The people looked and sounded like a unit, what a church should be, and surely what a church would have been like in these villages before the revolution.

It was a community, I realized – the kind of community that Father Dmitry had wanted to create. It was small and unpretentious, but it was itself and that was what mattered. When the worshippers lined up to take communion, a stocky man with swept-back hair gestured to me to join the queue in front of him. I declined, smiling.

'Go on, don't be scared,' he said with a smile of his own.

'No no,' I said, searching for a reason not to go. 'Um, I'm a Protestant.'

He shied away as if I had tried to kiss him, and spent the rest of the service on the other side of the room watching me in confusion. Candles were passed out from the front, and a kind-eyed woman pressed one on me.

'With the love of God,' she said, and I took it. I liked standing there with a candle, part of a little twinkling constellation of people joined together by friendship and trust in this church on a Sunday morning. It was simple and affecting, far more so than the grand processions and choreography of a cathedral, and I felt a little flicker of hope. Perhaps, far below the radar, such groups are operating all across Russia and will provide the trust and friendship Russians need to rebuild their society from the wreckage left by the KGB.

After the service, Father Vadim and I bundled into a minibus. He had no car, and a long way to get home, so a worshipper gave us a lift, through Unecha and down the long straight that heads east. The wind blew tendrils of snow across the tarmac ahead of us, and every passing car was trailed by a blizzard. Otherwise, it was a cold clear day.

Father Vadim's house was more untidy than anything I have ever seen. Boxes and paper and general stuff were strewn on every surface, but he clearly did not mind. He swept a space on a chair clear for me, then sat down too. His mother put the kettle on, then joined us.

She had, it transpired, worked in a library in Moscow and had asked Father Dmitry if he would give a lecture there. This was 1990, still Soviet times, and asking a priest to address a crowd was a brave thing to do.

'I had believed for about a year,' said Father Vadim, 'and that was when I met him. He was small and not as dramatic as I thought he would be. The first thing he made everyone do was pledge sobriety because our country is falling apart. He said that we had lost our sense of self and were drinking too much.'

Father Vadim's grey cat had got over its suspicion of me, and now sat on the table taking darts at my pen.

'This was his way to save the country. He was very worried for Russia, and he said spirits were the big danger. It was fine for me, I had not drunk for a few years anyway, and after this meeting I said I wanted to be christened, so he took me to his flat and christened me.'

Vadim went with him to church, and enjoyed it. He enjoyed the sense of community. At that time, Moscow was suffering from the severe economic policies at the end of communism. He said he did not really understand Father Dmitry's desire to launch into politics. He just wanted a monk's life, somewhere in a village, where things would be simpler.

There are a lot of souls that need saving. A book by three Russian sociologists describes how, in 1974, one in eight children born in villages were officially registered as disabled because of exposure to alcohol *in utero*. That sounds terrible enough, but the situation has now got so much worse that all the categories used by such previous studies have become useless.

'The situation is apparently past the point when diagnoses like "drinking", "binge drinking" and perhaps even "alcoholism" reflect the true meaning of the problem. What is going on today is more aptly described as "pervasive human degradation", "profound degeneration of a genetic pool", and so on. While such qualifications may *sound* harsh, they are not off the mark at all,' they wrote.

Father Vadim wanted to help and, when the chance came to serve in Father Dmitry's home village, he grabbed it.

'Our villages are dying. There is no help from the government. It is closing the schools, the medical centres. There are no farms, just a few people work and that's all. This drunkenness keeps growing, and people have lost their sense of life. People either leave to find work, or they get drunk,' he said. 'It used to be men who drank but now women have started to as well. This degradation is serious. You do not notice it so much in towns, but in villages there is nothing. In the 1980s there were children, schools, but now it's all gone. A house here would cost you 5,000 roubles. That's with a garden. In fact, offer someone your mobile phone and they would happily exchange it for a house. Only old people are left, and they're dying.'

I asked him what he thought of the government, which has, after two decades of doing nothing, finally launched policies to save the Russian population. Vladimir Putin, in his spell as prime minister, promised to stabilize the population at 143 million, but by the time he said it that number already looked unrealistic.

Putin has boasted of improvements to the birth rate – a 20 per cent increase in the number of children being born – and credited his government's policies for it. But most of that increase was really just an echo of the anti-alcohol campaign of the 1980s. The birth rate increased under Gorbachev, and that baby boom meant a bulge in the number of parents two decades later and thus more children. But the effect will be temporary. Soon the parenting generation will be those born after 1991, when the number of Russians born halved. To stabilize the population, those women would have to start having heroic numbers of children, and there is no sign of that happening.

The government needs to restrict alcohol sales but, mindful of what happened to Gorbachev when he tried to do so with vastly greater state resources behind him, it is cautious in doing so.

'We hope in God and for a miracle because nothing good now comes from our own brains. The government really does nothing, no one in the country believes in the government. I look at the future with pessimism.'

12

They don't care any more

So, did Father Dmitry have a choice? Could he have refused to surrender to the KGB? The question is an important one because, as I
have thought almost ever since I first heard of him, his personal experience closely mirrors that of his whole nation. When he betrayed his
own conscience, he did irreparable damage to his soul. Before, he was
a happy and confident man. Afterwards he was a miserable racist. The
transformation was total and was a result of that moment when he
decided to stop struggling, to seek compromise with people who
wanted nothing but his destruction.

Everything that followed – the sadness and the hatred – was a result
of that moment. It is important to understand that his misery was a
result of his own choice, because it takes us back to the misery of his
whole nation. If he could have acted differently, if he had a choice, it
means every Russian had a choice. That means that the depression of
individuals is not inevitable. If every Russian had a choice, there is
hope that some people took another path, and will continue to do so.

The simple answer to the question of whether he had a choice is:
yes, he did. And the proof for that is his old friend Gleb Yakunin, who
was arrested a few months before Father Dmitry on similar charges,
but who did not recant in 1980 and who won himself a five-year
prison term and five years in exile as a result. The life stories of the
two men could almost be a science-fiction story, in which someone
faces an important binary choice and we get to see all the consequences that follow from both available decisions. Father Dmitry
went one way; Father Gleb went the other.

Father Gleb and I arranged to meet in the office of For Human
Rights, a pressure group, in central Moscow. I was early and sat in the

lobby, surveying the chaos of a place where new-generation Russians scurried around while grizzled veterans of the Soviet-era struggle tapped away one-fingered at their keyboards.

Brown boxes were piled along the corridor, those on the bottom sagging under the weight of those above and slowly oozing their papers on to the floor. Wires ran along the walls and floor, linking extension cord to extension cord. Heaps of newspapers were covered in drifts of dust. One headline – 'How much of an armed force does Russia need?' – was all but illegible through the dirt. An alcove was full of a precarious heap of ring binders. If you had wanted to access the one labelled 'Outgoing 2008', you would have had to remove about a dozen others first or else risk them all collapsing on the floor. Some tinsel decorated a doorway. New Year's Eve had been just a few weeks previously, but the tinsel looked like it had been there far longer than that.

Yakunin arrived fifteen minutes late, bustling in off the street and greeting everyone boisterously. He led me downstairs, where the basement office was if anything more chaotic than the one above. We found space on a Formica-topped desk piled with broken electronic equipment, and he unloaded bread, pork, garlic, tea bags, sugar and more from a paper bag.

'There,' he said, when the kettle had boiled and my notebook was on my knee, 'let's talk.'

When he said 'let's talk', he meant that he would talk. He had a story to tell and did not intend to be interrupted. He and Father Dmitry met in the 1960s when, in the temporary liberal interlude that followed Stalin's death, they opposed changes to the governance of the Orthodox Church that made priests into employees of their parishioners – that is, of the local government – and thus increased state control over them.

In the end, only Yakunin and one other agreed to put their names to the letter of protest, and Yakunin lost his parish as a result.

Despite Father Dmitry's last-minute decision to keep his signature off the letter, the two men remained close. They were priests, they were neighbours, their wives got on; they had a lot in common. When Yakunin founded the Christian Committee for the Defence of Believers' Rights in 1976, Father Dmitry republished its statements in his self-typed newspaper.

'He was a pure Church person and said what he wanted. I was banned and only Dudko could speak so openly. Naturally, that meant Western journalists went to him, and when the KGB decided to crush the human rights movement, they added him too,' Yakunin said.

The KGB linked them together, and the KGB's favourite newspaper, the *Literary Gazette*, lambasted them both, along with Ogorodnikov, in 1977. Yakunin's arrest in November 1979 preceded Dudko's by a couple of months, and they were held in the same detention centre. It was there that Yakunin got the first hint that Father Dmitry might not endure. While his own interrogator attempted to break him down, Yakunin could hear voices coming through the wall.

Yakunin's interrogator noticed and said: 'So? Do you hear how your friend Dudko is talking to his investigator?'

At the time, Yakunin thought Father Dmitry was holding out, since the voices were loud and angry, but he was wrong. He was deeply disappointed by Dudko's recantation and television appearance, and by the subsequent changes to his character.

'There were always people who gave up, because they were scared. But with Dmitry Dudko, it was like a rebirth. He could have asked for forgiveness for his cowardice, but he didn't. Instead, he created a construction to explain it. It was like a psychological rebuilding of himself. He went on and on about how much he loved the KGB. It was almost as if he fell into a psychological hole.'

Yakunin was tried and convicted. He was under no illusions about the official Church's attitude to him. At his trial, two priests who represented the Orthodox Patriarchate abroad testified that his 'anti-patriotic activity' had turned the Christians of the world against the Soviet Union. Another witness said Yakunin could drink two bottles of vodka (Yakunin asked in return: 'Over what period?'), while another said Yakunin was an agent of imperialism, an opponent of peace, and deserved to be on trial. On hearing his sentence, Yakunin said: 'I thank God for the destiny I have been given.'

He was therefore in prison when Father Dmitry suffered the guilt and loneliness that allowed the KGB to remodel his character, and he was away in exile for the whole long process that changed his old friend from a believer in humanity to an anti-Semite. This is not to say that all was well in prison. Yakunin and others suffered torments.

Ogorodnikov later wrote that he had attempted suicide three times, in full knowledge of the fact that it was a mortal sin.

And their tormentors knew how to keep them twisting. In 1986, Ogorodnikov was tried again and forced to confront the world's indifference. 'An empty courtroom during my trial, where besides the KGB there were only the two of you,' he wrote to his mother, 'is symptomatic evidence of the loss of interest in my cause and the weakening of Christian activity.'

It is a testament to the strength of both Yakunin's and Ogorodnikov's characters that they survived. At last they heard that things were changing. A colonel in the KGB flew all the way to Yakutia to see Yakunin in exile, and they got drunk together. Yakutia was about as remote as you could get in the Soviet Union, so Yakunin realized something was up.

'He said they knew I was honest, and they did not need me to sign any papers. I could go back to Moscow and be a priest if only I stopped my political and human rights activities. I told them I had already been so long in prison I didn't mind staying a little longer,' he said, smiling. 'Then a couple of months passed and all political prisoners were amnestied.'

He was given a parish, but it was a different world that he had come back to. The dissidents had always hoped that, given the chance, everyone in Russia would be just like them: idealistic, democratic, honest. It did not turn out that way. The new freedoms did not spark a reckoning of the betrayals of the past as the dissidents had hoped, or an examination of the Russians' own sins, but rather an orgy of blaming minorities and foreigners. The change wrought in Father Dmitry had been visited on millions of other Russians, who shared his distrust of outsiders and his self-loathing.

Among the little group of believers who had discussed the reforms to the Church with Father Dmitry and Yakunin in the early 1960s was a priest called Alexander Men. Unlike them, however, he had stayed out of trouble. He had not felt the need to advertise himself, so the Soviet government had not bothered him, instead leaving him to inspire those around him with his gentle faith and unflinching honesty.

He was born a Jew, but had never felt any kind of discrimination from ethnic Russians in the 1970s, the time when Father Dmitry was preaching inclusiveness and urging everyone to stand together to oppose the collapse of Russian society. By September 1990, however, that had all gone.

'In 1975, fifteen years ago, I gave an interview which was published in Paris. They asked me whether there was any anti-Semitism in the Church. I said that I hadn't come across any, not on a mass scale. Fifteen years later and the picture has completely changed. I wouldn't say the same thing now. Anti-Semitism has become, unfortunately, one of the distinguishing features of the Church,' he told an interlocutor, who then asked if he himself had been a target.

'Of course, that goes without saying. I feel it. I have been a priest for a long time, thirty or so years, but this has only started to happen now. I feel it in the way people behave towards me, in the way they talk to me, in everything … There has to be a category of people who are held responsible for the sins of society. They are the personification of society's own sins.'

Men pointed out that, even if the anti-Semites were right and that it was Jews who had ordered that churches be dynamited and believers killed, nothing would have happened had Russians refused to obey. Obeying orders, he was saying, is not a defence.

'That means people are to blame. But it's a very difficult thing to admit and so you have to find someone else to blame. It's easy to swear at the Jews. A coward will always pick on someone defenceless.'

That was an austere message to give to the Russians, a nation that had been obeying unpalatable orders for seven decades.

'Make a comparative analysis of denazification in Germany and destalinization here and you'll understand.'

That interview seems as relevant now as it did when he gave it, perhaps even more so considering the Kremlin's current campaign against historians who publish works 'to the detriment of Russia's interests'. But he never got to see how prophetic he was. He was struck down from behind with an axe four days later while walking from his home to the train station. He was aged just fifty-five. His murder has never been solved, but it is easy to see a link between the racism he had suffered and his tragic end.

Yakunin rambled a lot during our conversation. It was hard to keep him on the topic of the 1980s. He preferred to skip through current events – Egypt, a new law in Russia, the unexpected cold, an album of chants he wanted to record – but he would come back to the 1980s in the end.

'In our camp there were fifty political prisoners and 250 guards. And we only had three real dissidents. Of the others, some had tried to cross the border, or to blow something up. They were not actual dissidents. Us dissidents were necessary to the KGB though, you see, and when they imprisoned us all they had no one left to fight.

'The thing that interests me is why they were so scared of us. When our information got to the West, they were scared. But look now, look at the things people write, and they don't care. They spit on it. That is the single big difference between now and then. They don't care any more.'

In 1990, after his release from the camps, Yakunin was elected to the Russian parliament. He was part of the liberal wing pushing for reforms and, when hardliners launched a coup to try to preserve the Soviet Union in 1991, it was natural that he should be part of the commission set up to investigate it. That gave him access to the KGB archives. It is hard to believe now, but in that brief window of reform, an uncompromising dissident priest was allowed free access to the deepest secrets of the state.

'They asked me which bit I wanted to see. I said Fifth Directorate, fourth section, which was the section devoted to the Orthodox Church. I wrote out all the most important facts for three months. I should have kept my mouth shut and worked more, but I could not.'

In January 1992, Yakunin publicly revealed the extent to which top Church figures had helped the KGB. He published their codenames, giving them a chance to own up to their identities: ABBAT (that was Metropolitan Pitirim); ANTONOV (that was Metropolitan Filaret); and ADAMANT (that was Metropolitan Yuvenali, Father Dmitry's bishop and the one who had moved him from parish to parish at the KGB's request). They refused to identify themselves, and their outraged boss, the patriarch, went to top officials demanding that Yakunin's access be ended.

Yakunin protested and wrote to the patriarch. 'If the Church is not cleansed of the taint of the spy and informer, it cannot be reborn,' he told him. He listed the codenames again, and singled out one unknown hierarch for particular attention.

'The most prominent agents of the past include DROZDOV – the only one of the churchmen to be officially honoured with an award by the KGB,' he wrote. The patriarch was right to panic about the damage Yakunin could do, since DROZDOV was in fact himself. The KGB's penetration had gone to the very top, and it is hardly surprising that the Church did not want to rid itself of the spies. If it did, there would be hardly anyone left. It was not just the odd rogue priest who had informed on his flock, but almost everyone. The rogues were the ones who had refused to help the KGB.

In this way, the Church was a true reflection of the whole of Russian society. The KGB and the Russian people had penetrated each other to such an extent that they could not be separated. The culture of betrayal and suspicion and distrust that the KGB relied on had become part of the national culture, poisoning politics in the 1990s and beyond: decades of corruption, murder and sordid sex scandals. If it cannot purge itself, however, the Russian nation will never rid itself of the illness that has driven people to alcohol. Russians need to trust each other again.

Amid the furore of the emerging truth of how far the KGB had penetrated the Church, Patriarch Alexy attempted to explain why he had decided to work for the security services. Like informers everywhere, he clearly knew deep down that he had acted wrongly, but he could not bring himself to do the honourable thing and resign. Instead, he told an audience in America that he had no choice but to co-operate, since otherwise the churchgoers would have had no priests, which would have been a disaster.

'I still now think with terror of what might have happened to my flock if by my "decisive" actions I had left it without the Eucharist, without being able to attend church, if I had left their children without Baptism and the dying without their final parting words. I would have committed a great, indelible sin, and out of concern for my own moral reputation I would have left the running of the diocese and betrayed my flock,' he said. In short, he had had to betray the Church in order to save it.

Yakunin continued his campaign. Eventually, therefore, in October 1993, he was defrocked. Even the Soviet Union had not disqualified him as a priest. It had taken his parish, but not his title. It took the spite of an Orthodox hierarchy on the defensive to throw him out. He maintained his campaign for a full inquiry into the Church, however, and in February 1997 the Church took the last remaining step open to it. He was officially excommunicated, a step usually reserved for someone who has committed acts of serious and unrepentant heresy. 'Let him be anathema before the whole people,' the Church said in a statement issued after a full synod.

It is a sign of how far the Church's values and those of the liberals had diverged that, while Yakunin was being thrown out, a priest called Ioann could remain metropolitan of St Petersburg despite anti-Semitism so virulent that he considered *The Protocols of the Elders of Zion* to be 'already in action'. A racist was a bishop. A KGB agent was patriarch. In a way, it is hardly surprising that Yakunin should be thrown out for being an honest man.

Western liberals who had praised Father Dmitry in the past were so disgusted by the change in him and the Church that they dropped any further interest. In a study of the modern Russian Orthodox Church published in Britain in 1986, Dudko had the second highest number of entries in the index: more than Stalin, or Solzhenitsyn, more even than Ukraine. In another study by the same author published ten years later, he was not mentioned once.

I asked Yakunin whether he regretted never having made up with Father Dmitry.

'You know, my mother and father are buried at the Friday Cemetery,' he began, and I worried he had headed off on another tangent. Then I remembered that Father Dmitry is buried in the Friday Cemetery, so I listened closely. 'I regularly go there to pray. One time, when I had finished, I needed a pee, so I went over to the wall, and I was peeing, and I looked up, and there was Dmitry Dudko, and I was pissing on him.'

He laughed.

'No, I never saw him again. It would have been like talking to a deaf mute. There would have been no point.'

As I walked away, I mused on what Yakunin had said, and I realized something I had not noticed before. I had spoken to almost all the people who had been closest to Father Dmitry, the core members of his old community, over the previous year or so. And almost none of them now had any contact with each other at all.

Yakunin never saw Father Dmitry after their arrest. Ogorodnikov never saw Yakunin, and asked me for his phone number. It was me who broke the news to Ogorodnikov that his old friend Sergei Fedotov had died the year before.

'What? Sergei? Tell me you're mistaken, tell me you're mistaken,' he said again and again, breaking off our talk to come back to it.

Father Vladimir never saw Father Alexander, and neither of them saw Yakunin. Father Dmitry's son Mikhail, when he heard I had seen Yakunin, who is his godfather, said: 'Well, I don't expect you'll hear much from him.' And so it went on. The KGB's destruction of the community had been so successful that now they just swapped gossip about how far the others had fallen.

'You know, apparently, he's involved in group sex,' one former disciple said about another I had spoken to. And that pretty much summed it up. Gossip and distrust had replaced solidarity and friendship. And if the KGB could do that to these staunch fighters and firm friends, just imagine what they did to the whole country. And that is how the Russian nation was divided and ruled.

SPRING?

13

Making a new generation

It was more than a year before I saw Yakunin again. As I walked down Moscow's Maly Kislovsky Lane to meet him, I could remember exactly how he had looked when we parted: dark-green hat pulled down over his forehead; black jacket tightly buttoned over a scarf; hands deep in his pockets against the cold; eyebrows together in what was almost a scowl.

Then it had been winter. Now, it was a balmy Moscow summer morning and he looked like a different man. His open-toed sandals and light shirt were part of the effect, of course, but more striking was his broad smile and clear forehead. He laughed as I walked up. I tried to apologize for being late, but he ignored me. He tucked his arm through mine by way of a greeting and marched me down the street.

We were going to buy teabags and biscuits but it took me a few minutes to realize that, since he began to speak immediately and did not slacken until we had reached the front of the queue in the shop and it was time to pay. I have rarely known glee so irresistible. He checked regularly that I was paying attention to him, but need not have worried. I was impatient for every new word.

'Did you see what happened here this winter? Did you see?'

I replied that I had, of course.

'The spirit of freedom has been released,' he said, with a smile of pure mischief. 'It is a new world.'

When we had last spoken, Moscow had been deep in a cynical, exhausted funk. Politics under Vladimir Putin was devious and venal but everyone I knew insisted that that did not matter. They hardly cared about government, they said. They wanted to talk about films and books: anything, in short, that did not involve the men in the Kremlin.

Politics boiled down to one question: when would Putin return to the presidency? He had stood down in 2008, having served the constitutional maximum of two consecutive terms, and become prime minister. His old friend Dmitry Medvedev, who had the advantages of being less charismatic and shorter than Putin, had taken over the top job. Would Putin stand for election again in 2012? Or would Medvedev serve another term before Putin took his old job back?

The meagre nature of the choice perhaps explains why it did not inspire great popular enthusiasm. In September 2011, Putin answered it: he was coming back. Medvedev, president of the largest country on earth, was forced to humiliate himself and stand down after a single term, despite having won with more than 70 per cent of the vote just three and a half years previously.

Putin, who made the announcement at the congress of his United Russia party, which dominated parliament despite lacking a clear ideology, presumably assumed that that was that. The question was answered: the one man whose vote counted had voted, and he would be back in his old job come March.

The first public sign that everything might not go to plan came on 20 November, when Putin attended a martial-arts bout. This was his territory, the kind of macho arena that he revelled in. He was famously a black belt in judo, and regularly had himself photographed bare-chested in the wilds, fishing or hunting. Martial-arts fans should have been his natural constituency. But when he stepped into the ring to congratulate the winner, they booed him. State television cropped the footage, but a raw video went viral on the internet.

This was just a fortnight before his United Russia party was to compete in parliamentary elections, and it was ominous. An opposition campaign was encouraging Russians to vote for anyone but United Russia, and had found a surprising level of support. Cynical, tired Muscovites suddenly gained inspiration. They flooded to the polls.

Panicking officials resorted to the crudest of fakery: stuffing ballot boxes with votes for United Russia; changing the official vote count between the polling station and the central collating authority. Even so, United Russia won less than half the vote and, thanks to cameras on mobile phones and ordinary people acting as observers, the frauds were detected so voters knew that its true tally had been far lower. There was no single headline-grabbing moment, just a steady drip of little incidents that cumulatively were far more damaging. Voters felt demeaned, and popular anger among ordinary middle-class Muscovites bloomed.

On the night of the poll, 6,000 people protested. That may not sound like much, but that made it already one of the biggest opposition protests since the 1990s. Yakunin was out of the country at the time but he made sure he was back for the big march on 10 December on Bolotnaya Square. Fifty thousand people or more turned out in the depths of the Moscow winter to demand fair elections.

'Before when people organized protests there were 200 people or 500 people, maximum 1,000. And then this just exploded. You cannot explain it rationally. It is the spirit of freedom, and I think it will be victorious. It has come to our country at last. I was in the protests, not at the front or anything but at the back. It was an amazing feeling, amazing.'

The leaders of the marches were mostly young creative Muscovites, skilled at using the internet to distribute information about fraud and about their plans. It was ominous for Putin. These were the very people who had benefited from the stability he had brought. Under his rule, living standards for all Russians had improved. He had raised pensions and state salaries and had made sure they were paid. He surely thought the trajectory he had set would win him loyalty for ever. But if Putin expected this new golden youth to be grateful to him, he had miscalculated. During the 2000s, they had linked up with contemporaries abroad, taken holidays in Europe and America. They felt themselves to be modern Europeans, yet they were being treated like trash.

A friend of mine, Alexei, told me, after he had attended the protest on Bolotnaya Square: 'I always thought I was the only one who thought the way I think, but there were thousands of us.' It was the same wonder expressed by Father Dmitry's disciples in the 1970s when they attended his church discussions. They had been all alone, and then suddenly realized they had the same desires as everyone else. The trust and hope the KGB had tried so hard to extinguish in the 1980s had bloomed once more.

Putin's response to the protesters was the same as that of his Soviet predecessors. He tried to disperse them, to turn them on each other: liberals against nationalists; believers against atheists. When it was his own turn to face election, in March 2012, he won comfortably with more than 62 per cent. But that was a total boosted by distant regions, ruled by local strongmen, who could provide him with tallies in excess of 80 per cent. In Chechnya, which is firmly controlled by Putin's handpicked ruler Ramzan Kadyrov, the president gained more than 99 per cent on a 99 per cent turnout. Other regions might not have been so extreme in their expression of loyalty, but they were not far off.

The regions were a sideshow, however. Moscow was what mattered, since it was the largest city, home to the most educated people, headquarters of Russia's largest companies and seat of the government. It is the only city to have grown consistently under Putin's rule. It is resented in the regions as a hungry parasite that sucks everything up and gives little back. If Putin was expecting gratitude, however, he was disappointed. Muscovites flooded into the polling stations both to vote and to act as observers. Petty fraud was no longer possible and Putin won less than half the vote, despite complete dominance of broadcast media in the run-up to the election.

'People were so disturbed by the violations in December that ten times as many of them came out as observers. This civilian control over the elections changed the situation radically,' said Dmitry Oreshkin, a Russian political analyst who has advised the Central Election Commission.

In St Petersburg, Putin's home city, there were fewer observers and officials had more room for manoeuvre. Oreshkin explained to me how they used a loophole intended for ships and remote science facilities: they set up sixty-nine new polling stations within just five days of the vote, meaning observers struggled to monitor them.

The turnout in these new stations was remarkably high at more than 90 per cent, of whom an equally remarkable 95 per cent voted for Putin. That added 100,000 votes to Putin's tally and independent observers calculated that, without these and other distortions, Putin could well have won less than half in St Petersburg too.

'It is a very important conclusion that the capital cities are prepared to reject the official resources and that makes the legitimacy of Putin's election very doubtful,' said Oreshkin. 'The cities are getting out of the control of his administrative resources. This is an irreversible movement.'

Putin might have won, but his subsequent actions smacked of panic: the maddened dash of a cow who treads on a wasps' nest. In weeks, his parliament passed laws restricting the right to protest and access to the internet. He recriminalized libel, meaning Russians could be jailed in future for criticizing him. Most demeaning, a new law would oblige non-governmental organizations that raise money abroad – and most do, as there are few independent cash sources in Russia – to register as 'foreign agents'. Putin had made much of the fact that the protesters were serving foreign interests, contrasting them with the patriots supporting his own cause.

And police harassed the protest leaders too. Ksenia Sobchak, a socialite and television personality who morphed into an opposition activist despite her father having been Putin's boss in the 1990s, had her flat raided in June 2012, her safe opened and all her money 'confiscated'. Anti-corruption blogger Alexei Navalny was charged with defrauding a state timber company, with a potential sentence of a decade in jail.

The faces of this wave of repression were, however, Nadezhda Tolokonnikova, Maria Alekhina and Yekaterina Samutsevich, three young women accused of being part of a formless punk collective called Pussy Riot. Their music, in truth, is not likely to win them many fans, but that did not matter. It was the bold nature of their protests that made them stand out. They had already swarmed on to Red Square with their guitars and trademark brightly coloured balaclavas. Then, on 21 February, after Patriarch Kirill of the Orthodox Church had directly intervened in politics by praising Putin as a 'miracle', they decided to go further. They ran into the Cathedral of Christ the Saviour in central Moscow (which was rebuilt after 1991, having been demolished by Stalin). There, they donned their balaclavas and jumped around in front of the icon screen. Set to music, the video featured the lyric 'Mother of God, drive out Putin'. On the internet, it was a sensation.

Officials decided that this was a case they could make an example of. The women had insulted the Orthodox Church and could thus be presented as non-patriotic. Arrested, they were charged with 'hooliganism motivated by religious hatred' and held in detention awaiting trial for five months. The charges carried a potential sentence of seven years. Putin, stung by the outcry abroad, appealed to the court to be merciful, and their final sentence was two years (though Samutsevich was later released on appeal). Two of them are young mothers, but were barred from seeing their children.

'Gera thinks it's like a Russian fairy-tale: her mother is a princess who has been captured by an evil villain and put in a cage ... Which, of course, is basically true,' Pyotr Verzilov, Tolokonnikova's husband, told a British journalist during the trial. Gera is their four-year-old daughter.

The trial was the blackest of farces. The judge blocked any petition from the defence, while allowing prosecutors any liberties they asked for. Lawyers for the girls said the case was worse even than those in Soviet times, while, for many observers, it was quite simply the 1960s all over again. The raft of restrictive laws was equivalent to 1967's Article 190, which banned 'knowingly false fabrications that defame the Soviet state and social system'.

The young women themselves made the parallel complete with dignified closing speeches that could have been lifted from the darkest pages of the 1970s.

'Katya, Masha and I are in jail but I don't consider that we've been defeated, just as the dissidents weren't defeated. When they disappeared into psychiatric hospitals and prisons, they passed judgement on the country,' said Tolokonnikova.

That made the women from Pussy Riot the new Sinyavsky and Daniel, the writers jailed in 1966 for publishing their works abroad. That trial too had been intended to demonstrate strength and firmness. It succeeded only in creating the dissident movement. This new protest movement was armed, not with carbon-copied statements passed from hand to hand, but with the whole internet. Its followers numbered not hundreds but hundreds of thousands.

'The Pussy Riot trial damages Russia's reputation no less than the trial of Andrei Sinyavsky and Yuli Daniel damaged the Soviet Union's reputation almost 50 years ago. The Sinyavsky–Daniel trial created a rift between the political leadership and the cultural and intellectual segments of society, one that lasted until the collapse of the Soviet Union,' wrote Konstantin Sonin, a professor and vice president of the

New Economic School, in his column in a Moscow daily. 'The Pussy Riot case has been a major blow to Russian society by effectively excluding this country from the list of civilized nations. Whatever shocking words the female punk rockers might have yelled in Moscow's main cathedral, how can that justify putting them in handcuffs, escorting them with police Rottweillers and jailing them before the trial as if they were dangerous criminals?'

I was not sure how Yakunin would react to Pussy Riot, given that they had behaved disrespectfully in an Orthodox church. Inevitably, however, he had an explanation all of his own, and looked deep into the Russian past to find it. In medieval times, the Russian people had few means to resist its government, he said. Perhaps the only one, in fact, was the Holy Fools – in Russian, *Yurodivie* – who claimed divine inspiration and spoke the truth fearlessly to their all-powerful rulers.

'These fools used to go around naked and they would piss in church, and demonstrate that priests were acting wrongly. They did it to the tsars too,' said Yakunin.

The most famous of all the Holy Fools was St Basil, who is said to have once upbraided Tsar Ivan the Terrible for not paying attention in church. He also offered the tsar meat during Lent, saying it did not matter whether he kept the religious fast or not, since he had committed so many murders. This public expression of the nation's private anger at its king won him the love of Muscovites. The great multi-coloured tulip-domed cathedral on Red Square, the most famous church in Russia, still bears his name. When he died, the tsar himself helped carry his coffin.

'This is what these girls were doing. They were telling the truth in the name of the people. They did not disrespect the church. They crossed themselves correctly, they did everything right. If they had sung "Praise Putin, give him a long reign" they would have been rewarded. But they did not do so. They told the truth.'

We had finally returned from the shop, and were sitting and drinking our tea and eating our biscuits. Yakunin holds his own religious services in the basement we were sitting in, as he tries to keep alive the spirit of challenge that the dissident priests of the 1970s represented. With Father Dmitry dead and compromised, and Father Alexander Men murdered, only Yakunin is left.

His movement is ever more distant from the official Orthodox Church. Under Putin, the Church has moved close to top officials. Patriarch Kirill lives in great splendour and regularly meets the president. That has inevitably made him a target for criticism, not least when a photo of him was digitally altered to remove his Breguet watch, worth many thousands of pounds. The watch was still visible in a reflection in the polished table.

Putin and the patriarch are undaunted, however. They have used the Church to harness the religious feelings of Russia's citizens behind the government. This was most obvious in October 2011 when one of Putin's oldest friends arranged for a piece of the Virgin Mary's belt to tour Russia. It was of course no coincidence that the relic should have arrived during the election campaign.

The man who arranged for the belt to visit Russia was Vladimir Yakunin (no relation of Father Gleb's), head of the huge Russian Railways company. He is also head of a shadowy religious organization called the St Andrew the First-Called Foundation, whose supervisory council includes leading figures from state television, the interior ministry, the railways company and the presidential administration.

The Virgin Mary's belt normally lives on Mount Athos, a rocky Greek peninsula studded with monasteries, with which the Russian Church has had close relations for centuries. The belt is said to aid fertility in women who gaze upon it, although it is hard to know how it gained this reputation as no women are allowed on Mount Athos. Even female animals are banned (except for chickens and, some say, cats).

Putin travelled to Vnukovo airport on 20 October 2011, to welcome the belt and its escorting monks, and met them again at the end of their fifteen-city tour. Archimandrite Ephraim, one of the belt's escorts, praised the faith of the 3 million people who had come to see the relic, and took the opportunity to ask for Putin to help Greece, which was still in the depths of economic crisis.

Putin sidestepped the request, and focused instead on the belt's miraculous properties for barren women. Ephraim confirmed that miracles had taken place: 'We are permanently receiving telephone calls, in which people say that a miracle has happened: "I have been married for ten years, and now I have a child." Twenty examples of such miracles have been recorded already. And there is already an agreement that, after the Virgin's Belt's trip around Russia, a book will be published about the miracles that have taken place.'

Such births would indeed be miraculous. The belt had arrived in the country just thirty-eight days previously and children had already been born. It is a testament to the new parents' faith that they were pleased, rather than traumatized, by the experience. Putin sounded suitably impressed.

'If this helps to solve our demographic issue, it would come in handy. In any case, I hope it will,' he said.

Gleb Yakunin, however, said the government had completely miscalculated the belt's powers. He pointed out that the belt had been making its progress around the country when Putin was booed at the martial-arts bout. According to him, Putin's humiliation before his supporters was the true miracle wrought by the Virgin Mary.

'Everything began when they brought the belt here. That was when the spirit of freedom was unleashed,' he said.

The ability to cure infertility is only one of the belt's minor qualities, he said. Far more important is its ability to protect a nation from its enemies. Yakunin said that, in bringing in the belt, Putin had undermined himself. He had not realized that he is in fact his own nation's enemy.

'It was an act of blasphemy because Putin is not a true believer, and now the belt is miraculously causing the nation to rise up,' he said. 'Whatever Putin does now it is too late. Business is opposed to him, the young people too. Trying to suffocate the movement and turn us into North Korea is just stupid.'

His delight in what had happened was overpowering. He laughed and nodded constantly, convinced that Putin had succeeded in defeating himself. He even seemed amused by the thought that he could be arrested once more, and sent back to the camps.

When Yakunin was sent to prison in 1981, he rode in a prison train, guarded and shackled. When I took the same line in 2012, I had one of the luxurious berths favoured by richer Russians and foreigners. I had been forced to change my ticket at the last minute, and all the cheapest berths were gone, meaning I was sharing a compartment with a well-tanned family from one of the oil towns of Siberia. They were returning home from holiday in Italy, where the weather had apparently been fantastic.

The father of the family discussed sport with great persistence, but I managed to fall asleep anyway and in the morning they were gone, their places taken by two brunettes and a blonde from Nizhny Novgorod. They were off to a training seminar organized by their bank, but their conversation centred on a serial killer on the prowl in their hometown. He prefers blondes, said the blonde.

This was the famous Trans-Siberian Mainline, and our train was heading for Beijing. My fellow passengers included two French women, a Brazilian man in tight shorts and at least a dozen Americans. Everyone disembarked at every stop and swarmed round the women selling pies, beer and soft drinks. The Americans were staying on the train all the way to China, a journey that would take them a week. I, however, reached the city of Perm that evening, swung my bag on to my shoulder and climbed down on to the platform.

When Yakunin travelled from Perm to his camp, he was locked in a metal cage in the back of a truck. Once again I had a more comfortable time, sitting in the front seat of a four-wheel-drive truck driven by Alexander Ogaryshev, a local opposition politician who had volunteered to show me around. We pulled out of Perm through heavy traffic and over the River Kama, a tributary to the Volga, and into the forest that stretches from here for thousands of kilometres to the north and east.

Alexander is a Perm native who trained as a lawyer at the interior ministry's academy in Nizhny Novgorod. That is an elite institution, and graduating should have led to a highly lucrative position in the police, where income from bribes can exceed official salaries many times over. He said, however, that he had been so revolted by the corruption, and the difference between the high ideals preached at the academy and actual police practice, that he quit and went into business with some friends.

'The corruption was total. They were just there to serve their own interests. Who paid more was all they cared about,' he had said a couple of days before we drove into the forest, as we sat over coffee.

'If I went to the station, they were all drinking. They respected nothing. The police should serve the state, they should want to be honest and to help people. They should not be serving just for the chance to make money.'

He and his friends owned a network of casinos until the government made casinos illegal in 2009. Casinos still exist, of course, and there was one disguised as an internet café opposite my hotel, but now they are run by corrupt officials who are immune to the law. Alexander and his friends moved into the restaurant business in response, and he now owned three venues across Perm. We sat in one of them while he told me about winter 2011–12. He had driven all the way to Moscow to take part in the protests, a journey of more than 1,000 kilometres. On arriving there on 10 December, he went straight to Bolotnaya Square without having slept.

'Our hope was that finally something could be changed in the country. Previously people just wanted to leave. I had this sense there that we could change things. I can sell up and leave at any time. I have a friend in Germany. For the first time, however, there was hope that we could change things, instead of this apathy. We need to keep this going. The protest was like a great unification. There were all these creative people with slogans that they invented themselves. The most creative people support the opposition, it was wonderful.'

The Perm region itself did not see any particular protests against United Russia's election. That may be because the party gained only 36 per cent there, which was down among the lowest levels in Russia, so there was not much to protest against.

The lack of protests is unlikely to be because Perm residents are too cynical and apathetic to take action, however. They are descended from generations of exiles, and it has been a favoured dumping ground for the Russian government's unwanted citizens for generations. Elmira Polubesova, a fifty-three-year-old activist from a liberal pressure group called Solidarity whom we were sitting with, boasted that Perm's tradition of exile made it an island of freedom in an oppressive sea.

'Judging by my own children, they have a chance to go to Canada but they say they want to stay here, they want to create conditions for a family, to change things. In Soviet times it was prestigious to be employed by someone, to have worked somewhere for forty years. The situation was such that you had to stay put, people were scared to leave or to speak out because they could lose their pension.

But now people have changed, they work for themselves. The generation that was repressed is dying. Even I did not experience the repression that my mother had, and when people have not been personally affected they are not scared to decide things for themselves.'

A ten-minute drive from the restaurant in Alexander's four-wheel-drive was the puppet theatre, a shabby beige building closed for the summer. In the 1930s it had a different function: a detention centre for those suspected of counter-revolutionary crimes. In almost any other Russian city, its past would have been forgotten. In Perm, however, a group of local activists had persuaded the theatre's management to let them set up a small museum round the back. Alexander Kalikh, a lean middle-aged man, is in charge of the project and he had agreed to show us around.

We walked across the courtyard to a brick annexe, opened a steel door and ducked inside. Incongruously, puppets hung on the walls alongside the displays about the repressions of the Stalin years. This was still a theatre after all. Kalikh said he was planning to reopen a bricked-up window that had looked on to the courtyard, and through which prisoners had once spoken to their relatives.

'No one kept here was aware that they would be taken to be shot but many people still alive remember seeing their relatives for the last time through that window.'

A few officials were even assisting him in his efforts to commemorate the past, he said, including the Federal Prisons Service, which had provided a genuine grille from an old window. He speculated that officials from the Service might have a guilt complex through working for the organization that had imprisoned so many people.

'The FSB is different, however. They haven't helped us in twenty years, they must have an order not to. The local government does help us a little, but that's because this is Perm, you know, it would not happen in other places.'

Schoolchildren now come to the building not just for the puppet performances, but to learn about how the secret police arrested people on token charges, penned them up and then shot them. The museum has lists of the people who were kept here, and can always find people who lived on the same street as the visiting children.

'We can show them the route the prisoners took to get here. That means for young people history is before their eyes. They have to sense that all this happened close to them, that it was not somewhere completely different. And we can show them that the times have not really changed. Look at the similarities between Stalin and Putin, now there has been a whole series of repressive reforms: to NGOs, to libel, to protest. Whose methods are these? Your rights mean nothing, we do not even know what will happen in a year.'

On the way out, he pointed to a poster on the wall with a quote from the poet Yevgeny Yevtushenko that loosely translates as 'If we forget, we are cattle. If we remember, we're a nation.' As a slogan, it is defiant and proud. If you surrender to officials' demands to forget their victims, you are collaborating in the crime.

The Perm region was home to three of the last camps for political prisoners in the Soviet Union. Perm-35, Perm-36 and Perm-37 were nicknamed the Perm triangle. Perm was a major centre of the weapons industry in Soviet times and was thus closed to foreigners, which made it a good place to keep dissidents.

Its glorious weapon-building past is attested to by a gigantic Order of Lenin in the centre of town, awarded in 1971 for its 'great successes in the development of industrial production'. The fruits of that production are on show in a museum on the outskirts. Visitors can see everything from a tsarist-era cannon to a ballistic missile that could fly 9,600 kilometres and deliver a 0.6-megaton atomic device. More powerful missiles have been made since, but were not on display.

Alexander Ogaryshev and I were on our way to Perm-36. Perm-35 and Perm-37 (where Yakunin served his term) still operate as prisons and are thus closed to visitors. Perm-36, however, the last point in the triangle, was abandoned. Former prisoners and members of Memorial, a charity devoted to historical research and human rights, took it over in 1992. At first they just wanted to preserve it, so future generations could see what a functioning camp had looked like. Having patched it up, however, they were faced with the question of what to do with it.

The obvious solution was to open it to visitors, which is what they did. It remains the only functioning museum on the territory of the gulag anywhere in Russia, which means it is the closest equivalent Russia has to the memorial at Auschwitz. Perm-36 may not have been one of the most terrible islands in Solzhenitsyn's archipelago, but it remains a unique memorial to the inhumanity of the twentieth century, and deserves to be far better known.

Driving there from Perm took about two hours, a distance considered insignificant by locals but deeply monotonous for those not used to the forest. The trees were occasionally birch with white trunks and light-green leaves, but normally pines, all orange trunks and dark needles. Sometimes fields opened out on either side of the road, and they heralded a village of single-storey houses huddled together. When the turning to Perm-36 finally appeared to the right of the road it was a relief.

We passed through the village of Kuchino, which seemed largely abandoned, then Makhnutino, which looked little better. The road was gravel, and we trailed a cloud of dust that billowed around us when we stopped at the police checkpoint. This was the weekend of the year when Perm-36 organizes a festival. Organizers expected 10,000 visitors and the police were taking a close interest. Among the blue-shirted officers, however, were volunteers in red T-shirts with the words 'Territory of Freedom' on the back, and they waved us through.

The camp headquarters was a two-storey cream building on a bluff above the River Chusovaya. The river curved away around a broad flat field. Sand banks stretched alluringly out into the water, offering the chance of a swim. Swallows swooped to sip the river, and fish left ripples on its smooth surface. The prisoners, of course, saw none of this. They arrived in closed trucks and were ushered immediately behind the camp's high fences and barbed wire. Often they had no clear idea of where they were. According to a camp legend, one intake of prisoners included an ornithologist who was able to judge by the birds he heard that they were near the Ural Mountains. Previously, no one had known.

The headquarters is the only building in the camp above a single storey, and most of the others are brick and timber barracks overshadowed by green watchtowers armed with searchlights. These were where the prisoners lived for the duration of their sentences.

We were among the first people to arrive for the three-day festival, and the camp was still largely deserted. We joined a tour run by a local pensioner called Sergei Spodin, who guided his group of eight with great skill and knowledge. The camp, he said, had included both living quarters and working quarters, where prisoners were expected to earn their keep. Outside the barracks were multiple rings of fences and barbed wire. Inside the barracks were informers paid with privileges like an extra tea ration.

'In forty-one years there was not a single escape. The system worked very well.'

Between this Tough Regime section of the camp and a second section, where prisoners lived in the even harsher Special Regime conditions, was a shooting range where the guards practised.

'There was shooting day and night. As you can imagine, this had a significant effect on people's psychology, because everyone knew they were not practising to shoot rabbits but to shoot people. This is a quiet region and you could hear the shooting 10 or 20 kilometres away. Everything was done to try to break people's spirits.'

Despite the guards' best efforts, when Yakunin arrived in the Perm triangle in 1981 the dissidents were as defiant as ever. They had evolved a highly complex game to play with their jailers. Their aim was to publicize their plight and to smuggle information to the West, whence it would be broadcast back on foreign radio. This would embarrass the Soviet government, which insisted it protected its citizens' human rights. The jailers' aim was to break the dissidents' spirits, to make them recant as Father Dmitry had done. Failing that, they just wanted to interrupt the flow of news updates.

Yakunin's arrival was heralded by an immediate flurry of reports on his progress in the underground *Chronicle of Current Events* (even now, he refused to tell me how the news reached the outside world).

'Not long before Yakunin's arrival in the camp all the Bibles were confiscated. On Yakunin's arrival, his Bible was also confiscated,' said the *Chronicle*'s issue number 62, dated July 1981.

On 4 May 1981, it said, Yakunin and a group of others had started a hunger strike to protest against the Soviet Union's failure to fulfil its international commitments to protect the human rights of its citizens. The hunger strike, Yakunin told me, had been the one weapon of the dissidents.

'We wrote these statements for anniversaries and so on, and we were always smuggling them out. We organized hunger strikes and the guards hated it. They would beat us but they couldn't stop us,' he said, with a chuckle. 'We wanted to show we were not broken, that we were taking part in the struggle in as far as we could.'

Throughout the 1980s, the jailed dissidents risked their health and sometimes their lives by forcing themselves to go for extended periods without food. Sakharov went on hunger strike for the right of his wife to have medical treatment abroad, Yakunin for the right to have a Bible, others just to show they were alive. This was in itself a sign of how much the camps had changed since Stalin's days. In the 1930s, a hunger strike would have led inevitably to death, since no one cared whether prisoners ate or not. Now, thanks to the pressure exerted by Western states, officials were under orders to keep the dissidents alive, and that gave the prisoners a lever to exert pressure on their guards.

There was always something to go on hunger strike for, if only for the right to be officially considered a political prisoner. Anatoly Marchenko died in 1986 after a three-month hunger strike aiming to secure the release of political prisoners.

Other prisoners looked for less terrible ways to make their points. Vladimir Bukovsky, a poet imprisoned in the 1970s, described the lengths prisoners would go to to irritate their jailers, whose time could be wasted almost indefinitely by exploiting the bureaucratic complaints procedure.

As he wrote in his memoirs:

We had been schooled by our participation in the civil rights movement, we had received an excellent education in the camps, and we knew of the implacable force of one man's refusal to submit. The authorities knew it too. They had long since abandoned any idea of basing their calculations on communist dogma. They no longer demanded of people a belief in the radiant future – all they needed was submission. And when they tried to starve us into it in the camps, or threw us into the punishment cells to rot, they were demanding not a belief in communism, but simply submission, or at least a willingness to compromise.

Bukovsky and his comrades had no intention of compromising. They reacted to every departure from strict procedure by writing an official complaint, and they could write up to thirty letters of complaint a day. They patiently sent them higher and higher up the chain of command, then branched out sideways in ever more elaborate directions.

> It is best to address your complaints not to run-of-the-mill bureaucrats, but to the most unpredictable individuals and organizations, for instance to all the Deputies of the Supreme Soviet, or of the Soviets at republican, regional or city levels, to newspapers and magazines, to astronauts, writers, artists, ballerinas, to all the secretaries of the Central Committee, all generals, admirals, productivity champions, shepherds, deer-breeders, milkmaids, sportsmen, and so on and so forth.

The guards came, if not to respect this kind of activism, at least to fear it and the extra work it created. Complaints could trigger committees of investigation, which had to be responded to, and it was best to avoid generating them. Although political prisoners had no special status in the camp system, they won the right to be addressed with the respectful plural form of the word 'you' and by their first name and patronymic. In any other prison, inmates were treated like rats.

This peculiar ritualized battle has been all but forgotten in Russia today. If you have not read the history of the dissident movement, and do not understand the complex relationship between the officials' equal but opposite desires to punish the prisoners while avoiding publicity, it makes no sense at all. Spodin, however, as he guided us around Perm-36, spoke of the prisoners like the heroes they were.

'Everything was done to break their spirits, to demean them, but they resisted.'

Further down the track was the Special Regime camp, which made the ordinary Tough Regime barracks seem luxurious. Here the cells were gloomy, their windows fitted with downward-slanting slats so prisoners would never see outside. The cell walls were plastered with uneven concrete – called 'fur' in prison slang – to make them ugly and uncomfortable to lean against. The exercise yard is a square of three paces by three paces. Its walls are three metres high, and topped with a mesh of barbed wire, meaning inmates here would never see anything but sky and walls.

'When I was a teenager, I thought this was a warehouse,' said Spodin. 'There were never any people, it was so quiet, it was only later I realized it was a camp. Our parents used to say people were locked up because of the war. They never told us these were political prisoners or anything.'

As we walked out of the barracks and back into the open air, Spodin described his own family's experiences of repression. His father's parents came from Ukraine and were sent to the Urals in 1934 during the collectivization campaign. Some of his father's siblings remained behind, and he had aunts and cousins in Ukraine whom he had never met. His family was lucky, however: at least the children had been able to remain with family members.

'The state often isolated the parents and raised the children itself. The state wanted to create a culture of informers,' he said.

His confession unlocked something in the other members of the tour, and people began to volunteer details about their own past.

'My grandmother was also repressed,' said a burly man in a blue T-shirt.

'My family was from Ukraine too, but was sent here,' said a woman in a red dress.

This is the kind of experience the museum directors want to provide for everyone. They want to make ordinary people realize that the country's history is their history too, and that it stretches forward to today. As we walked out, we saw a group of nine officers from the OMON, Russia's riot police, all in uniform. They were beginning a tour of their own. These are the government's enforcers, and their image is of mindless, brainwashed thugs. Yet here they were, standing patiently while a young woman explained the repressive system of the Soviet state.

'Those are the kind of comrades who really need this place,' said the burly man in the blue T-shirt, with an emphasis on the word 'comrades'. Everyone laughed.

The director of the museum is Viktor Shmurov, a heavyset man with a salt-and-pepper beard. He is a historian and was the first person to spot the unique possibilities of the Perm-36 site. Since it dates back to the Stalin years, it has the wooden barracks and facilities of the original gulag camps, which is why he was so keen to preserve it.

He and his friends, short of cash and building materials, even managed to get the camp's old sawmilling equipment working. They ran a timber business in the early 1990s, ploughing the profits back into the camp. The Russian word for a saw bench – *pilorama* – gives its name to the yearly festival.

'This has been a gradual process. We were building the museum for a long time, and it was hard. We wanted to present it in a positive way,' he said. In 2005, on the tenth anniversary of the museum's opening, they organized a concert.

'I don't like speeches, congratulations, things like that, but we invited a lot of bards and poets to perform. They went on to the stage, it was a beautiful concert and that is how Pilorama started.'

Two years later, they brought in political experts and activists to hold discussions and the shape of the festival was created: music, film and free conversation, all on a site where previously none of these things had been possible.

'Here are thousands of free people who behave absolutely as free people,' he said. 'If Pilorama is ever cancelled, it will show things have got very bad here, something will be rotten in Denmark. But I have no doubt that we will continue.'

One festival does not equal political freedom, but it is a start. If the winter of protests does lead to Russia's sclerotic politics becoming a little livelier, it could have an important impact on Russia's population crisis. Estonia had similar health problems to Russia (though not quite as bad) when part of the Soviet Union. After independence, the life expectancy of the average Estonian man initially sank, but then soared to all-time highs. You can see a similar pattern in other communist countries that have joined the European Union: Romania, Hungary, Slovakia. Prosperity and democracy does seem to be a good way to wean a population off massive alcohol abuse.

The Pilorama discussion sessions inevitably focused on the winter election season, with highly technical statistical presentations showing how fraud had been committed, and what ordinary citizens could do to stop it. The mobilization of thousands of Muscovites to observe the polls had forced electoral officials to behave more honestly, the experts explained, proving it with graphs and photographs. In the December election, the results from Moscow followed no conceivable statistical logic. It was clear officials had falsified the returns. By March, however, the curve was almost identical to that seen in a Western European election. Officials had been forced to record accurate results. It was a heady demonstration of the power of free citizens to affect their own destiny.

Every one of the sixty chairs was full, and another thirty or forty people were standing at the back.

It is a mark of the importance of the event that a group of young people from a Kremlin-linked youth group attempted to sabotage the discussions, asking aggressive questions and accusing the speakers of serving foreign interests. Sergei Kovalyov, a human rights veteran who served time in Perm-36 in the 1980s, fielded the remarks with admirable restraint, considering one of the young men was wearing a hammer and sickle T-shirt. I could not help wondering what would happen if a man of a similar age wore a swastika into Auschwitz.

'It would be very good if we had decommunistication, like they have had denazification,' said Kovalyov after he had finally extricated himself from the discussion. 'You see the support that there still is for the Soviet Union, and among people that were not even born at its height. They were all born after the death of Stalin, and even after Khrushchev. The oldest among them is probably only forty. There are some people among them you can talk to, but their emotions keep getting in the way.'

He was on his way to the toilet when I interrupted him. It is a rectangular building in the corner of the camp, where inmates had squatted at twelve squalid concrete holes above a noisome pit of slurry. I asked him if it was not peculiar to be using the same toilet again after all these years away.

'That was the only toilet, and you had to walk from the barracks over there. It is a long way, particularly in the cold, and many of the old men had dirtied their clothes before they reached it. Think how long it would take someone if he had a walking stick,' he said. 'In fact, if you don't stop asking me questions, I risk the same fate.'

The popular weekly *Arguments and Facts* had launched a publicity campaign against Pilorama, running an interview with a former prison guard who rubbished the dissidents' claims to have been treated badly here. Vladimir Kurguzov is chairman of the Council of Veterans of Perm-35, by which he means the people who served as guards over the dissidents, rather than the dissidents themselves. His testimony was intended to be aggressive but was unintentionally rather sad, revealing an old man who has been left behind by events. He boasted of the dissidents he had jailed, including Kovalyov, and then described seeing Kovalyov again.

'Do you remember me?' he had asked. Kovalyov said he did not.

'That cannot be. I abused you in Perm-35 and 36, how can you not remember your major oppressor? I worked here for days on end, everything came through me. So why don't they remember the main monster?' he replied. He may have been trying to be sarcastic, but was clearly offended by how history had flipped round. He had been in a position of power, and was now one of life's losers, while Kovalyov is fêted around the world.

He insisted that conditions in the camp had actually been very pleasant, that the dissidents ate better than most people in the country and had had nothing to complain about.

'They were in the warm and dry, they ate at a table with a table-cloth, having previously looked at a menu. Apart from that their books were published abroad. When they needed new glasses, they declared a hunger strike or refused to work. Therefore, people did not die in our camp, like they did in Kolyma,' he said.

It was a telling comment, with its total incomprehension of the motivation of people he had seen every day for years. He seemed unable to understand that it was the fact of being locked up that was the problem, not the conditions. If you have been imprisoned for writing a poem, no amount of tablecloths is going to make you happy about it. The difference between this Kurguzov and the likes of Kovalyov is – ironically, considering the positions they used to occupy – that between a slave and a free man.

Kurguzov, like the young men sent to disrupt the Pilorama discussions, insisted that the festival was funded from abroad (it is, in fact, mostly supported by the local government) to harm the image of Russia. That is an argument that only works if you look the wrong way down the telescope. If you turn it round you see, not the shameful fact of the camp, but the heroic resistance of the inmates. The attendees of the festival preferred to focus on the trust and respect among the former prisoners, rather than the whining of their former guards.

The festival had erected a stage in the centre of the camp, and the performers could look down the length of the barracks to the front gate. I had wondered who would play for the finale, expecting an earnest bard with a guitar and a songbook of protests. Fortunately, the organizers knew their audience better than that, and out came Markscheider Kunst, a Russian ska band with a horn section exuberant even by the magnificent standards of the St Petersburg music scene.

Their two drummers whipped out their irresistible rhythm, while the saxophone and trumpet sent a torrent of glorious brass through the old cells, between the bars, over the fences and into the forest beyond. No evil spirit of the past could withstand such joyful playfulness, and the crowd whooped along. A young woman at the front jumped up and down, her long glossy dark hair whipping back and forth in time with the music.

They are not a political band, but it was hard not to notice the lyrics to their anthemic 'Krasivo Sleva'. 'Winter is ending, we'll start again from the beginning, winter is ending, winter is ending,' they sang, and once again the horns blasted out their glorious crescendo.

The night before, my tent had been one of hundreds by the river in a field noisy with music, laughter and singing. Beneath all those sounds though, from the other tents, from all directions, had come the muffled but unmistakable sounds of young Russians getting busy making a new generation.

Postscript

It was 28 June, the anniversary of Father Dmitry's death, and I went looking for his grave in Moscow's Friday Cemetery.

I cut left and right, trending downhill along paths pushed through the mass of granite. Graves were piled together in vast numbers. It looked impossible that there could be room for as many people below the ground as were commemorated above it. Fifty-year-old graves were wedged up against ones from last week.

Close to the ragged wall that separated the cemetery from, by the sound of it, a major highway, a crowd of fifty or so people were already gathered. A young woman, seeing my camera, showed me through and pointed out Dudko's grave – 24 February 1922 to 28 June 2004. His life had coincided, more or less, with that of the Soviet Union.

Here was a mixed crowd: women in headscarves, young and old; men in open-necked shirts, some bearded, most not. There was Father Mikhail Dudko, Father Alexander and Father Vladimir, all in the sweeping robes of their office. They donned pectoral crosses. Father Mikhail slipped a golden cloth around his neck, and the service began.

The light-blue fences placed around many of the graves interrupted the unity of the congregation, which was forced to cram itself in where it could. But the Orthodox chant was glorious for all that. Father Mikhail's cracked voice led the chant in a strained falsetto; then the lovely many-level response mingled itself with the wind in the trees.

The Old Slavonic chanting had its usual lulling effect. The antiquated language made it easy to concentrate on the purity of the sound, not the meaning of the sentences, rather like going to see the opera in a language you do not speak. Father Alexander took over after a while, his nostrils were flared slightly and his bushy beard did not obscure the pure good looks that Russian soldiers have in World War Two newsreels.

'Dear fathers, brothers and sisters. Today, we honour the memory of Father Dmitry. Today, we have made a pilgrimage to this holy place where Father Dmitry, his body is buried. His soul is always with us, because he did a lot for us, he strengthened us, he united us. Is this not true? In the hardest conditions of persecution, he supported us. And thanks be to God that we are once more together,' the priest said, warming to his theme. 'He was a true father, he worried about his children. That's how he was, and this affected us also. He gathered us in, and treated our spiritual diseases. He had a particular faith, a particular spirit. We honour him with kind memories, bright memories, we pray for him.'

A mutter of prayer passed through the worshippers, whose attention was completely fixed on the priest. He passed the gold cloth to Father Vladimir, and the chant renewed itself. White incense smoke swirled among the gravestones. The crowd begged with their sweet voices for forgiveness from God in the manner that Russians have prayed for centuries, ever since the first king in long-ago Kiev adopted the faith of the Greeks.

The wind sighed in the trees, and the sunlight danced on the gravestones. The horrible heat of the day did not penetrate down here. The chanting lulled me again as it faded in and out. Today's Moscow might be a bustling city of banks and billboards and Bentley showrooms, but this felt like the Russia that had endured for centuries before banks were even thought of.

When the ceremony was over, a small group of women came over to quiz me gently on who I was and what I was doing. I explained my interest in Father Dmitry, and my concern over the falling population, and they began to tell me about how they had met him and what he meant for them and how much he had cared about the dying Russian nation.

'When I first went to his house, I was amazed, just by what it looked like at first. There was this terrible mess, but that was just on the surface. His whole family, well, they paid no attention to these domestic things. I completely did not understand. If you had something, you had it; if not, not; for me it was really strange. They lived in a sort of non-material way. That was the first thing,' one woman called Ksenia told me.

A second woman chipped in: 'When you entered their family, you entered a different world.'

Ksenia again: 'That's where it all started.'

And the second woman interrupted: 'It was like the earth opened.'

Ksenia confirmed that: 'Yes, it opened, and I began to, I'm talking about myself, I began to grow. There were all these discussions, that went deeper, deeper, deeper.'

Another woman, with a drawn middle-aged face, a few strands of hair falling out of her headscarf, stepped towards me. It was not easy to approach because of the narrow paths between the graves, but she was determined. She wanted, she said, to tell me her story.

She had been married, she said, only a short time when her husband began to drink. He drank vodka every day, and came home staggering and violent. All her attempts to stop him had come to nothing, and her life was horrible. That was when she met Father Dmitry.

'I saw him, and, how to say, he was like, he shone, he glowed with light, you could shut your eyes and see him; this was love, he glowed with love. He was white-haired, his hair was all like this,' she said, waving her hands around above her head with a broad smile. She had met him, she said, in the late 1980s when Father Dmitry was holding prayer meetings at which he made lists of the people present and made them promise not to drink. It was the dam he erected against the vodka engulfing the country and the misery engulfing himself.

'I want to tell you what happened with me,' she said. 'So listen. When I went to him, I wrote down my question, and he used to answer all the questions that we wrote down. I used to go there, and it became winter, and it was dark and my son said he could not let me go alone, and would come with me to escort me. I said to him that he needed to relax, that he was always working, that he came home late, that he could not come, but he said he wanted to come with me. And he started to come too, and I said to the priest: "I don't drink but my husband drinks and I have come for him. I want you to write him down on your list."'

Father Dmitry refused, saying that her husband had to come himself to pledge sobriety. She went home and begged and begged her husband, but he refused and refused.

'Until one beautiful day I asked him and he agreed. This was like a miracle. We get to the train station, he doesn't turn back. We get to the bus stop, he doesn't turn back. He gets to the library and he doesn't turn back,' she said, her eyes gleaming.

They had sat at the back of the library where Father Dmitry held his meetings, and she had gripped her husband's hand. He was distrustful of the gathering, as if it was some kind of cult.

'He swore at everyone, using all these swear words. Do you know these words in Russian? Yes? Well, he was using them all. The believers understood it was not him speaking, that evil was speaking. He swore, he was swearing, and he said he could not stand it. He said that he had had it up to here. And I'm being quiet, and not saying anything – let him swear.'

Father Dmitry came up to her husband and looked at him: 'I will give you five years. Five years. Five years not to drink.'

Her husband said: 'I can't survive.'

'You will survive.'

'I won't survive.'

'You will survive.'

'Father,' he said, 'I will drink.'

'No, you won't.'

'I have drunk for twenty years. What have I not drunk? Anything that burns I've drunk. I will drink.'

'No, you won't.'

She laughed a beautiful musical laugh, and her face had dropped a decade or more. She looked young: 'The priest was like this, and my husband was like that.'

Two times Father Dmitry said with such certainty: 'No, you won't.'

They went home, and her husband calmed down and no more was said about it.

'Then the next day my husband left to go to work, and to think that my husband after twenty years could come home from work sober. What a thought. The time comes. It's four, five, and I'm waiting, and everything's shaking inside, could it be possible? I wasn't worried that he would drink, of course he would drink, he always drank, but that he would go against God. This was very important to me, it was like a sin. I was thinking about how I had forced him to commit a sin. Five o'clock, six o'clock, seven o'clock. And he appears,' she paused for dramatic effect, loving her story.

'And I look at him. And he's sober. Sober!'

Her husband had told her an incredible story: 'The bus broke down, we stopped on a bridge, the lads ran off and bought some wine, and said, "Seryoga, pour it out," and I said, "I do not drink." And they said, "What?" And I said, "I do not drink. I went to a priest, and the priest gave me five years of no drinking." They gave me a glass, but I said no.'

The woman laughed with joy.

'He said no. No! And he's been like this ever since. Ever since. It was a miracle. It is a miracle. A miracle. Father Dmitry saved him. He wanted to save the whole Russian people like that, one at a time. That was what I wanted to say. God bless you.'

Sources and Bibliography

For my demographic data I have relied on the website of Russia's Federal Service of State Statistics (www.gks.ru), which publishes figures at fascinating levels of detail. I have used the monthly figures (which tend to show a lower total), rather than the census data, mainly because they allowed me to follow changes over small periods of time in very specific places, which is crucial to how I came up with my ideas. I have used www.mortality.org, for reliable life-expectancy and other statistics.

I have used and appreciated *Russia's Peacetime Demographic Crisis* by Nicholas Eberstadt (Washington, DC, 2010). He seems to make a good case, but I have also followed the online discussion about whether he has gone too far in his gloomy prognostications.

I have used newspaper archives in London and Moscow, as well as periodicals from elsewhere, for contemporary views on Dmitry Dudko. Among the most useful have been *Russkaya Mysl* (*Russian Thought*, 8 March 1979; 12 April 1979; 29 February 1980), the *Keston News Service* (26 June 1980), *Khronika Tekushchikh Sobytii* (the *Chronicle of Current Events*, multiple issues, available on www.memo.ru), *The Times* (of London, multiple issues), the *New York Times* (multiple issues) and those papers included in Google's mercifully digitized news archive.

I have scoured the libraries of Moscow and London, and corresponded with libraries further afield, in an attempt to find everything ever written by Dmitry Dudko. He was a prolific writer, so this has not been easy. I never found a copy of *Vrag Vnutri* (Frankfurt, 1979) but, otherwise, I am confident I have read the vast majority of his work. Here is a list of the books and articles that most informed this book.

Our Hope (New York, 1977) is the English translation of *O Nashem Upovanii* (Paris, 1975).
Podarok ot Boga (*A Present from God*, Moscow, 1997) is the closest thing he wrote to an autobiography.

The *Collected Works* published by the Moscow Patriarchate (Moscow, 2004) include in Volume 1: 'Vernost v Malom' ('Faithful over a Few Things'); 'Poteryannaya Drakhma' ('The Lost Coin'); 'Vyyavlenie Iskusnykh' ('Exposure of the Skilled'). Volume 2 contains: 'Na Skreshchenii Dorog' ('At the Meeting of the Roads'); 'Kak Istolkovat Pritchi' ('How to Interpret Parables'); 'Propoved Cherez Pozor' ('Preaching through Shame'). Volume 3 contains: 'Khristos v nashei Zhizni' ('Christ in our Life'); 'Liturgiya na Russkoi Zemle' ('Liturgy on Russian Land'); 'V Ternie i pri Doroge' ('Among the Thorns and along the Wayside').

I pieced together his self-published newspaper *V Svete Preobrazheniya* (*In the Light of the Transfiguration*) from an unpublished collection in the Russian State Library; from the *Vestnik Russkogo Khristianskogo Dvizheniya* (*Bulletin of the Russian Christian Movement*, no. 127, 1978 and no. 129, 1979); from *Volnoe Slovo* (*Free Word*, no. 33); and from 'Propoved Cherez Pozor' in the *Collected Works*.

Religion in Communist Lands (Volume 1, nos. 4–5; Volume 4, no. 2) contains accounts of his sermons.

Other writings are in:

Vestnik Russkogo Khristianskogo Dvizheniya (no. 118, 1976; no. 120, 1977)
Russkoe Vozrozhedenie (*Russian Renaissance*, no. 2, 1978; nos. 7–8, 1979)
Izvestia (21 June 1980)
Journal of the Moscow Patriarchate (no. 7, 1980)
Den (*Day*, including 21–7 June 1992; 15–21 November 1992; 1–9 January 1993; 7–13 February 1993; 23–29 May 1993; 1–7 October 1993)
Zavtra (*Tomorrow*, March 1994; March 1995; September 1994; November 1995; April 1996)
Nash Sovremennik (*Our Contemporary*, November 2002)

The 1960s and 1970s were the heyday of the dissidents' hand-printed samizdat ('self-published') literature. Some of these were smuggled into the West, printed in book form and then smuggled back (tamizdat: 'published there'). Many were also translated and published in English. They include:

Elena Bonner, *Alone Together* (London, 1986)
Vladimir Bukovsky, *To Build a Castle* (London, 1978)
Natalya Gorbanevskaya, *Red Square at Noon* (London, 1972)
Natalya Gorbanevskaya, *Selected Poems with a Transcript of her Trial and Papers Relating to her Detention in a Prison Psychiatric Hospital* (Oxford, 1972)

Karel van Het Reye (ed.), *Letters and Telegrams to P. M. Litvinov* (Dordrecht, 1969)

Dina Kaminskaya, *Final Judgement: My Life as a Soviet Defence Lawyer* (London, 1983)

Leopold Labedz and Max Hayward (eds.), *On Trial: The Case of Sinyavsky (Tertz) and Daniel (Arzhak)* (London, 1967)

Pavel Litvinov, *The Demonstration on Pushkin Square* (London, 1969)

Pavel Litvinov, *The Trial of the Four* (London, 1972)

Anatoly Marchenko, *My Testimony* (London, 1969)

Anatoly Marchenko, *From Tarusa to Siberia* (Strathcona, 1980)

Anatoly Marchenko, *To Live Like Everyone* (London, 1989)

Zhores Medvedev, *The Rise and Fall of T. D. Lysenko* (London, 1969)

Zhores and Roy Medvedev, *A Question of Madness* (New York, 1972)

Viktor Nekipelov, *Institute of Fools: Notes from the Serbsky* (New York, 1980)

Alexander Ogorodnikov, *A Desperate Cry* (Keston, 1986)

Andrei Sakharov, *Moscow and Beyond* (New York, 1991)

Harrison E. Salisbury (ed.), *Sakharov Speaks* (London, 1974)

Igor Shafarevich, *Russophobia* (samizdat, from 1981)

Gennady Shimanov, *Notes from the Red House* (Bromley, 1974)

Gleb Yakunin and Lev Regelson, *Letters from Moscow: Religion and Human Rights in the USSR* (Keston, 1978)

I have also relied on secondary literature for information on Russia, the Soviet Union, demographics, religion, totalitarianism and other themes covered in this book. These are the ones I have found most useful.

Olga Afremova, *Otets Dmitry Dudko* (*Father Dmitry Dudko*, Moscow, 1992)

Ludmilla Alexeyeva, *Soviet Dissent* (Middletown, Conn., 1985)

Mordechai Altshuler, *Soviet Jewry on the Eve of the Holocaust: A Social and Demographic Profile* (Jerusalem, 1998)

Christopher Andrew and Vasili Mitrokhin, *The Mitrokhin Archive: The KGB and the World* (London, 2005)

Anne Applebaum, *Gulag: A History* (London, 2003)

Anne Applebaum, *Iron Curtain: The Crushing of Eastern Europe, 1944–56* (London, 2012)

Yitzhak Arad, *The Holocaust in the Soviet Union* (Lincoln, Nebr., 2009)

Edwin Bacon and Mark Sandle (eds.), *Brezhnev Reconsidered* (Basingstoke, 2002)

Samuel H. Baron, *Bloody Saturday in the Soviet Union, Novocherkassk 1962* (Stanford, 2001)

Gal Beckerman, *When They Come for Us We'll Be Gone: The Epic Struggle to Save Soviet Jewry* (Boston, 2010)

Anatoly Belov and Andrei Shilkin, *Diversiya bez dinamita* (*Sabotage without Dynamite*, Moscow, 1973)

Philip Boobbyer, *Conscience, Dissent and Reform in Soviet Russia* (London, 2005)

Michael Bourdeaux, *Risen Indeed: Lessons in Faith from the USSR* (London, 1983)

Anthony Burgess, *A Clockwork Orange* (London, 2011)

Alex Butterworth, *The World that Never Was: A True Story of Dreamers, Schemers, Anarchists and Secret Agents* (London, 2011)

William C. Cockerham, *Health and Social Change in Russia and Eastern Europe* (London, 1999)

Robert Conquest, *The Harvest of Sorrow: Soviet Collectivisation and the Terror-Famine* (London, 1986)

Alexander Dallin, *German Rule in Russia 1941–45: A Study in Occupation Politics* (London, 1981)

R. W. Davies and Stephen G. Wheatcroft, *The Years of Hunger: Soviet Agriculture 1931–1933* (New York, 2004)

Judith Deutsch Kornblatt, *Doubly Chosen: Jewish Identity, the Soviet Intelligentsia, and the Russian Orthodox Church* (Madison, Wis., 2004)

Jared Diamond, *Collapse: How Societies Choose to Fall or Survive* (London, 2011)

Sidney D. Drell and Sergei P. Kapitza, *Sakharov Remembered: A Tribute by Friends and Colleagues* (New York, 1991).

Peter J. S. Duncan, *Russian Messianism: Third Rome, Revolution, Communism and After* (London, 2000)

Nicholas Eberstadt, *Russia's Peacetime Demographic Crisis* (Washington, DC, 2010)

Jane Ellis, *The Russian Orthodox Church: A Contemporary History* (London, 1986)

Jane Ellis, *The Russian Orthodox Church: Triumphalism and Defensiveness* (Basingstoke, 1996)

John Fennell, *A History of the Russian Church to 1448* (London, 1995)

Murray Feshbach, *Ecological Disaster: Cleaning Up the Hidden Legacy of the Soviet Regime* (New York, 1995)

Murray Feshbach and Alfred Friendly Jr, *Ecocide in the USSR: Health and Nature under Siege* (London, 1992)

Orlando Figes, *A People's Tragedy* (London, 1996)

Orlando Figes, *The Whisperers* (London, 2007)

Orlando Figes, *Just Send Me Word* (London, 2012)

Harvey Fireside, *Soviet Psychoprisons* (New York, 1979)

Sheila Fitzpatrick, *Stalin's Peasants: Resistance and Survival in the Russian Village after Collectivization* (New York, 1994)

Chrystia Freeland, *Sale of the Century* (London, 2005)

Masha Gessen, *The Man without a Face* (London, 2012)

Graeme Gill and Roger D. Markwick, *Russia's Stillborn Democracy? From Gorbachev to Yeltsin* (Oxford, 2000)

Yves Hamant, *Alexander Men: A Witness for Contemporary Russia* (Torrance, Calif., 1995)

Stephen Handelman, *Comrade Criminal: Russia's New Mafiya* (New Haven, 1995)

Albert Heard, *The Russian Church and Russian Dissent* (London, 1887)

Mikhail Heller and Aleksandr Nekrich, *Utopia in Power: The History of the Soviet Union from 1917 to the Present* (London, 1986)

David Hoffman, *The Oligarchs* (London, 2011)

Robert Horvath, *The Legacy of Soviet Dissent: Dissidents, Democratisation and Radical Nationalism in Russia* (London, 2005)

Grigory Ioffe and Tatyana Nefedova, *Continuity and Change in Rural Russia: A Geographical Perspective* (Boulder, Col., 1997)

Grigory Ioffe, Tatyana Nefedova and Ilya Zaslavsky, *The End of Peasantry? The Disintegration of Rural Russia* (Pittsburgh, 2006)

David Joravsky, *The Lysenko Affair* (Chicago, 1986)

Oleg Kalugin, *Spymaster: My 32 Years in Intelligence and Espionage against the West* (London, 1994)

Ryszard Kapuscinski, *Imperium* (London, 2007)

Halik Kochanski, *The Eagle Unbowed: Poland and the Poles in the Second World War* (London, 2012)

Stephen Kotkin, *Steeltown USSR: Soviet Society in the Gorbachev Era* (Berkeley, 1991)

Stephen Kotkin, *Magnetic Mountain: Stalinism as a Civilization* (Berkeley, 1995)

Stephen Kotkin, *Armageddon Averted: The Soviet Collapse 1970–2000* (Oxford, 2008)

Richard Lourie, *Sakharov: A Biography* (London, 2002)

Wolfgang Lutz, Sergei Scherbov and Andrei Volkov (eds.), *Demographic Trends and Patterns in the Soviet Union before 1991* (London, 1994)

A. Malenky, *Magnitogorsk: The Magnitogorsk Metallurgical Combine of the Future* (Moscow, 1932)

Nick Manning and Nataliya Tikhonova (eds.), *Health and Health Care in the New Russia* (Aldershot, 2009)

David Marples, *The Collapse of the Soviet Union, 1985–91* (Harlow, 2004)

Mervyn Matthews, *Patterns of Deprivation in the Soviet Union under Brezhnev and Gorbachev* (Stanford, 1989)

Catherine Merridale, *Night of Stone: Death and Memory in Russia* (London, 2000)

Fyodor Mochulsky, *Gulag Boss* (Oxford, 2011)

George Orwell, *Nineteen Eighty-Four* (London, 1949)

Richard Overy, *Russia's War* (London, 2010)

Boris Pasternak, *Dr Zhivago* (London, 1959)

Donald Rayfield, *Stalin and his Hangmen* (London, 2004)

Keith Richards, *Life* (London, 2011)

T. H. Rigby (ed.), *The Stalin Dictatorship: Khrushchev's 'Secret Speech' and Other Documents* (Sydney, 1968)

Elizabeth Roberts and Ann Shukman (eds.), *Christianity for the Twentieth Century: The Life and Work of Alexander Men* (London, 1996)

Abraham Rothberg, *The Heirs of Stalin: Dissidence and the Soviet Regime 1953–1970* (Ithaca, NY, 1972)

Angus Roxburgh, *The Strongman* (London, 2012)

Joshua Rubenstein and Alexander Gribanov (eds.), *The KGB File on Andrei Sakharov* (London, 2005)

Theo J. Schulte, *The German Army and Nazi Policies in Occupied Russia* (Oxford, 1989)

John Scott, *Behind the Urals: An American Worker in Russia's City of Steel* (Bloomington, Ind., 1973)

Simon Sebag Montefiore, *Young Stalin* (London, 2007)

Robert Service, *Stalin: A Biography* (London, 2004)

L. Sitko, *Intalia: Stikhi i vospominaniya byshikh zaklyuchennihk Minlaga* (*Intalia: Poems and Remembrances of Prisoners of the Mineral Camp*, Inta, 1995)

Timothy Snyder, *Bloodlands* (London, 2011)

Alexander Solzhenitsyn, *Cancer Ward* (London, 1968)

Alexander Solzhenitsyn, *Arkhipelag Gulag* (*The Gulag Archipelago*, Moscow, 1990)

Francis Spufford, *Red Plenty* (London, 2011)

William Taubman, *Khrushchev: The Man and his Era* (New York, 2003)

Olga Semyonova Tian-Shanskaia, *Village Life in Late Tsarist Russia* (Bloomington, Ind., 1993)

William Tompson, *The Soviet Union under Brezhnev* (Harlow, 2003)

Mark Trofimchuk, *Akademia u Troitsy* (*Academy of the Trinity*, Sergiev Posad, 2005)

Judyth L. Twigg (ed.), *HIV/AIDS in Russia and Eurasia* (Basingstoke, 2006)

Tim Tzouliadis, *The Forsaken: From the Great Depression to the Gulags: Hope and Betrayal in Stalin's Russia* (London, 2008)

Anatoly Vaneyev, *Dva Goda v Abezi* (*Two Years in Abez*, Moscow, 1992)

Timothy Ware, *The Orthodox Church* (London, 1993)

Frank Westerman, *Engineers of the Soul* (London, 2010)

Stephen White, *Russia Goes Dry: Alcohol, State and Society* (Cambridge, 1996)

Michael Wieck, *A Childhood under Stalin and Hitler: Memoirs of a 'Certified' Jew* (London, 2003)

Venedikt Yerofeyev, *Moskva–Petushki* (Moscow, 1989)

Venedikt Yerofeyev, *Moscow Stations* (London, 1998)

These are specific references, listed by chapter, to works mentioned in the text.

INTRODUCTION: WE WILL BURY YOU

The reference to the king rejecting Islam comes from Heard's *Russian Church and Russian Dissent*. The statistics on relative alcohol consumption come from Eberstadt, *Russia's Peacetime Demographic Crisis*. The figures for the increase in Russia's consumption of alcoholic drinks from 1940 to 1984 come from White, *Russia Goes Dry*.

The 'we will bury you' comment and the background to Khrushchev saying it are from Taubman's biography of the Soviet leader.

The information on Sinyavsky and Daniel comes from *On Trial*, edited by Labedz and Hayward. The Alexeyeva book quoted is her excellent *Soviet Dissent*.

Transparency International's corruption perceptions index is available on the organization's website cpi.transparency.org, and the Levada Centre's survey is on www.levada.ru along with a fascinating array of other investigations.

CHAPTER 1: THEY TOOK OUR GRANDFATHER'S LAND

The quotes from Father Dmitry are mainly taken from his *Podarok ot Boga*.

The eyewitness account of pre-revolutionary village life comes from Tian-Shanskaia's *Village Life in Late Tsarist Russia*. Other useful books on peasant life include the early parts of Figes's *A People's Tragedy*, plus the early chapters of the following books on the famine.

These are Conquest's *The Harvest of Sorrow*, Davies and Wheatcroft's *The Years of Hunger* and *Stalin's Peasants* by Fitzpatrick. Snyder's *Bloodlands* is magnificent for collectivization, famine and the violence of the war, while Ioffe and Nefedova's *Continuity and Change in Rural Russia* was also a major source.

The fate of the Jews is described in Altshuler's *Soviet Jewry on the Eve of the Holocaust* and Arad's *The Holocaust in the Soviet Union*. The general origins and effects of anti-Semitism are touched on in Butterworth's *The World that Never Was*. Accounts of the mass rape inflicted by Soviet soldiers when they captured towns in World War Two are legion. Among them are those in Applebaum's *Iron Curtain*.

CHAPTER 2: A DOUBLE-DYED ANTI-SOVIET

For details on Stalin's deal with the Orthodox Church, see Service's biography of the dictator, as well as the books by Jane Ellis. The quote asking where all the priests have gone is from Trofimchuk, *Akademia u Troitsy*, the Sergiev Posad seminary's official history.

The details of production of food on private plots come from Ioffe and Nefedova's *Continuity and Change in Rural Russia*. The quote expressing amazement about Hagia Sophia is from Heard's *The Russian Church and Russian Dissent*. The details about Pavlik Morozov are from Orlando Figes's *The Whisperers*. The narrative of the gulag is largely taken from Applebaum's *Gulag*.

The Lenin comment is from Volume 35 of his collected works, as quoted in Andrew and Mitrokhin, *The Mitrokhin Archive*, which is also the source for the details on KGB penetration of the Church.

CHAPTER 3: FATHER DMITRY WAS K-956

Details on the gulag are from Applebaum's *Gulag* and from Solzhenitsyn's *Gulag Archipelago*.

CHAPTER 4: THE GENERATION OF CHANGE

For information on the protest against the invasion of Czechoslovakia, see Gorbanevskaya's *Red Square at Noon*. The Khrushchev secret speech can be found in Rigby's *The Stalin Dictatorship*. The Leonid Plyushch quotes come from Fireside's *Soviet Psychoprisons*. Information on writers' roles under Stalin can be found in Westerman's *Engineers of the Soul*.

The Father Dmitry quotes here are taken from *Our Hope*, a collection of his sermons published in the West in English (and in Russian as *O Nashem Upovanii*). A description of the debris of Father Dmitry's first church, following its demolition, is in the introduction to Bourdeaux's *Risen Indeed*.

The 1972 sermon is from *Religion in Communist Lands*, Volume 1, nos. 4–5. The other descriptions are from 'An Eyewitness Account' in *Religion in Communist Lands*, Volume 4, no. 2; and from an article by Anatoly Levitin-Krasnov found in the Memorial archives and originally published in *Vestnik Russkogo Khristianskogo Dvizheniya* in 1974.

The lonely struggle of Soviet Jews for emigration is described in Beckerman's *When They Come for Us We'll Be Gone*. The letter by the 'Jewish woman' is by L. A. Gold and is dated 5 May 1974. It comes from the Memorial archives.

CHAPTER 5: REDS ADMIT BAN OF REBEL PRIEST

The details of shops selling meat, fruit and vegetables versus shops selling alcohol come from White's *Russia Goes Dry*, as do most references to alcohol statistics in this chapter. The quotes from *Moskva–Petushki* are taken from the English-language version published in 1998 by Faber & Faber under the title *Moscow Stations*.

The quotes from the sermon preached in Kabanovo are from the *Vestnik Russkogo Khristianskogo Dvizheniya*, no. 118 from 1976. The quotes from Father Dmitry's confessions, here and elsewhere, are from his notebooks published as 'Na Skreshchenii Dorog' in the *Collected Works*.

Details on the number of abortions and government policy towards them come from Lutz, Scherbov and Volkov (eds.), *Demographic Trends and Patterns in the Soviet Union before 1991*, from Eberstadt's *Russia's Peacetime Demographic Crisis*, from Feshbach and Friendly's *Ecocide in the USSR*, and from Feshbach's *Ecological Disaster*.

The Sakharov quote is from his essay 'Progress, Coexistence and Intellectual Freedom', which I found in Salisbury (ed.), *Sakharov Speaks*. The protests by Shafarevich and by Yakunin and Regelson were published in *Religion in Communist Lands* in 1976 and are available online at www.biblicalstudies.org.uk.

CHAPTER 6: THEY BEHAVED LIKE FREE MEN

The Father Dmitry quotes here are from his self-published newspaper *V Svete Preobrazheniya*. A little more on his car crash in 1975 can be found in *Religion in Communist Lands*, but it remains a mysterious incident.

Details on the Helsinki Accords and the formation of the Helsinki Groups are from Andrew and Mitrokhin, *The Mitrokhin Archive*, Beckerman's *When They Come for Us We'll Be Gone* (which is also my source for the quotes from Shcharansky), Tompson's *The Soviet Union under Brezhnev*, Horvath's *The Legacy of Soviet Dissent* and Lourie's biography of Sakharov.

The Amalrik quote is from Boobbyer, *Conscience, Dissent and Reform in Soviet Russia*.

The text of the interview with the *New York Times* was published in *Russkoe Vozrozhdenie*, no. 2, 1978. The press-conference transcript is in *Letters from Moscow: Religion and Human Rights in the USSR* by Yakunin and Regelson.

Details on the abuse of psychiatry come from Fireside's *Soviet Psychoprisons*, from Rothberg's *The Heirs of Stalin*, from the Medvedevs' *A Question of Madness*, from Alexeyeva's *Soviet Dissent*, from Shimanov's *Notes from the Red House*, from Nekipelov's *Institute of Fools* and from Gorbanevskaya's *Selected Poems*.

The story of the Soviet Union's support of Lysenko's quack biology can be read in Joravsky's *The Lysenko Affair* and Medvedev's *The Rise and Fall of T. D. Lysenko*.

CHAPTER 7: IDEOLOGICAL SABOTAGE

Andropov's war against the dissidents is dealt with well in Andrew and Mitrokhin, *The Mitrokhin Archive*.

CHAPTER 8: IT'S LIKE A PLAGUE

Keith Richards's autobiography *Life* is well read on the audiobook, mainly by Johnny Depp. Of many audiobooks I have listened to on long train journeys, it may be my favourite.

For Poland's experience during and after the Soviet invasion, I relied on Kochanski's *The Eagle Unbowed* and on Applebaum's *Iron Curtain*. Mochulsky's *Gulag Boss* is not entirely reliable, since it was written much later as a justification of his own role in the camps, but is the best we have.

CHAPTER 9: THE UNWORTHY PRIEST

Details on the Podrabineks' trials can be found in the *Chronicle of Current Events*, and other reactions to Father Dmitry's recantation of his views can be seen in Google's news archive. I have not been able to find a video recording of Father Dmitry's television appearance, so I have relied on contemporary observers' descriptions of his appearance.

CHAPTER 10: THE K G B DID THEIR BUSINESS

The quotes from Father Dmitry are from his *Podarok ot Boga,* 'Vernost v Malom' and *V Svete Preobrazheniya.*

The quote accusing the KGB of killing the 'spiritual father' is from the *Chronicle of Current Events*. Father Dmitry wrote about Divnich in *Nash Sovremennik.*

CHAPTER 11: I LOOK AT THE FUTURE WITH PESSIMISM

The Gorbachev anti-alcohol campaign is described in White's *Russia Goes Dry,* and its spectacular demographic effects are dealt with at length by Eberstadt in *Russia's Peacetime Demographic Crisis.* The corrupt privatization deals and crooked 1996 presidential elections are well described in Freeland's *Sale of the Century* and Hoffman's *The Oligarchs.*

The three Russian sociologists are Ioffe, Nefedova and Zaslavsky, and their book describing degradation in the countryside is *The End of Peasantry? The Disintegration of Rural Russia.*

CHAPTER 12: THEY DON'T CARE ANY MORE

Details of Ogorodnikov's torments in the 1980s can be found in his *A Desperate Cry.* That covers more ground than my account of his life, which more or less ends in the mid-1970s. The life story of Alexander Men is described in Roberts and Shukman (eds.), *Christianity for the Twentieth Century.* He was a fascinating and humane man, who deserves to be better known. The details of KGB infiltration of the Orthodox Church are from Andrew and Mitrokhin's *The Mitrokhin Archive,* and from Ellis's *The Russian Orthodox Church: Triumphalism and Defensiveness.*

CHAPTER 13: MAKING A NEW GENERATION

Some of the finest writing on the winter protests in Moscow was by Julia Ioffe in the *New Yorker*. The British journalist mentioned in the account of the Pussy Riot trial is Tom Parfitt, whose coverage of the winter of protests for the *Daily Telegraph* was also superb. Other journalists whose work I appreciated include Miriam Elder of the *Guardian* and Shaun Walker of the *Independent*.

'Krasivo Sleva' is found on the Markscheider Kunst album of the same name. I would recommend St Petersburg ska as something purely joyful to anyone who needs cheering up.

Acknowledgements

Thanks to Helen Conford at Penguin for editing sensitively but forcefully. Thanks also to Lara Heimart, my editor at Basic, for her faith in me, and to my agent Karolina Sutton at Curtis Brown.

This book has involved a lot of time sitting in libraries and travelling in Russia, and I am very grateful to the Society of Authors' Authors Foundation for giving me the John Heygate award, which helped pay for me to do both.

I have shamelessly trespassed on people everywhere I have gone. I have been bought drinks, given food, told stories and driven to places I could not otherwise have reached. Through this, I have come to a far greater understanding of Russian culture than I previously possessed, and for that understanding and that hospitality I am profoundly grateful.

In Moscow, thanks to Amie Ferris-Rotman, Antoine Lambroschini, Tom Parfitt and Simon Ostrovsky for having me to stay. Thanks also to Tanya and Kirill Podrabinek for their generosity. In Perm, thanks to Alexander Ogaryshev, and to Masha, Kolya and Slava. In Abez, thanks to Alexander and Natasha Merzlikin and their family. In Inta, thanks to Yevgeniya Kulygina and to Nikolai Andreyevich. In Unecha, thanks to Tamara Fyodorovna and her family. In Bryansk, thanks to Yuri Solovyov for his insights.

In Cambridge, thanks to the extraordinary Marina Voikhanskaya. An evening with her inspired two very different books.

Massive thanks to Xenia Dennen, Michael Bourdeaux and Larisa Seago, all formerly or currently working at the Keston Institute. Their patience and help allowed me to obtain documents I could never otherwise have found.

Staff members at the State Public Historical Library of Russia and the Russian State Library (the Lenin Library) in Moscow were helpful far beyond the call of duty and cheerfully subverted their own photocopying rules when faced with a bit of pleading. The people at Memorial in Moscow were magnificent and shared their huge archive with me. I also appreciated the services of the British Library and the London Library.

Every person mentioned in the text is identified by his or her own name, apart from my friend Misha in the Introduction, whose name I have changed.

To create a clear narrative, I have taken some liberties with the order in which conversations happened. Days, weeks or months after an interview, other conversations often provoked new questions. That means that many of the interviews presented as single events are actually composites of several different encounters.

Naturally, journeys of discovery do not proceed in a simple linear fashion (or they don't for me anyway), so some conversations have been moved backwards or forwards to suit the narrative. The content of all conversations is of course presented faithfully. These are the interviewees whose insights were most important to me. I am grateful to all of them.

Max Adler, Solikamsk; Vasily Afonchenko, Bryansk; Ludmilla Alexeyeva, Moscow; Nikolai Andreyevich, Inta; David Badaryan, Inta; Yulia Boretskaya, Inta; Semyon Boretsky, Inta; Alexander Daniel, Moscow; Mikhail Dudko, London and Moscow; Vladimir Dudko, Berezina; Irina Flige, London; Natalya Gorbanevskaya, Moscow; Maria Gureva, Bryansk; Alexander Kalikh, Perm; Lidiya Khodunova, Berezina; Alexei Kolegov, Syktyvkar; Alexei Kovalyov, Unecha; Sergei Kovalyov, Perm; Yevgeniya Kulygina, Inta; Zhores Medvedev, London; Alexander Merzlikin, Abez; Natasha Merzlikina, Abez; Michael Meylec, Perm; Father Mikhail, Inta; Alexander Ogaryshev, Perm; Alexander Ogorodnikov, Moscow; Dmitry Oreshkin, Perm; Vladimir Petrovsky, Moscow; Alexander Podrabinek, Moscow; Kirill Podrabinek, Moscow; Tanya Podrabinek, Abez and Moscow; Elmira Polubesova, Perm; Lev Regelson, Moscow; Vladimir Sedov, Moscow; Alexander Semyonov, Moscow; Zoya Semyonova Sr, Moscow; Zoya Semyonova Jr, Moscow; Viktor Shmurov, Perm; Vasily Shpinkov, Kazashchina; Alexander Skaliukh, Perm; Yuri Solovyov, Bryansk; Sergei Spodin, Perm; Oleg Sukhanov, Sergiev Posad; Alexander Tefft, London; Father Vadim, Staraya Guta; Anna Vasilyevna, Berezino; Nina Vasilyevna, Berezino; Marina Voikhanskaya, Cambridge; Maria Volkova, Berezina; Gleb Yakunin, Moscow; Olga Zagorskaya, Inta.

Index

Abez gulag camp/town 58–61, 66, 67, 68–71, 155, 156, 157, 159–66, 168

abortion 85, 95, 99

Achkasova, Olga 66

Afghanistan, Soviet invasion (1980) 131, 135, 177

agriculture 19, 20, 21, 22, 28, 29, 34, 48, 191
  collectivization 11, 18, 23, 24, 25–6, 29, 34–5, 37, 69, 145
  home grown food 31, 37
  see also famine

Akhmatova, Anna 60, 70

alcoholism *see* drinking

Alexeyeva, Ludmilla 8, 9

Alexy I, Patriarch 44–5

Alexy II, Patriarch (KGB codename DROZDOV) 45, 222–3

Amalrik, Andrei 113

Andreyevich, Nikolai 61, 62, 63, 64, 66, 67–8, 70, 71, 147, 148, 151, 154

Andropov, Yuri, as head of KGB 7, 112, 138–9, 140, 177

Arguments and Facts 247–8

Armenia 62, 63

Arsenevo (village) 182, 187, 191

Arteyev family (of Abez) 165–6

atheism 88, 90, 96–7

Marxism as 82, 85, 86
  see also religion

Austria 7

Badaryan, David 62–4

bankers/businessmen 210

St Basil 234

Baydino (village) 182, 187, 188–91
  Father Dmitry in 182, 188, 189–90, 192–6

BBC 82, 88, 102, 110, 114

Berezina (village) 20, 21, 24, 28–9, 31, 32, 33, 110, 211, 213–16

Berezino (village) 14–18, 20

Berezovsky, Boris 210

birth control 99
  abortion 85, 95, 99

birth rates *see* population crisis

Boretsky, Semyon 151–3, 159

Boretsky, Yulia (wife of Semyon Boretsky) 151, 153

Brezhnev, Leonid 7, 75, 86, 95, 99, 100, 112, 177, 206
  his 'developed socialism' concept 75
  Helsinki Agreement (1975) and 112–13

brick making 152, 153

Britain 82
  see also BBC

271